"In *The Way of Dante*, Richard Hughes Gibson does not teach us about Dante; rather through Dante, we learn more about the reality of sin, ourselves, and God. By uniting Williams, Lewis, and Sayers's writings on *The Divine Comedy*, Gibson grants readers a blessed opportunity of a cotaught Great Books seminar, a dialogue of the dead orchestrated with vitality around one of the tradition's eternal poets!"

**Jessica Hooten Wilson,** Fletcher Jones Chair of Great Books at Pepperdine University

"This is the book for which many readers of Charles Williams, Dorothy Sayers, and C. S. Lewis have been waiting, and one that richly fulfills their anticipations. With solid scholarship and yet a light touch, the author shows how interest in Dante held this trio of writers together as a network, motivating, critiquing, quoting, and promoting each other as readers of the medieval poet. With keen insight and a lively manner that belies the difficulty of the task, the author clearly demonstrates how the complex relations between Williams, Sayers, and Lewis allow the many-sidedness of Dante to emerge today—as poet, storyteller, humorist, and theologian. Always illuminating and interesting, this book is essential reading for all who value the writings of these three modern interpreters of Dante."

**Paul S. Fiddes,** professor of systematic theology at the University of Oxford and principal emeritus and senior research fellow at Regent's Park College

THE WAY OF DANTE

THE WAY OF

# DANTE

Going Through Hell, Purgatory, and Heaven with
C. S. Lewis, Dorothy L. Sayers, and Charles Williams
AFTERWORD BY NICOLE MAZZARELLA

## RICHARD HUGHES GIBSON

ivp
Academic
An imprint of InterVarsity Press
Downers Grove, Illinois

**InterVarsity Press**
P.O. Box 1400 | Downers Grove, IL 60515-1426
ivpress.com | email@ivpress.com

InterVarsity Press® is the publishing division of InterVarsity Christian Fellowship/USA®. For more information, visit intervarsity.org.

All Scripture quotations, unless otherwise indicated, are taken from The Holy Bible, New International Version®, NIV®. Copyright © 1973, 1978, 1984, 2011 by Biblica, Inc.™ Used by permission of Zondervan. All rights reserved worldwide. www.zondervan.com. The "NIV" and "New International Version" are trademarks registered in the United States Patent and Trademark Office by Biblica, Inc.™

While any stories in this book are true, some names and identifying information may have been changed to protect the privacy of individuals.

Quotations from Dorothy L. Sayers are used by permission of David Higham Associates LTD.

The publisher cannot verify the accuracy or functionality of website URLs used in this book beyond the date of publication.

Cover design: Faceout Studio, Tim Green
Interior design: Daniel van Loon
Image: © Andrew_Howe / iStock via Getty Images

ISBN 978-1-5140-1338-0 (print) | ISBN 978-1-5140-1339-7 (digital)

Printed in the United States of America ∞

**Library of Congress Cataloging-in-Publication Data**
Names: Gibson, Richard Hughes author
Title: The way of Dante : going through Hell, Purgatory, and Heaven with C.
   S. Lewis, Dorothy L. Sayers, and Charles Williams / Richard Hughes
   Gibson.
Description: Downers Grove, IL : InterVarsity Press, 2025. | Series: Hansen
   lectureship series | Includes bibliographical references and index.
Identifiers: LCCN 2025021037 (print) | LCCN 2025021038 (ebook) | ISBN
   9781514013380 paperback | ISBN 9781514013397 ebook
Subjects: LCSH: Dante Alighieri, 1265-1321–Influence | Sayers, Dorothy L.
   (Dorothy Leigh), 1893-1957–Criticism and interpretation | Lewis, C. S.
   (Clive Staples), 1898-1963–Criticism and interpretation | Williams,
   Charles, 1886-1945–Criticism and interpretation | Hell in literature |
   Heaven in literature | Theology in literature | LCGFT: Literary
   criticism | Essays
Classification: LCC PQ4381 .G53 2025 (print) | LCC PQ4381 (ebook) | DDC
   851/.1–dc23/eng/20250506
LC record available at https://lccn.loc.gov/2025021037
LC ebook record available at https://lccn.loc.gov/2025021038

32  31  30  29  28  27  26  25  |  12  11  10  9  8  7  6  5  4  3  2  1

For Brett Foster (1973–2015),

*better craftsman,*

and Timothy Larsen,

*a Light in the Dark Wood*

*I am convinced, then, that we need never be afraid to read into the great images of Dante all the fullness of significance which they can be made to contain—so long, of course, as our interpretation does not involve a degradation of the image and is not incongruous with the general purpose of his allegory. A great poem is not the perquisite of scholars and critics and historians: it is yours and mine—our freehold and our possession; and what it truly means to us is a real part of its true and eternal meaning.*

DOROTHY L. SAYERS,
"DANTE'S IMAGERY: I—SYMBOLIC" (1947)


*It has taken Christendom that long to catch him [Kierkegaard] up; it took it fifty to catch up St. Thomas, and it has not caught up Dante yet.*

CHARLES WILLIAMS, THE DESCENT OF THE DOVE (1939)


*Dare I confess that after Dante even Shakespeare seems to me a little factitious?*

C. S. LEWIS, "DANTE'S SIMILES" (1940)

# CONTENTS

# SERIES PREFACE

G. WALTER HANSEN

## THE KEN AND JEAN HANSEN LECTURESHIP

I was motivated to set up a lectureship in honor of my parents, Ken and Jean Hansen, at the Wade Center primarily because they loved Marion E. Wade. My father began working for Mr. Wade in 1946, the year I was born. He launched my father's career and mentored him in business. Often when I look at the picture of Marion Wade in the Wade Center, I give thanks to God for his beneficial influence in my family and in my life.

After Darlene and I were married in December 1967, the middle of my senior year at Wheaton College, we invited Marion and Lil Wade for dinner in our apartment. I wanted Darlene to get to know the best storyteller I've ever heard.

When Marion Wade passed through death into the Lord's presence on November 28, 1973, his last words to my father were, "Remember Joshua, Ken." As Joshua was the one who followed Moses to lead God's people, my father was the one who followed Marion Wade to lead the ServiceMaster Company.

After members of Marion Wade's family and friends at ServiceMaster set up a memorial fund in honor of Marion Wade at Wheaton College, my parents initiated the renaming of Clyde Kilby's collection of papers and books from the seven British authors—C. S. Lewis, J. R. R. Tolkien, Dorothy L. Sayers, George

MacDonald, G. K. Chesterton, Charles Williams, and Owen Barfield—as the Marion E. Wade Collection.

I was also motivated to name this lectureship after my parents because they loved the literature of these seven authors, whose papers are now collected at the Wade Center.

While I was still in college, my father and mother took an evening course on Lewis and Tolkien with Dr. Kilby. The class was limited to nine students so that they could meet in Dr. Kilby's living room. Dr. Kilby's wife, Martha, served tea and cookies.

My parents were avid readers, collectors, and promoters of the books of the seven Wade authors, even hosting a book club in their living room led by Dr. Kilby. When they moved to Santa Barbara in 1977, they named their home Rivendell, after the beautiful house of the elf Lord Elrond, whose home served as a welcome haven to weary travelers as well as a cultural center for Middle-earth history and lore. Family and friends who stayed in their home know that their home fulfilled Tolkien's description of Rivendell:

> And so at last they all came to the Last Homely House, and found its doors flung wide. . . . [The] house was perfect whether you liked food, or sleep, or work, or story-telling, or singing, or just sitting and thinking best, or a pleasant mixture of them all. . . . Their clothes were mended as well as their bruises, their tempers and their hopes. . . . Their plans were improved with the best advice.[1]

Our family treasures many memories of our times at Rivendell, highlighted by storytelling. Our conversations often drew from images of the stories of Lewis, Tolkien, and the other authors. We had our own code language: "That was a terrible Bridge of Khazad-dûm experience." "That meeting felt like the Council of Elrond."

---

[1] J. R. R. Tolkien, *The Hobbit* (Unwin Hyman, 1987), 50-51.

One cold February, Clyde and Martha Kilby escaped the deep freeze of Wheaton to thaw out and recover for two weeks at my parents' Rivendell home in Santa Barbara. As a thank-you note, Clyde Kilby dedicated his book *Images of Salvation in the Fiction of C. S. Lewis* to my parents. When my parents set up our family foundation in 1985, they named the foundation Rivendell Stewards' Trust.

In many ways, they lived in and lived out the stories of the seven authors. It seemed fitting and proper, therefore, to name this lectureship in honor of Ken and Jean Hansen.

## ESCAPE FOR PRISONERS

The purpose of the Hansen Lectureship is to provide a way of escape for prisoners. J. R. R. Tolkien writes about the positive role of escape in literature:

> I have claimed that Escape is one of the main functions of fairy-stories, and since I do not disapprove of them, it is plain that I do not accept the tone of scorn or pity with which "Escape" is now so often used: a tone for which the uses of the word outside literary criticism give no warrant at all. In what the misusers of Escape are fond of calling Real Life, Escape is evidently as a rule very practical, and may even be heroic.[2]

Note that Tolkien is not talking about escap*ism* or an avoidance of reality but rather the idea of escape as a means of providing a new view of reality, the true, transcendent reality that is often screened from our view in this fallen world. He adds:

> Evidently we are faced by a misuse of words, and also by a confusion of thought. Why should a man be scorned, if, finding himself in prison, he tries to get out and go home? Or if, when he cannot do

[2]J. R. R. Tolkien, "On Fairy-Stories," in *Tales from the Perilous Realm* (Houghton Mifflin, 2008), 375.

so, he thinks and talks about other topics than jailers and prison-walls? The world outside has not become less real because the prisoner cannot see it. In using Escape in this [derogatory] way the [literary] critics have chosen the wrong word, and, what is more, they are confusing, not always by sincere error, the Escape of the Prisoner with the Flight of the Deserter.[3]

I am not proposing that these lectures give us a way to escape from our responsibilities or ignore the needs of the world around us but rather that we explore the stories of the seven authors to escape from a distorted view of reality, from a sense of hopelessness, and to awaken us to the true hope of what God desires for us and promises to do for us.

C. S. Lewis offers a similar vision for the possibility that such literature could open our eyes to a new reality:

> We want to escape the illusions of perspective. . . . We want to see with other eyes, to imagine with other imaginations, to feel with other hearts, as well as with our own. . . .
>
> The man who is contented to be only himself, and therefore less a self, is in prison. My own eyes are not enough for me, I will see through those of others. . . .
>
> In reading great literature I become a thousand men yet remain myself. . . . Here as in worship, in love, in moral action, and in knowing, I transcend myself; and am never more myself than when I do.[4]

The purpose of the Hansen Lectureship is to explore the great literature of the seven Wade authors so that we can escape from the prison of our self-centeredness and narrow, parochial perspective in order to see with other eyes, feel with other hearts, and be equipped for practical deeds in real life.

---

[3]Tolkien, "On Fairy-Stories," 376.
[4]C. S. Lewis, *An Experiment in Criticism* (Cambridge University Press, 1965), 137, 140-41.

As a result, we will learn new ways to experience and extend the fulfillment of our Lord's mission: "to proclaim freedom for the prisoners and recovery of sight for the blind, to set the oppressed free" (Lk 4:18).

**Figure I.1.** Domenico di Michelino, *Dante, Florence and the Divine Comedy* (1465), Cathedral of Santa Maria del Fiore, Florence, Italy

# INTRODUCTION

"AND NOW," DOROTHY SAYERS confided to a friend in early July 1946, "I've got this lecture on Dante to write. What on earth made me say I'd do it?"[1] When I encountered Sayers's remark in fall 2023, I could relate. I was then teaching three courses, including one on Tolstoy and Dostoevsky, whose weekly page count was wearing even me down; working on multiple other writing projects, some with looming deadlines; nursing an Achilles injury that would soon require surgery; driving children hither and yon; cooking dinner for my equally beleaguered spouse; vacuuming occasionally; and in so many other ways feeling that there was far too much going on to allow me to deliver the ninth installment of the Ken and Jean Hansen Lectureship at the Marion E. Wade Center.

What had I been thinking when I pitched a three-part lecture series on Dante's influence? The previous Hansen lecturers had shown a wise frugality in their topics, discussing one or, at most, two of the seven writers whose books and papers are collected by the Wade. I, meanwhile, had made the prodigal proposal to examine how three Wade authors—Sayers and her friends Charles Williams and C. S. Lewis—gathered around Dante (whom I counted an honorary fourth). My worries were compounded by the fact that my archival labors revealed daily how thoroughly

---

[1] Quoted in Barbara Reynolds, *The Passionate Intellect: Dorothy L. Sayers' Encounter with Dante* (Kent State University Press, 1989), 98.

Dante had infiltrated my trio's reading and writing lives. Every visit to the Wade seemed to dredge up new material, which then inevitably hinted of other apposite artifacts lurking in the vault. As the date of the first lecture, in mid-January 2024, approached, I felt short on time and long—far too long—on bibliography.

I tracked down the lecture in question—an inquiry into Dante's craft as a storyteller through a close inspection of *Inferno* XXVI—and took heart from its evidence that Sayers survived her ordeal unscathed. In fact, the event was such a success that her hosts, the faculty of the Cambridge Society for Italian Studies' summer school, invited her to return the following year to deliver two more lectures. In them, she again took Dante as her subject ("Dante's Imagery: Symbolic" and "Dante's Imagery: Pictorial"). Flipping through Sayers's three published collections of critical writing on Dante, I discovered that the overwhelming majority of their contents had originally been invited talks.[2] In the span of nine years—concluding only with her death in 1957—she lectured on Dante publicly more than ten times and, as she would undoubtedly admit, did so privately on many more occasions. This connected her—it dawned on me—with my other two Wade authors. Months earlier, I had at great peril to my eyesight inched my way through the nearly indecipherable notes that Williams made for "lectures on Dante 1933–1941" (as the three folders in question are marked at the Wade). And Lewis had been long known to me as a lecturer on Dante by way of *The Discarded Image* (1964), originally a "course of lectures given more than once at Oxford" to bring students up to speed on the medieval model of the universe, and through his two talks to the Oxford Dante

---

[2]Those collections would be *Introductory Papers on Dante* (1954), *Further Papers on Dante* (1957), and the posthumously published *The Poetry of Search and the Poetry of Statement* (1963), the last of which, as the name suggests, mixes Sayers's addresses on Dante (or addresses on other topics that became Dante seminars) with topics such as the Faust legend and poetic language.

Society (which have long ranked among my favorite pieces of Dante criticism).[3]

Set against this background, the Hansen series now appeared a rite of passage. If my authors had lectured, so too must I lecture. And how much damage could I really do? My series would, after all, be gesturing back to true founts of wisdom—my three authors' writings on Dante and, beyond them, the wellspring, Dante himself. Whatever brambles I might place in my audience's path, the right road would remain in plain view.

Reviewing Sayers's lectures didn't just work on my courage, though. Her words also reminded me that this was going to be *fun*. Having taught the *Divine Comedy* (hereafter we'll do as Dante did and just call it the *Comedy*) for many years, I know that *fun* is not a word commonly associated with Dante—either the man or the reading thereof. Yet from her life-altering, total-immersion plunge into the *Comedy* in 1944 (see chapter two) until her dying day, Sayers insisted on it. "I was prepared to find him a GREAT POET, and of course a GREAT RELIGIOUS POET, all in solemn capital letters," Sayers reported to Williams in the wake of that momentous reading, "but I was not prepared to find him good company, and I was certainly not prepared to find myself continually saying with a chuckle, 'Dear, funny Dante!'"[4] To open the lecture "The Comedy of the Comedy" (1949), Sayers told her audience that she had toyed with the idea of inserting the sentence "George was curled up comfortably in the big arm-chair, chuckling over *The Divine Comedy*" into a story to test the degree of Dante snobbery in the land. "The game," she explained, "would be to see how many reviewers and correspondents could be lured into accusing me of gross illiteracy." She anticipated that high-minded readers would "solemnly [point] out that the work in question, so far from being

---

[3]C. S. Lewis, *The Discarded Image* (Cambridge University Press, 1964), vii.
[4]Dorothy L. Sayers to Charles Williams, September 14, 1944, in *LDS*, 3:77.

a humorous piece, was a Great Religious Poem, permeated from end to end by Awful Sublimity and unmitigated Grimth."[5]

Williams and Lewis, the Wade archive revealed, encouraged revolt against such false cultural pieties. After Sayers bombarded him with dispatches as she raced through the *Comedy*, Williams suggested that his employer, Oxford University Press, might publish them as a booklet under his editorial supervision. "I do very much want people," he implored her, "to get all you say about the laughter and lightness and fun—even—of Dante. We want to break up the hideous monstrosity of the catholic [*sic*] mystical poet which they envisage as part of their solemn culture."[6] Williams's words here betray his sense that calling Dante a "mystic" was a distraction from the real issue. In his 1943 study of Dante, *The Figure of Beatrice*, he writes in this vein:

> We do not know if [Dante] was a "mystic," nor is it our business; and the word, having been mentioned, may now be dismissed. The present point about the work of this great poet is that it refers us not to a rare human experience but to a common; or rather it begins with one that is common [namely, romantic love] and continues on a way which might be more common than it is.[7]

The "hideous monstrosity" is the false vision of Dante as a dealer in arcana, one whose experience has nothing to do with ours. In fact, the "way" Dante tread, Williams always stressed, is open to future travelers. (As I discuss in chapter five, Sayers came around to the idea of Dante as a particular sort of mystical poet by building on Williams's thought and, in acknowledgment of that debt, named Williams as a member of the same order.) Alas, Williams's death the following spring would doom their collaboration on a Dante booklet, yet Lewis immediately stepped in with an offer that

---

[5]Dorothy L. Sayers, "The Comedy of the Comedy," in *IPD*, 151.
[6]Quoted in *LDS*, 3:77. A facsimile is also available in DSP, folder 116.
[7]*FB*, 11.

allowed Sayers to disseminate key ideas from her correspondence with Williams (again, see chapter two).

Upon receiving her acceptance of that offer, Lewis applauded her suggestion that she write on the "narrative power" of the *Comedy*. Writing to Sayers on May 25, 1945 (only ten days after Williams's death), Lewis told her, "I am sure you've struck the right subject. And the learned need it more than anyone else for, as you must know yourself, the last thing they ever dream of noticing in a great narrative poem is the narrative."[8] Four days later, he added:

> The reason why they [the learned authorities] don't like either the narrative element or low comedy is that these have obvious immediate entertainment value. These prigs, starting from the true proposition that great art is more than entertainment reach the glaring *non sequitur* "entertainment has no place in great art"— like people who think music can't be "classical" if there is a catchy tune in it.[9]

The following year, Sayers would begin that first lecture on Dante referenced above by echoing Lewis's diagnosis of the learned prejudice against entertaining stories:

> *The Divine Comedy*—and let us not forget it—is a poem which tells a story. It is easy enough for superior persons to scorn the story-teller's art and patronize his unsophisticated audience. Story-telling (so they say, and I will not deny it) is a knack often possessed by very vulgar and illiterate writers; the eagerness to know what happened next is (no doubt) a mark of the eternal child in us all.

---

[8] C. S. Lewis to Dorothy L. Sayers, May 25, 1945, in *CLCSL*, 2:654.
[9] C. S. Lewis to Dorothy L. Sayers, May 29, 1945, in *CLCSL*, 2:657-58. This was a hallmark of Lewis's literary criticism. In his late work *An Experiment in Criticism*, he makes his case as follows: "If entertainment means light and playful pleasure, then I think it is exactly what we ought to get from some literary work—say, from a trifle by Prior or Martial. If it means those things which 'grip' the reader of popular romance—suspense, excitement and so forth—then I would say that every book should be entertaining. A good book will be more; it must not be less." C. S. Lewis, *An Experiment in Criticism* (Cambridge University Press, 1961), 91-92.

> Good story-telling often results—discreditably—in popularity
> and large sales, and is therefore a thing to be condemned by the
> high-minded; and it is all the more disconcerting to discover that
> good story-telling is one of the conditions of earthly immortality.[10]

Dante, Sayers goes on to declare, "is an incomparable story-teller,"
and as such, he may be enjoyed by anyone who appreciates a
well-told tale. No doctorate is required for admission to his art.
The medieval poet—who, we must recall, wrote his epic in the
local tongue of Tuscany rather than the international language
of learning, diplomacy, and culture, Latin—had intended to be
a popular author: "Dante wrote to be read by the common man
and woman, and to distribute the bread of angels among those
who had no leisure to be learned."[11] She dedicated years of her
life to the distribution of that bread, her lectures being spinoffs of
the main project: composing a translation of the *Comedy* that the
"common reader" (her phrase) could take up and read with delight.
As she worked, happily, to that end, Sayers had regular recourse to
Williams's work on Dante and repeated contact with Lewis—who
proved an at once admiring and critical reader in the best sense.

## A COHORT OF DANTE READERS

Early on, I envisioned my three writers as free agents working in
parallel. Accordingly, my game plan for the lectures had been to
reveal their respective, and separate (so I assumed), responses to a
favorite author through comparison and contrast. The inadequacy
of that scheme became obvious once I installed myself at the
Wade. I was surprised and more than a little amused to discover
that I had even underestimated the height of the pillar on which
they set Dante's bust. Williams called the Florentine "a genius
of the greatest power" and "the greatest European poet" (to

---

[10]Dorothy L. Sayers, "The Eighth Bolgia," in *FPD*, 102.
[11]Dorothy L. Sayers, introduction, in *IPD*, xiii.

which he added, parenthetically, "greatest as poet, not only as metaphysician").[12] Lewis named Dante among the "candidates for the supreme poetical honors of the world" in 1936, and then, four years later, clarified, "I think Dante's poetry on the whole the greatest poetry I have read"—ranking Dante above Homer, which even Dante hadn't done.[13] Sayers, not to be outdone, called Dante a "universal poet, speaking prophetically of God and the Soul and the Society of Men in their universal relations."[14] Moreover, Dante appeared to her not just (as we have heard) *an* "incomparable" storyteller but *"the most* incomparable story-teller who ever set pen to paper."[15]

Once I dug beneath the bibliographical topsoil of my trio's best-known titles, once I was reading their private correspondence, minor works, and footnotes, I saw that they crisscrossed over Dante to a far greater degree than I had imagined. Across a range of documents and years, I witnessed how they motivated each other to read (or revisit) Dante; how they studied and at times critiqued each other's stances on and, in Sayers's case, renderings of Dante; how they quoted each other's remarks on Dante; and how they promoted each other's Dantean endeavors in public addresses and print publications. Simple comparison and contrast wouldn't suffice under these conditions. The archive had not presented me with three parallel processes; it was handing over a dense clump of relations.

As my first Hansen lecture closed in on me, and the stacks of archival materials looming over me reached fearful heights, I

---

[12]*HCDH*, 90, 106.

[13]C. S. Lewis, *The Allegory of Love: A Study of Medieval Tradition* (Oxford University Press, 1936), 155; Lewis, "Dante's Similes," in *Studies in Medieval and Renaissance Literature*, ed. Walter Hooper (Cambridge University Press, 1966), 76.

[14]Dorothy L. Sayers, introduction, in *The Divine Comedy 1: Hell*, trans. Sayers (Penguin, 1949), 10.

[15]ATYS, 2, italics added.

realized that the problem facing me—the dizzying number of Dantean connections between them that I had turned up—was in fact the solution. At the Wade, I stumbled upon the chief historical claim of this book: that *Sayers, Williams, and Lewis must be understood as a cohort of Dante readers whose invocations of Dante—public and private, conspicuous and covert—comprise a network of allusions, quotations, and citations.* Now, in calling them a cohort, let me stress at the outset that I do not mean to suggest that they always thought the same way about Dante. They did not. In fact, they broke on some major issues (as subsequent chapters will detail). Yet differences of opinion were surely a feature rather than a bug in these exchanges. The three benefited, moreover, from each party's distinct fascinations with Dante's work—Sayers, once again, with Dante's gifts for narrative and humor, Lewis with Dante's cosmos and the improbably pleasurable linguistic brew he concocted to describe it, and Williams with Dante's portrayal of romantic love's religious potential and the thickness of the poet's allegory. Shared reverence for Dante enriched my trio's friendships; disagreements and distinct angles on Dante kept their conversations interesting.

## A CHAPTER IN THE *COMEDY*'S BIOGRAPHY

Over the last few decades, and especially of late, humanities scholars have dedicated themselves to recording the biographies of books, or even particular copies of books, as well as in readers' lives in books. Unsurprisingly, Dante's literary legacy has received this kind of attention—with Joseph Luzzi's recent *Dante's Divine Comedy: A Biography* serving as a compact case in point. *The Way of Dante* argues that the Sayers-Williams-Lewis cohort's activities represent a notable chapter of that biography. To put it another way, this book doesn't just present the subject of Dante as a window into my trio's thinking and relationships; it also proposes that my trio's writings teach us important lessons about the *Comedy*. Sayers, Williams, and Lewis matter as Dante critics, I am arguing. Their "chapter" in the *Comedy*'s reception history is notable in three respects: the audiences, the vehicles, and the fullness of their Dantean ventures. The remainder of this introduction sets up these themes of the book, followed by a brief outline of the chapters ahead.

To explain the first, Luzzi's chapter on the generation under consideration here is helpful. Luzzi focuses on a different set of Dante enthusiasts—modernists T. S. Eliot, W. B. Yeats, James Joyce, Ezra Pound, and company. These writers were my trio's contemporaries, and their paths occasionally overlapped (all three knew Eliot, for example, Williams making an especially strong impression on him). Yet Luzzi's portrait of the modernist Dante presents a striking contrast to Sayers's, Williams's, and Lewis's dealings with the Florentine poet. All extolled Dante—but for very different reasons.

Tellingly, the modernists made a habit of pasting bits of Dante into their work without translation or reference. A well-known example (cited by Luzzi) is the block of Italian verses—sans attribution—sitting in the epigraph of Eliot's "The Love Song of J. Alfred Prufrock." Eliot expects you to recognize them (or maybe he doesn't?) as the words of the false counselor Guido da Montefeltro in *Inferno* XXVII. In the lines Eliot quotes, Guido consents to speak with Dante based on his belief that no one gets out of hell. Very inviting! Reflecting on Eliot's move, Luzzi observes, "Unlike the Romantics, who aimed at emotional authenticity and affective connection with their readers, Eliot and his fellow Modernists wished to separate sophisticated literary production from mainstream cultural consumption."[16] "Difficulty and complexity," he continues, "were the aesthetic buzzwords of the Modernist

---

[16]Joseph Luzzi, *Dante's Divine Comedy: A Biography* (Princeton University Press, 2024), 126.

movement, pushing its adherents to chart new artistic ground even if the output risked lapsing into the opaque and unintelligible." Dante was an inspiration for the modernists because his poetics were experimental, his meanings obscure. He too was difficult.

This book argues that Sayers, Williams, and Lewis were working in the opposite direction. While Williams and Lewis were members of the Oxford Dante Society, and Sayers had occasion to talk shop with the *dantisti* (as serious Dante scholars are called), they did not, for the most part, address their writing to Dante insiders. Rather, they endeavored to bring readers, auditors, students *into* Dante's poem, Dante's mentality, Dante's cosmos. They were in the business of making Dante available to newcomers. That project had its own difficulties, as Sayers pointed out on several occasions. Nowhere was she more candid than her 1954 address to a group of educators, "On Translating the *Divina Commedia.*" The target audience of her translation, she explained, consisted of people who were certainly literate but not "(in the old sense of the word) educated"—as in not steeped in the Greco-Roman classics and their medieval and early modern respondents. This vast "new reading public" included "boys and girls in the upper forms," "university students of all types," and "the intelligent suburban housewife and office-worker who snatch their culture at odd moments." The task of the Dante translator was no doubt daunting:

> Somehow we have to capture this elusive and ill-prepared "common reader," and persuade him or her to embark on a 14,000 line poem by a writer six hundred years dead, of whom all that is generally known is that he has a great reputation for obscurity, believed that the sun went round the earth, and took a vindictive delight in describing the torments of a physical Hell in which no enlightened person believes.[17]

---

[17]Dorothy L. Sayers, "On Translating the *Divina Commedia*," in *PSPS*, 94.

Sayers goes on to suggest various stratagems—beginning with "write readable English"—to help the common reader to overcome his or her (and the *her* mattered very much to Sayers) apprehensions and pick up the poem. Sayers trusted that Dante—that "incomparable" storyteller and singer—would take it from there.

Williams and Lewis wrote about, gestured toward, and slyly passed Dante over to the "common reader," too. My trio's Dantean enterprises were largely directed at nonspecialists (such as the public lectures noted earlier), and their adaptations of Dante's ideas, characters, and locales took, for the most part, popular forms (such as the thriller and science fiction). Reading *un*translated bits of Dante in modernist poetry made such readers feel the distance between themselves and Dante. My cohort sought to bridge that distance.[18] This book argues, therefore, that Sayers, Williams, and Lewis were each, after their own fashion, translators of Dante to their generation.

## A FEW WORDS ON DIFFICULTY

This is not to say that my writers were never themselves difficult. The complaint has often been made about Williams's writing, and this issue must be dealt with up front since it will come up in the chapters ahead. Lewis in fact called Williams on it publicly and privately, and his perspective is illuminating. His 1939 review of *Taliessin Through Logres*, Williams's collection of *modern* Arthurian poetry, begins on exactly this note: "The only reason for reading a difficult poem is some assurance that it contains goodness great enough to outweigh the evil of its difficulty."[19] Lewis then engages in cost-benefit analysis to show that the good of the book

---

[18]To be fair to Eliot, he made efforts of his own in this respect, earning him a few cameo appearances in subsequent chapters.

[19]C. S. Lewis, "A Sacred Poem," review of *Taliessin Through Logres*, by Charles Williams, *Theology* 38 (1939): 268.

does outweigh its evils.[20] Those evils include traits that Lewis associated with modernist poetry—obscurity, harshness, "talk of jakes and latrines." Yet Lewis argues that Williams's difficulty is in the service of something different than the modernist variety, and so warns against "modernist misunderstanding" of Williams's work: "He has got all necessary 'disillusionment' over before the poem begins," Lewis asserts, "so that no more can be said on that well-worn theme, and we can proceed at once to something positive." Lewis goes on to list several positives: "We find throughout [Williams's poems] an understanding of health, of discipline, and (above all) of courtesy, which are rare at the present time. No poem expresses more charity or less indulgence. But perhaps its greatest gift to us is what I have called the quality of Glory."[21]

To read Williams is thus to be *brought to life*, and, as that last phrase suggests, to be put in touch with something higher. Reviewing the posthumous edition of *Taliessin Through Logres* in 1946, Lewis uses Eliot as a foil:

> In reading Mr Eliot one seems to be listening to a voice that is always on the point of dying away—no poetry can more powerfully convey the sense of stillness, hushed expectancy, vacancy, death. In Williams, on the other hand, we are conscious of soaring energy, as if huge masses were being hurled to great heights, or as if we ourselves were being repeatedly flung up (into sunlight) on the crests of waves.[22]

---

[20]Lewis argues that the "greatest" of the collection's difficulties is actually "the most legitimate": its symbolism. He then explains the nature of that symbolism—essentially, an experience that gradually accrues multiple associations—by way of a contrast with allegory, that is, one-to-one correlation between image and concept, which rehashes a distinction he had made in *The Allegory of Love* (Lewis, "Sacred Poem," 270). I consider these matters at length in chapter 3.

[21]Lewis, "Sacred Poem," 275.

[22]C. S. Lewis, review of *Taliessin Through Logres*, by Charles Williams, *Oxford Magazine* 64 (1946): 248.

The effect reminded Lewis of Dante. Reflecting on Williams's Arthurian poetry after his death, Lewis argued that it was identifiable as "the work of a man who has learned much from Dante (the Dante of the *Paradiso*)."[23] As subsequent chapters will make clear, this was a very high compliment indeed. Lewis kept coming back to *Paradiso*, fascinated by its seemingly impossible "mixture of intense, even crabbed, complexity of language and thought with . . . *at the very same time* a feeling of spacious gliding movement, like a slow dance, or like flying."[24] Difficulty—whether in Williams or Dante—was worth it if the reader took flight. In 1939, Lewis's review announced the connection right away. "A Sacred Poem," Lewis titled the piece, alluding to Dante's famous characterization of the *Comedy* as *il poema sacro* in *Paradiso* XXV.

## DANTE DIFFUSION

The second notable feature of my trio's approach to Dante was recognized by Sayers in relation to Williams specifically. In her 1955 lecture "Charles Williams: A Poet's Critic" (note the date: ten years after Williams's death), Sayers posited that "All [Williams's] books illuminate one another, for the same master-themes govern them all, so that it is impossible to confine any one theme to a single book."[25] She then used the example of Williams's boundary-blurring "commentary" on Dante:

> For example, his most impressive commentary on Dante's dream of the Siren is to be found, not in *The Figure of Beatrice*, but in those chapters of *Descent into Hell* which deal with Mrs. Sammile and the Succubus; and to read that novel with the chapters on the *Inferno* is to enrich one's understanding of the whole conception

---

[23]C. S. Lewis, preface, in *Essays Presented to Charles Williams* (Oxford University Press, 1947), vii.

[24]C. S. Lewis to Arthur Greeves, January 13, 1930, in *CLCSL*, 1:875, italics original.

[25]Dorothy L. Sayers, "Charles Williams: A Poet's Critic," in *PSPS*, 74.

of Hell, both in Williams and in Dante. The mystical theology of
the Affirmative Way needs to be studied in *The Place of the Lion*
and in the *Taliessin* poems, and its imaginative treatment there
compared with its more formal exposition in the Dante volume.[26]

Many of the topics mentioned here—the Affirmative Way, the
two novels, the *Taliessin* poems—will reappear later in this book.
My concern now is Sayers's overarching claim: that Williams's
criticism of Dante and his fictional and poetic reworkings of and
reactions to Dante bleed into each other. To grasp what Williams
made of Dante, and Dante of Williams, we must—Sayers advises
us—be prepared to scuttle between the poetry, the fiction, and the
criticism shelves in the library. We also need to read his lectures, his
notebooks, his letters. Dante is all over the place. Moreover, Sayers
goes on to point out, Williams put Dante in conversation with not
just the usual suspects (Virgil, Ovid, Aristotle, Aquinas, the Bible)
but also later writers such as William Wordsworth, Samuel Taylor
Coleridge, George Benard Shaw, Coventry Patmore, George Fox,
John Keats, Søren Kirkegaard, Robert Browning, Alfred Lord
Tennyson, Gerard Manley Hopkins, and so on. Williams, Sayers
argues, "[breaks] down Dante's isolation and [treats] him quite
freely as a poet among other poets. I do not think that this had ever
been done for Dante in quite the same way before."[27] We must be
ready to encounter Dante at any time while reading Williams, and
to find the medieval poet discoursing productively with anyone
and everyone Williams had read.

I make the same claims on Sayers's and Lewis's behalf. Some of
their sharpest critical insights on Dante appear in creative works
and private missives, and their critical writing shows the same
ecumenism concerning Dante's conversation partners. In *A Preface
to Paradise Lost* (1942), for example, Lewis argues that Dante may

---

[26]Sayers, "Charles Williams: A Poet's Critic," 74-75.
[27]Sayers, "Charles Williams: A Poet's Critic," 80.

be "in one capacity" the companion of the poets Homer, Virgil, and Wordsworth (Wordsworth's inclusion on that list suggesting the influence of the book's dedicatee, Williams).[28] On the other hand, Lewis continues, Dante is "the father" of science fiction writers Jules Verne and H. G. Wells—and, we may add, the author of the Space Trilogy. I have suggested that we must zip around my trio's Dante writing network. Now I am proposing that we must also range freely *within* each author's oeuvre to understand the fullness of their encounters with Dante.

## THE FULLNESS OF DANTE

That word *fullness* requires a bit of parsing, for the way in which I am using it clarifies what this book does and does not offer. *Fullness* here does not mean "totality." A complete concordance of Dante references in Sayers's, Williams's, and Lewis's works would be thicker than the book you are holding and would interest only a handful of die-hards. In fact, exhaustive coverage of Dante's influence on even one of my three authors would require a weighty tome, as the book-length studies of Sayers's later-in-life "encounter with Dante," the influence of the *Comedy* on Lewis's novels, and Lewis's "medieval mind" (in which Dante factors prominently) show.[29] Thus, this book bears witness to the breadth of Sayers's, Williams's, and Lewis's interactions with Dante, but it is far from comprehensive.

The sense of fullness that concerns us here is the one Lewis invokes in his autobiography *Surprised by Joy* (1955) when he writes of recalling "a place and time at which I had tasted the lost Joy with unusual fullness." Lewis is speaking of the *experience* of

---

[28]C. S. Lewis, *A Preface to Paradise Lost* (Oxford University Press, 1942), 111.

[29]Those studies would be Reynolds's *Passionate Intellect* (1989), Marsha Daigle-Williamson's *Reflecting the Eternal: Dante's Divine Comedy in the Novels of C. S. Lewis* (Hendrickson Academic, 2015), and Jason Baxter's *The Medieval Mind of C. S. Lewis: How Great Books Shaped a Great Mind* (IVP Academic, 2022).

fullness—of having one's heart, senses, or even whole being filled to capacity. The scene in question offers helpful exposition of this experience. Walking over hills on a misty morning, eagerly awaiting the delights stored in new volumes of Richard Wagner's *Der Ring des Nibelungen* that he had received as Christmas presents, awash in sensations ("the coldness and loneliness of the hillside, the drops of moisture on every branch, and the distant murmur of the concealed town"), Lewis felt "a longing (yet it was also fruition) which had flowed over from the mind and seemed to involve the whole body."[30] This "joy" (as Lewis described the longing) was a paradoxically satisfying unsatisfaction—a desire that is desirable for itself and yet also beckons beyond itself. Ultimately, it beckoned Lewis beyond the world.

That is the sort of fullness my trio experienced when reading Dante. The *Comedy* was the ultimate readerly satisfaction. "I should describe [*Paradiso*] as feeling more *important* than any poetry I have ever read," Lewis told Arthur Greeves in early 1930. Williams and Sayers would have concurred.[31] And yet, though Dante filled their hearts and minds to capacity, they knew that the *Comedy* was only a way station on a journey whose end the poem itself dared to depict: paradise. "What the blissful know," Sayers explained to the audience of her lecture "The Meaning of Heaven and Hell" (1948), "is Reality, the ultimate reality of every good thing that they have imagined, filling them through and through with itself—and inexhaustible."[32] The *Comedy* was at once at a poetic feast and a mouthwatering foretaste of the real paradise, and Sayers, Williams, and Lewis read it with every expectation of meeting Dante there.

Now, those last statements must be qualified immediately, lest I appear to be reinstating the false idol that Sayers toiled to cast

---

[30]C. S. Lewis, *Surprised by Joy* (Geoffrey Bles, 1955), 158.
[31]Lewis to Greeves, January 13, 1930.
[32]Dorothy L. Sayers, "The Meaning of Heaven and Hell," in *IPD*, 54.

down—the *Comedy*, once again, as a "Great Religious Poem permeated from end to end by Awful Sublimity and unmitigated Grimth." It *is* a Great Religious Poem, all three members of my cohort agreed. (In *A Preface to Paradise Lost*, Lewis says so directly: "The *Comedy* is a religious poem"; and his reasoning is sound: It is "a poetical expression of religious experience."[33]) It is often sublime. It has its moments of "grimth" (a word of Sayers's coinage).[34] In the first volume of her translation—*Hell* (1949)—Sayers admits it: "Dante is sublime, intellectual, and, on occasion, grim," and "we need not forget" it.[35] Yet, she continues, "we must also be prepared to find him simple, homely, humorous, tender, and bubbling over with ecstasy." In the same section, she characterizes the *Comedy* first as "the record of an intimate personal experience" (as was "every line he wrote," Sayers believed) and then as "a great Christian allegory." It contains multitudes.

Each of my authors testified memorably to its multiplicity. In *The Discarded Image*, Lewis names the *Comedy*—alongside Thomas Aquinas's *Summa Theologiae*—as a supreme illustration of the medieval effort to "[bring] huge masses of heterogenous material into unity."[36] The *Comedy* is, he argues, as "unified and ordered as the Parthenon or the *Oedipus Rex*, as crowded and varied as a London terminus on a bank holiday." Responding to fan mail on her *Hell*, Sayers remarks that the medievals didn't

---

[33]Lewis, *Preface to Paradise Lost*, 128.

[34]She appears to have first deployed *grimth* in *The Documents in the Case* (1931), a detective novel cowritten with Robert Eustace: "We saw the New Year in with dancing and the usual imbecile festivities. Mrs. H. thanked me with tears of excitement in her eyes—it was pathetic—like giving sweets to a kid. Even H. was a little moved from his usual grimth." But the word became strongly attached to Dante—or at least other people's visions of Dante: "Something has *got* to be done about the legend of Dante's grimth!" she wrote to Barbara Reynolds in 1947. "The legend is so universal that when I first read the *Comedy* I couldn't believe my eyes, and began to wonder whether it was my ignorance of Italian that made me find things funny which were really not meant to be." Dorothy L. Sayers to Barbara Reynolds, October 16, 1947, in *LDS*, 3:332.

[35]Sayers, introduction, in *Divine Comedy 1: Hell*, 10.

[36]Lewis, *Discarded Image*, 10.

"pigeon-hole" as moderns do; they "mixed their intellect, feelings, philosophy, romance, politics, science and religious beliefs, oratory, small-talk, and contemporary gossip into one magnificent and variegated Christmas pudding."[37] Dante's gift, in turn, was to "combine all that vast array of ingredients into anything so simultaneously light, rich, and palatable." In *He Came Down from Heaven* (1938), Williams riffs on the Latin maxim *quot homines tot sententiae*—"there are as many opinions as there are people"—to attest to Dante's thematic range: *tot homini quot Dantes*—there are as many Dantes as there are humans.[38]

The Parthenon, the bustling railway station, the Christmas pudding, the everyman figure: The *Comedy* offers all of these things at once. There is much to inspire awe and dread in it, as my cohort's writings testify, but it is also an entertaining story featuring memorable characters, snappy dialogue, and brilliant word painting. Here learned allusion rubs elbows with vulgarity. Dante arranges meetings for himself with such grandees as Homer, Justinian, Saint Peter, and Adam (the first man) as well as the subjects of local scandal, infamous malefactors, and his buddies Casella and Belacqua. He walks with devils (tremulously), receives the searing care of angels, and gains temporary admission to the assembly of the blessed. My trio's works acknowledge this immense variety of moving pictures, encounters, and tones that Dante incorporated into his *Comedy* and grant readers license to do with the poem as they had done: to wonder at it, of course, but also to puzzle over its layers and secrets, to delight in its imagery and music, even to chuckle at its humor. (Perhaps Sayers chuckled a bit too much at times, Lewis thought.)

In *An Experiment in Criticism*, Lewis makes a pertinent distinction between "receiving" and "using" a work of art. When

---

[37]Dorothy L. Sayers to Richard Church, April 3, 1950, in *LDS*, 3:498.
[38]*HCDH*, 67.

we receive a work, he argues, "we exert our senses and imagination and various other powers according to a pattern invented by the artist," while when "using" art "we treat it as assistance for our own activities." He likens the user to one who adds a motor to a bicycle and then speeds along a familiar route. The person who receives a work of art, by contrast, is like one who is "taken for a bicycle ride by a man who may know roads we have never yet explored."[39] Dante was, and is, such a guide. He leads readers through the three realms of the afterlife, reporting firsthand on the deepest depths of depravity and the highest heights of ecstasy. To recall one of Lewis's most famous formulations from the same book, the *Comedy* offers "an enlargement of our being" to those who join Dante on the way.[40]

Sayers, Williams, and Lewis held grand receptions for Dante in their works. They strove to clear away hurdles (to borrow an image from Sayers) that might prevent their contemporaries from making the journey.[41] The members of my trio were convinced that powerful things could go on once readers—whether religious or irreligious at the outset—got inside Dante's cosmos because powerful things had happened to them there. They had been quickened by the *Comedy*.[42] Their labors were animated by the wish that others would encounter the *Comedy*'s beauties, sublimities, shock, peace, wit, wisdom—in a word, its fullness. Reading Dante just might change your life. It changed theirs.

---

[39]Lewis, *Experiment in Criticism*, 88.

[40]Lewis, *Experiment in Criticism*, 137.

[41]Sayers, introduction, in *IPD*, xviii.

[42]I borrow the word *quicken* from the passage in *A Preface to Paradise Lost* in which Lewis acknowledges that "in some very important ways" *Paradise Lost* is *not* "a religious poem" (unlike the *Comedy*, as we have seen). "If a Christian reader has found his devotion quickened by reading the medieval hymns or Dante or Herbert or Traherne, or even by Patmore or Cowper," Lewis writes, "and then turns to Paradise Lost, he will be disappointed." Lewis was, of course, speaking to his own experience being an avowed lover of medieval hymns, the poetry of Dante and George Herbert, and Thomas Traherne's prose.

## THE PLAN OF THE BOOK

My title phrase, *The Way of Dante*, is borrowed from Williams, who used it to describe both Dante's spiritual and artistic journey and the spiritual and artistic opportunities that the poet opens up for readers. Williams was himself borrowing language from Dante. Across his career, Dante often invoked the image of the "way"—his terms are *via* and *cammino* (or *cammin*). The most familiar instance appears in the opening line of *Inferno*: *Nel mezzo del cammin di nostra vita*, literally, "In the middle of the way/road/journey of our life." Sayers rendered it thusly for emphasis: "Midway this way of life we're bound upon."[43] Dante is putting his own allegorical spin on the familiar metaphor of life as a journey. "Midway" on the journey we all make, he is called to undertake another, the way narrated in the *Comedy*, in order to see where our journeys may terminate. That is the way that famously begins in a dark wood, circles down to the bottom of hell, circles up the terraces of Mount Purgatory, and ascends through the celestial spheres, before terminating in a house call on God in the Empyrean.[44]

These two Dantean ways—that of following Dante in one's own journey through life and that of following Dante through the *Comedy*—give this book its shape. In the ensuing chapters, I trace

---

[43]Sayers, *Divine Comedy 1: Hell*, 71.

[44]Dante enlists the language of the "way" throughout the *Comedy*. At the beginning of *Inferno*, Dante, having awoken in the infamous dark wood, struggles up a hill, his progress impeded by strange beasts. At this point, his way is "high and wild" (*alto e silvestro*, II.142). He then descends into hell in the company of the shade of the Roman poet Virgil, a course he calls "a long way and an evil path" (*la via è lunga e 'l cammino è malvagio*, XXXIV.95). As Dante and Virgil wind their way up the mountain in *Purgatorio*, the path is recast as "our sacred way" (*nostro cammin santo*, XX.142), which is to say it more obviously appears as the *pilgrimage* it has been from the first. Now penitential exertions bring spiritual benefits. In *Paradiso*, Dante is guided by Beatrice through the planetary spheres. At last, he arrives at the Empyrean, where the blessed behold God directly. That terminus his last guide, Bernard of Clairvaux, rightly names the "perfect consummation" of his arduous *cammino* (*Acciò che tu assommi / perfettamente . . . il tuo cammino*, XXXI.94-95). The way of Dante is in this sense an unforgettable travelogue, as Williams, Sayers, and Lewis all reported in their Dante criticism.

the two ways in alternating movements. The first—appearing in chapters one, two, four, and six—examines Sayers's, Williams's, and Lewis's interrelations as readers of Dante, professional critics of Dante, and creative writers responding to Dante. The second—appearing in chapters three, five, and seven—plots a course through the *Comedy* under my trio's supervision. Along the way, we will see Sayers, Williams, and Lewis swapping Dante allusions, disagreeing about how to use the word *allegory*, and learning some tricks from Dante about how to depict glorified bodies ("Beatrician encounters," Williams dubbed them). They will teach us about the parallels between Dante's hell and modern life, the Way of the Affirmation of Images (Williams's term), and strategies to make glory and holiness attractive to modern readers (the "problem of glory," as I'm designating it), among many other things.

That brings us to the matter of this book's audience. *The Way of Dante* is, first and foremost, a work of literary criticism. It has much to offer those interested in my *quartet* of authors—Sayers, Williams, Lewis, and their cicerone, Dante. At the same time, this book is a study of issues that artists have always wrestled with, including the spiritual dimensions of the creative process, the transmission of images over time and their revivification in new contexts, fellowship with one's contemporary artists, and commerce with the dead. For this reason, each of my Hansen lectures was followed by an artist's response, whether a performance, a meditation, or a mixture of both. The book ends on this note. In the afterword, novelist and contemplative Nicole Mazzarella traces the way of the artist through the terraces of *Purgatorio*. She translates the passage up Dante's mountain of "reconciliation and recollection" (as Williams calls it) into a liturgy for makers. Mazzarella homes in on a figural reference point of all the terraces—Mary, that unique bearer of the divine image (as

Sayers would point out)—and raises questions for contemplation. This is, admittedly, an unorthodox sendoff for an academic study. But a liturgical finale affirms my trio's convictions that the *Comedy* has lost none of its power to speak to the soul and that, with a little help, modern pilgrims can find their footing on the way of Dante.

# ABBREVIATIONS

ATYS    Sayers, Dorothy L. ". . . And Telling You a Story." In *Essays Presented to Charles Williams*. Oxford University Press, 1947.

CLCSL   Lewis, C. S. *The Collected Letters of C. S. Lewis*. Edited by Walter Hooper. HarperCollins, 2004

DSP     Dorothy L. Sayers Papers. Marion E. Wade Center. Wheaton College, Wheaton, IL.

FB      Williams, Charles. *The Figure of Beatrice: A Study in Dante*. Faber & Faber, 1943.

FPD     Sayers, Dorothy L. *Further Papers on Dante*. Methuen, 1957.

HCDH    Williams, Charles. *He Came Down from Heaven*. Heinemann, 1938.

IPD     Sayers, Dorothy L. *Introductory Papers on Dante*. Methuen, 1954.

LDS     Sayers, Dorothy L. *The Letters of Dorothy L. Sayers*. 5 vols. Edited by Barbara Reynolds. Dorothy Sayers Society, 1995–2002.

PSPS    Sayers, Dorothy L. *The Poetry of Search and the Poetry of Statement*. Victor Gollancz, 1963.

**Figure 1.1.** Illustration for Canto 1, Dante Alighieri, *La Commedia* (Venice, 1491)

# 1

## THREE PREHISTORIES

"THE ENJOYMENT OF THE *DIVINE COMEDY* is a continuous process," T. S. Eliot declares in his 1929 monograph *Dante*. "If you get nothing out of it at first, you probably never will; but if from your first deciphering of it there comes now and then some direct shock of poetic intensity, nothing but laziness can deaden the desire for fuller and fuller knowledge."[1] That Eliot had uttered a fine sentiment, all three of my authors would surely have agreed. They each felt that "direct shock of poetic intensity" while reading the *Comedy*, and that experience indeed inspired in them "the desire for fuller and fuller knowledge" of the poem.

Unsurprisingly, Sayers had her own, more colorful, way of putting it. "The trouble with Dante," she told her friend James Welch, the BBC's director of religious broadcasting, "is that, if one gets a taste for him, one is liable to become a Dante-addict." She playfully continued: "He acts like a drug—or rather, like an attack of rabies; the people who are bitten rush madly about biting all their friends. Beware of him. If you once come under the spell he will haunt your imagination, lay violent hands on your theology, intrude into your sermons, and seep through your most casual conversation like a dye."[2] I cite Sayers's description of Dante mania not only for its color; the date is also notable. She wrote these words in 1946, less

---

[1]T. S. Eliot, *Dante* (Faber & Faber, 1929), 16.
[2]Dorothy L. Sayers to James Welch, July 25, 1946, in *LDS*, 3:249.

than two years after she had come under Dante's spell at the age of fifty-one. As I will discuss below, there is every reason to believe she had made contact with Dante before, likely several times, but had not previously felt the "shock of poetic intensity." The enjoyment of the *Comedy*, Sayers's experience teaches us, may be a *dis*continuous process. Or perhaps the continuous part—the seeping of Dante into one's bloodstream—may begin only after multiple exposures. The reading life is rarely so neat as the stories we like to tell about it.

Therein lies the chief lesson of this chapter: Varied are the on-ramps, some longer and bumpier than others, to the way of Dante. The stories of how Sayers, Williams, and Lewis made Dante's acquaintance involve different timelines, contexts, and life stages, and those stories provide helpful framing for my trio's respective responses to Dante on display throughout this book. After examining the prehistories of their experiences with Dante before they met on the path in this chapter, I turn in the next to their convergence on the way.

## SAYERS: THE LONG WAY

Reviewing Williams's *The Figure of Beatrice* shortly after the book's release in 1943, critic Desmond MacCarthy named Dante among the greats with whom "we become acquainted" without reading directly, "so numerous are the channels through which their spirit seeps into the minds of men."[3] To this Sayers would add—the minds of *women*, too. In her 1955 address "On Translating the *Divina Commedia*," Sayers recalled that in the last decades of the nineteenth century "all decently educated" middle- and upper-class Britons "could be counted on to take an intelligent interest in Dante, or at least not look perfectly blank at the mention of his name." Thus, most houses in the social world into which she was born held copies of the *Comedy* (in Italian or English translation), "very often handsomely illustrated"

---

[3]Quoted in Barbara Reynolds, *The Passionate Intellect: Dorothy L. Sayers' Encounter with Dante* (Kent State University Press, 1989), 18.

with the "refined" engravings of John Flaxman or the "theatrical" ones of Gustav Doré. Yet even at that point, Sayers informed her audience, the "cultural swing-over from Italian to German had begun, and by the date of my own schooldays it was complete." "We had all heard of Dante;" she continued, "but we read Goethe and Schiller."[4]

In her first report to Williams on her rapid march through *Comedy* (she had at that point just escaped *Inferno* and begun her ascent of *Purgatorio*) in mid-August 1944, Sayers hinted that she had made previous attempts to read the poem but hadn't taken to it.[5] One month later, having completed the epic, Sayers further revealed that her prior acquaintance with Dante had come "from quotations and allusions in books of general literature and religious essays and so on—the sort of thing one comes across in the course of reading at large about this and that." She had received by osmosis "some of the set pieces," such as the doomed lovers Paolo and Francesca from *Inferno* V (a subject popular among nineteenth-century artists), and catchphrases, including *Vergine madre, figlia del tuo figlio* ("Virgin mother, daughter of your Son" [*Paradiso* XXXIII.1]). She was aware of "the tortures and the demons, and the politics, and the boiled popes."[6] In other words, Sayers knew *some* Dante in the way many readers do—as a matter of general cultural literacy.

These admissions to Williams help to explain Dante's presence in her writing prior to 1944. His first appearance in Sayers's oeuvre occurs in fact in her debut novel, the mystery *Whose Body?* (1922), in which her gentleman detective Lord Peter Wimsey is presented as a collector of early printed editions of Dante.[7] In *The Mind of the Maker*

---

[4]Dorothy L. Sayers, "On Translating the *Divina Commedia*," in *PSPS*, 93.

[5]Sayers explains that she had in her possession an edition in which the Italian faces an English crib on the opposite page and that, as Reynolds explains in a note, she "had previously dipped into this edition but had not had the resolve to persevere either with the Italian or the translation." Dorothy L. Sayers to Charles Williams, August 16-17, 1944, in *LDS*, 3:45-47.

[6]Sayers to Williams, August 16-17, 1944, in *LDS*, 3:76.

[7]The rare books in question likely caught her attention when they were displayed two years earlier during London's celebrations of the sixth centenary of Dante's death. For a detailed

(1941), to cite another Dante cameo, she quotes the *Comedy* in Italian to illustrate that unlike "mechanical inventions and scientific formula," new works of art do not necessarily supersede the old, juxtaposing Eliot's line "you who were with me in the ships at Mylae" from *The Waste Land* (1922) with Piccarda Donati's phrase in *Paradiso* III, *en la sua voluntade è nostra pace* ("and His will is our peace" [III.85]), one of Dante's best-known sound bites.[8] This was not a harsh burn on Eliot, mind you; he would have heartily agreed with Sayers's ensuing argument that "the later in date leaves the earlier achievement unconquered and unchanged." The comedy of the situation is that Eliot *had* read Dante thoroughly, while Sayers had not.[9]

With her characteristic good humor, Sayers could laugh at herself about this incongruence. In that first report to Williams on the *Comedy*, Sayers disclosed that the immediate stimulus to making a serious go at it was a moment of embarrassment. Having read Williams's *The Figure of Beatrice* (1943) and Lewis's *A Preface to Paradise Lost* (1942), and "re-read the greater portion" of *Paradise Lost* as a result of the latter, she "cheerfully remarked to a friend that Milton was a thunderingly great writer of religious epic, provided it did not occur to you to compare him with Dante." Her friend, however, confessed that she had never read Dante, and this disarmed Sayers: "I then became aware that I had never read Dante either, but only quoted bits of him and looked at Doré's illustrations to the *Inferno*. It then came to my mind that perhaps I had better read Dante, or else I might find myself condemned to toddle around for ever among the Hypocrites."[10]

---

discussion of the event and the books that Sayers references, see Barbara Reynolds's chapter "A Mind Prepared," in *Passionate Intellect*.

[8]Dorothy L. Sayers, *The Mind of the Maker* (Methuen, 1941), 33.

[9]In fact, Sayers had very likely come across the words from *Paradiso* that she quotes here while reading Eliot, who cites them on several occasions in his creative and critical writing. In his *Dante* monograph, which she read in late 1947 or early 1948, he references them as "words which even those who know no Dante know" (*Dante*, 52).

[10]Sayers to Williams, August 16-17, 1944, in *LDS*, 3:45.

Admittedly, there's something suspicious about Sayers's claim that she wanted to avoid a punishment that shows up thousands of lines into a poem she hadn't yet read. But the embellishment, if it is one, speaks to her wish to impress Williams—whose insight into Dante she would never doubt—with a good story. And the tale of her expedition through the epic *was* a good story, Williams confirmed. At last, Eliot's "direct shock of poetic intensity" ran right through her, changing the course of her professional life.

## WILLIAMS: DANTE'S FELLOW TRAVELER

Biographically speaking, Williams presents the opposite problem: When we look back to his earliest literary remains, he seems already to know all about Dante or at least Dante's way. In her 1955 lecture "Charles Williams: A Poet's Critic," Sayers informed her audience that Williams's "introduction to the *Commedia* took place, he told me, when he was hurriedly correcting the proofs of Cary's translation for the Oxford University Press, and his immediate reaction was: 'But this is true.'"[11] The letter that Sayers appears to be referencing—dated September 7, 1944—is a bit more ambiguous than she suggests, as Williams may not (at a distance of several decades) have been recollecting his very first encounter with the *Comedy* but rather an experience akin to the one Sayers had just reported in her letters in which he had "rushed" (his term) through the *Comedy*. In his early days at Oxford University Press (where he began to work in 1908), he explains in the letter, he and another editor "spent three days" reading the proofs in question. He goes on to say that he "must have known the *V.N.* [*Vita Nuova*] when I was first in love, and I thought then, as I've thought since, that it was wholly accurate."[12]

---

[11]Dorothy L. Sayers, "Charles Williams: A Poet's Critic," in *PSPS*, 73.
[12]Charles Williams to Dorothy L. Sayers, September 7, 1944, DSP, folder 116.

Nonetheless, Sayers captured an essential truth about Williams in that remembrance: that he viewed Dante as independent verification of what he had experienced. In a 1953 letter to Barbara Reynolds, Sayers offered further insights:

> The great power of Charles Williams is that for him *time*, in a sense, did not exist. If truth is eternal, it is true then and now—in 14th-century Florence or in 20th-century Wimbledon. He had that in common with the medievals, to whom Ancient Rome and Bethlehem were as near as Paris or Bologna. He insists to [Dante translator] J. D. Sinclair, in a correspondence I have seen, that what critics *will* not allow or understand is that "the thing does happen." He is talking of the "Beatrician experience."[13]

Later chapters will have much to say about the mechanics of Beatrician experiences. At present, it is enough to observe that such experiences involve glimpsing the eternal through the medium of the beloved—romantic love as a gateway to the divine. Sayers's important insight for us now is that Williams did not so much as step onto Dante's path as meet Dante on the path he was already traveling. In the 1955 address, she rightly pointed out that for Williams "the solidarity of human society lay visibly extended, not only in space, but also in time." Accordingly, Williams "came to Dante prepared to hail him across the negligible gap of six centuries as a fellow-poet, a fellow-lover, and a fellow-Christian."[14] On the matter of love, Williams did not historicize.

A case in point is Williams's first book, *The Silver Stair* (1912), a sequence of eighty-four love sonnets.[15] Critics have suggested

---

[13]Dorothy L. Sayers to Barbara Reynolds, April 9, 1953, in *LDS*, 4:91, italics original.

[14]Sayers, "Charles Williams: A Poet's Critic," 72.

[15]In a 1926 lecture, Williams would summarize *The Silver Stair* as follows: Its first part introduces a "young man thoroughly discontented with the world who suddenly and for the first time falls in love"; the second shows him "discontented with the ordinary result of love. He feels it in a way that urges him *away* from marriage as much as towards it; because he feels *love*. Love as a being not as a name"; the third is "a kind of ode in praise of Love as God and Man; of Its passion in the world, wherein the prostitutes of the street carry

multiple influences, such as W. B. Yeats, from whose *The Shadowy Waters* Williams took the book's epigraph, and Victorian poet Coventry Patmore, who had likened God's fierce love for the soul to the human lover's desire for the beloved.[16] The book also exhibits conspicuous debts to Dante Gabriel Rossetti ("More like Rossetti than anyone else," declared Sir Walter Raleigh, professor of English literature at Oxford), particularly his collection of translations *The Early Italian Poets: From Ciullo D'Alcomo to Dante Alighieri* (1861). Rossetti offered Williams models of the Italian sonnet, the form used throughout *The Silver Stair,* and how the language of courtly love might mix with modern English. Rossetti's practice of adding descriptive titles to the translated poems—such as "He solicits his Lady's Pity"—Williams likewise imitated (e.g., "He appoints time and place for meeting his lady").

As Rossetti's subtitle indicates, at the center of the collection is Dante, his *Vita Nuova* being its longest work. *Vita Nuova* was Dante's first book, a chain of love poems—plus commentary—that chronicles Dante's initial encounters with Beatrice, the growth of his love, and the temptations (ultimately overcome!) to look elsewhere after her death. Dante's characterizations of Beatrice are suffused with theological language, so much so that some passages later caught the Inquisition's eye (such as, for example, when the poet speaks of her as "the destroyer of all evil and queen of all good" and "my beatitude").[17]

---

Its cross, and the abominable stories of the smoking-room and the snigger buzz like flies about Its wounded Head . . . —of its Resurrection, and Its final communication of Itself to Its elect." Charles Williams, "Me," CW MS-144, pp. 5-6, Charles Williams Papers, Marion E. Wade Center, Wheaton College, Wheaton, IL.

[16]For information on Patmore's influences, the circumstances of the book's publication, and its major themes, see Grevel Lindop's chapter on *The Silver Stair* in his biography *Charles Williams: The Third Inkling* (Oxford University Press, 2015), 27-39.

[17]Cleric anxieties about that language amused Williams, who mentions it in *FB*. For an accessible survey, see Joseph Luzzi's chapter "*Comedia Proibita,*" in *Dante's Divine Comedy: A Biography* (Princeton University Press, 2024), 37-58.

Three decades later, in *The Figure of Beatrice*, Williams argued
that Dante only gradually realized in *Vita Nuova* that the Lord Love
of his allegory—the personification of Eros—could be identified
with God.[18] In *The Silver Stair*, Williams makes the connection
immediately, signaling that he wasn't simply developing an idea
he found in Dante but taking heart from Dante's example (just as
Sayers perceived). The two-part prologue distils the message thus:

> His ambush in a pebble's heart, His fleet
>> Passage in light and shadow of leaves, O soul,
>>> Hast thou escaped; wilt thou deny thy clay
>> If thereupon He stablish [*sic*] His control
> In mortal eyes that snare it, mortal feet
>> That tread the windings of salvation's way?[19]

On view here is the earliest expression in print of what in time
Williams would refer to as his "romantic theology," in which the
beloved presents a pregnant "image" of God that draws the soul to
its source (what Sayers above called the "Beatrician experience").
As these lines suggest, Williams also recognized that God may
seek to "ambush" our souls through natural imagery—the pebble,
the leaves' light show—making the "snare" of romantic love only
one of many divine plots to set us on "salvation's way."

Like so many of Williams's works, *The Silver Stair* is permeated
with curious locutions (including *deifical, lupanar,* and *littly*)
and features some odd plot twists (and none odder than the fact
that the lover ultimately renounces marriage). Yet such oddities
should not distract us from the book's evidence that from the first
Williams's writing career was bound up with Dante—his *fellow*
love poet.

---

[18]*FB*, 76: "I do not press that Love should here be taken as allegorically equal to Christ;
I am inclined to think that this develops in the *New Life* but is certainly not there at
the beginning."

[19]Charles Williams, *The Silver Stair* (Herbert and Daniel, 1912), vi.

## LEWIS: PARADISE FOUND

Lewis took a different track. In this case, early contact with Dante is easily located. Already in 1917, we find the teenage Lewis informing his father that he had read the first two hundred lines of *Inferno* in Italian "with much success."[20] A year and a half later, while convalescing from his injuries in the Great War, Lewis took up Dante again—now *Purgatorio*—though this time allowing himself to use an edition featuring an English crib opposite the Italian. "So 'ave the mighty fallen," he joked with his friend Arthur Greeves.[21]

Of *Paradiso*, the first trace in Lewis's papers appears in a letter to Greeves composed in the first days of 1930. Lewis reports on a four-day visit to Owen Barfield, during which they spent the mornings reading Aristotle's *Ethics* and (after a postprandial walk) read *Paradiso* "for the rest of the day" (the reading and conversation being so good that the two friends stayed up until 4 a.m. at one point). I have already quoted a snippet from his awestruck description of *Paradiso* in the introduction. Now we should hear it in full:

> [*Paradiso*] has really opened a new world to me. I don't know whether it is really different from *Inferno* (B. [Barfield] says it's as different as chalk from cheese—heaven from hell, would be more appropriate!)—or whether I was specially receptive, but it certainly seemed to me that I had never seen at all what Dante was like before. Unfortunately, the impression is one so unlike anything else that I can hardly describe it for your benefit—a sort of mixture of intense, even crabbed, complexity of language and thought with (what seems impossible) *at the very same time* a feeling of spacious gliding movement, like a slow dance, or like flying. It is like the stars—endless mathematical subtilty of orb, cycle, epicycle and ecliptic, unthinkable & unpicturable, & yet at the same time the freedom and liquidity of empty space and the

---

[20]C. S. Lewis to Arthur Greeves, February 8, 1917, in *CLCSL*, 1:275.

[21]C. S. Lewis to Arthur Greeves, October 6, 1918, in *CLCSL*, 1:403.

triumphant certainty of movement. I should describe it as feeling
more *important* than any poetry I have ever read.[22]

He confessed that he wasn't sure that his friend would like it,
however, given how thoroughly Catholic it was (Greeves had been
raised among the low church Plymouth Brethren and, after much
wandering, ended up a Quaker): "It is seldom homely: perhaps not
*holy* in our sense—it is too Catholic for that: and of course its blend
of complexity and beauty is very like Catholic theology—wheel
within wheel, but wheels of glory, and the One radiated through the
Many."[23] We will return to the profound critical insights contained
in this passage in chapter six (when *Paradiso* specifically is under
examination). For present purposes, the importance of these words
lies in their testimony to Lewis's new receptivity to Dante and, in
turn, his sense that his previous readings had missed the mark badly.
The scales had fallen from Lewis's eyes.

Three decades later, in *An Experiment in Criticism*, Lewis
insisted, "In good reading there ought to be no 'problem of belief,'"
and he cited as examples Dante and Roman poet and philosopher
Lucretius (who portrays the universe as "a meaningless dance of
atoms").[24] He read both, he recalls, "when (by and large) I agreed
with Lucretius. I have read them since I came (by and large) to
agree with Dante. I cannot find that this has much altered my
experience, or at all altered my evaluation, of either." He argues,
in turn, that a "true lover of literature" should imitate "an honest
examiner" who gives "highest marks" to the best performance
regardless of whether the examiner agrees with the writer's
views.[25] Yet Lewis's experience in 1930 suggests that "agreeing"—

---

[22]C. S. Lewis to Arthur Greeves, January 13, 1930, in *CLCSL*, 1:857, italics original.
[23]Lewis to Greeves, January 13, 1930, in *CLCSL*, 1:857, italics original.
[24]C. S. Lewis, *An Experiment in Criticism* (Cambridge University Press, 1961), 86; Lewis,
   *Surprised by Joy* (Geoffrey Bles, 1955), 164.
[25]Lewis, *Experiment in Criticism*, 86.

or at least moving toward agreement—with Dante *did* alter his experience of the *Comedy*.

The eye-opening sessions with Barfield sit right in the middle of the great revolution in Lewis's spiritual life recounted in the last chapters of *Surprised by Joy* (1955). There Lewis narrates two conversions—first to theism in the Trinity term (or spring) of 1929, which was accompanied by a return to church attendance, and then to Christian orthodoxy in September 1931. Biographers have raised questions about Lewis's chronology, and not without cause.[26] Thankfully, we don't need to iron out all the wrinkles here. My point is simply that the tenor of Lewis's enraptured account of *Paradiso* squares with *Surprised by Joy*'s picture of him in early 1930 as one increasingly alive to spiritual matters, including the claims of texts he'd previously read for pleasure or study. The autobiographer characterizes the shift by portraying himself as a fox "dislodged from the Hegelian Wood" of his old philosophical beliefs being pursued by a "pack" of hounds, including Plato, George Herbert, George MacDonald, J. R. R. Tolkien, Barfield, and, yes, Dante.[27]

But no remark is more telling than his instructions to Greeves— shared at the end of January 1930—concerning the reading of *Paradiso*, Lewis's enthusiasm having piqued Greeves's interest. *Paradiso* can't be consumed, he told his friend, "in long stretches (with one's feet on the fender) for the general atmosphere and conduct of the story," that is, as one might read a novel.[28] Instead, one should "read a small daily portion, in rather a liturgical manner, letting the *images* and the purely intellectual conceptions sink well into the mind" (italics in original). Lucretius never received this treatment.

---

[26]For more on the challenges of matching the events of Lewis's "inner world" narrated in *Surprised by Joy* "with the events of the world outside," see Alister McGrath's treatment of the date of Lewis's conversion in *C. S. Lewis: A Life* (Tyndale House, 2013).

[27]Lewis, *Surprised by Joy*, 212.

[28]C. S. Lewis to Arthur Greeves, January 30, 1930, in *CLCSL*, 1:876.

**Figure 2.1.** Jean-Jacques Feuchère, *Dante Meditating on the Divine Comedy* (1843)

2

# MEETING ON THE WAY

### A STORY IN SIX COMBINATIONS

CHAPTER ONE TRACED OUR three pilgrim-readers' respective routes to Dante. The present chapter brings them together on the way. My approach here is best described as eavesdropping. Using biographical and bibliographical data, we will intrude on them as they read Dante, we will look over their shoulders as they read each other's remarks on Dante, we will overhear them conversing about Dante, and we will thereby watch a cohort of Dante readers take shape.

## 1. WILLIAMS READS LEWIS (OR, *THE ALLEGORY OF LOVE* AFFAIR)

Our story begins with the concurrent perusal of books. On February 26, 1936, Lewis raved to Greeves that Williams's "*Christian fantasy*" (Lewis's phrase) *The Place of the Lion* (1931) was at once "a most exciting fantasy" and "a deeply religious and (unobtrusively) a profoundly learned book."[1] Two weeks later, on March 11, he sent the author fan mail touting the novel as "one of the major literary events of my life—comparable to my first discovery

---

[1]C. S. Lewis to Arthur Greeves, February 26, 1936, in *CLCSL*, 2:180, italics original. He considered it "good preparation for Lent, for it shows me (through the heroine) the special sin of abuse of intellect to which all my profession are liable, more clearly than I ever saw it before. I have learned more than I ever knew yet about humility."

of George Macdonald, G. K. Chesterton, or W[illiam] Morris."[2] The resonances were so deep that he felt he had to write: "A book sometimes crosses one's path which is so like the sound of one's native language in a strange country that it feels almost uncivil not to wave some kind of flag in answer." Williams was delighted because he had been planning to do the very same thing. "If you had delayed writing another 24 hours," he replied the next day, "our letters would have crossed. It has never before happened to me to be admiring an author of a book while he at the same time was admiring me. My admiration for the staff work of the Omnipotence rises every day."[3]

The book on Williams's desk was Lewis's soon-to-be-published study of medieval love poetry, *The Allegory of Love,* to which Williams had gained early access thanks to his editorial position at Oxford University Press, Lewis's publisher. In fact, as Lewis would learn weeks later, Williams played an important role in one of the last steps of its production. When Lewis submitted the manuscript to the press in 1935, he called it *The Allegorical Love-Poem.* His editor, John Mulgan, didn't think the title promising, however, so he asked the author for alternatives, and Lewis proposed the following:

> *Britomart, or, The Allegorical Love Poem*
>
> *The Baptism of the Gods: A Study of the Erotic Allegory of the Middle Ages*
>
> *Cupid Catechumenus: An Essay in the History of the Medieval Allegories of Love*
>
> *The Age of Busirane, or, The Allegorical Love Poem*

Deeming all of these "ridiculous," Lewis wrote again a few days later—March 19, 1936—to announce that *The House of Busirane*—after a character who symbolizes "unlawful love" in Edmund

---

[2] C. S. Lewis to Charles Williams, March 11, 1936, in *CLCSL*, 2:183.
[3] Quoted in *CLCSL*, 2:184.

Spenser's *The Fairie Queen*—should be the title "if you think the original (and truthful) one too forbidding."[4] Mulgan consulted Williams, who was at work on marketing materials for the book, and the two settled on *The Allegory of Love*. It offered, Mulgan wrote to Lewis on March 30, "a better idea of the general and philosophical nature of your book."[5] One of Williams's first acts of friendship, then, was to save Lewis from his worst literary instincts.

*The Allegory of Love* lays claim to uncovering one of the rarest of historical occurrences: a "real change in human sentiment."[6] In eleventh-century France, Lewis argues, poets "discovered or invented, or were the first to express, that romantic species of passion which English poets were still writing about in the nineteenth," "[effecting] a change which has left no corner of our ethics, our imagination, or our daily life untouched."[7] Lewis goes so far as to propose that "Compared with this revolution, the Renaissance is a mere ripple on the surface of literature." Poetic allegory—whose origins Lewis traces back to late Rome—would be the chief engine of its publicity. The attraction of such a study to the author of *The Silver Stair* will be obvious. Two years later, in *He Came Down from Heaven*, Williams pronounced *The Allegory of Love* "one of the most important critical books of our time."[8] He reveled in the fact that Lewis had shown this "revolution" in erotic love to be "a historic fact," which Williams gleefully knit into his way of telling the history of Christianity.[9]

---

[4]Quoted in Elizabeth Knowles, "Eleven Case Studies of the OUP Publication Process," in *The History of Oxford University Press*, ed. William Roger Lewis (Oxford University Press, 2013), 3:407.

[5]Quoted in Knowles, "Eleven Case Studies," 407.

[6]C. S. Lewis, *The Allegory of Love: A Study of Medieval Tradition* (Oxford University Press, 1936), 11.

[7]Lewis, *Allegory of Love*, 4.

[8]*HCDH*, 64.

[9]Williams writes, "All these alterations"—to the human condition caused by Christianity— "filled men's pre-eminent moments with new nourishment and new repair. The imagination of the world and of heaven had changed. Of all these alterations one affected perhaps more

He took this academic work, moreover, as a flashing sign that Lewis shared his convictions regarding the potential for romantic love to serve a serious religious purpose. And he was picking up on a real thread—albeit a slight one—in the book. Early on, for example, Lewis observes that while the "love religion" on display in courtly love poetry often took the form of a "parody of the real religion," it could (but normally did not) "become something more serious than a parody."[10] It could even find "a *modus vivendi*"—in the sense of arrangement that allows rivals to coexist—"with Christianity and produce a noble fusion of sexual and religious experience." Lewis then cites the example of Dante. Again, a little later in the book, he writes, "When *Frauendienst*"— chivalry toward women—"succeeds in fusing with religion, as in Dante, unity is restored to the mind, and love can be treated with a solemnity that is whole-hearted."[11]

In his reply to Lewis's letter, Williams revealed that he had already composed, and failed to publish, "a little book called *An Essay in Romantic Theology*" due to the disapproval of the bishop of Oxford. *The Allegory of Love* gave fresh grist to that mill: "I still toy with the notion of doing something on the subject, and I regard your book as practically the only one that I have ever come across, *since Dante*, that shows the slightest understanding of what this very peculiar identity of love and religion means."[12] Williams felt he had found a kindred spirit among the living—just as he had in Dante among the dead. He enclosed with his reply a copy of his *Poems of Conformity* (1917), whose contents express

---

than all the rest (except for the central dogmas) the casual fancies and ordinary outlook of men and women. As a historic fact the change has been described in words better than any I could find by Mr. C. S. Lewis" (*HCDH*, 63-64).

[10]Lewis, *Allegory of Love*, 21.

[11]Lewis, *Allegory of Love*, 42.

[12]Quoted in *CLCSL*, 2:174, italics added. Regarding the essay in question, its content, development, and abandonment, see Charles Williams, *Outlines of a Romantic Theology*, ed. Alice M. Hadfield (Eerdmans, 1990).

the same convictions about love, erotic and divine, aired in *The Silver Stair*.

Lewis, however, was not like-minded in this regard, and one can almost hear him sighing behind the opening words of his reply: "This is going to be a complicated matter."[13] He acknowledges that *The Allegory of Love's* "respectful treatment" of the sort of "romanticism" dear to Williams's heart must have indeed resonated with his correspondent and even seemed "to you almost like a trap." But, Lewis continues, he is a "native in a quite distinct, though neighbouring, province of the Romantic country." He defines the boundary as follows: "There is a romanticism which finds its revelation in love, which is yours, and another which finds it in mythology (and nature mythically apprehended) which is mine. Ladies, in the one: gods in the other—the bridal chamber, or the wood beyond the world." It is the second romantic impulse that made *The Place of the Lion*—a novel in which Platonic archetypes run riot in our world—so compelling to Lewis. To put it in Dantean terms, the journey of love launched in *Vita Nuova* for the one, the cosmic journey launched in *Paradiso* for the other.[14]

That reply could have been the end of the matter. But Williams was not deterred. He accepted Lewis's invitation—made in the first letter and repeated in his second—to meet and was soon a regular at the "informal club called the Inklings" that Lewis advertised in his first letter.[15] Williams's biographer, Grevel Lindop, insightfully

---

[13]C. S. Lewis to Charles Williams, March 23, 1936, in *CLCSL*, 2:175.

[14]Though the two men would have insisted that both journeys have the same destination; see chap. 7.

[15]C. S. Lewis to Charles Williams, March 11, 1936, in *CLCSL*, 2:173. After reviewing Lewis and Williams's initial exchange, Paul Fiddes writes that the "'inward' journey" that the two men "[took] together over the next nine years might . . . be mapped as negotiating a route between frontiers, involving some adjustment of adjoining districts within a larger country." Fiddes, *Charles Williams and C. S. Lewis: Friends in Co-Inherence* (Oxford University Press, 2021), 9. Fiddes's book is required reading for anyone who wants to understand their relationship and is particularly illuminating regarding Williams's notion of coinherence and Lewis's translation of that idea in his mature writings.

observes that Williams offered what Lewis "most valued in a friend: enough agreement to make profound and affectionate communication possible, and enough disagreement to provide endless fodder for debate."[16] Dante served all their purposes: a poet at home in both of their provinces of the romantic country, a shared love, an inexhaustible topic of debate.

## 2. LEWIS READS WILLIAMS (AND RECOMMENDS HIS BOOK)

The Dantean "romantic theology" Williams advertised to Lewis was not suppressed for long, appearing first in a long chapter on Dante in *He Came Down from Heaven* (1938) and finding its fullest expression in print, five years later, in *The Figure of Beatrice*. Williams had been refining the latter book's core ideas—about love, about Dante, about the imagination, about the development of the artist—over two decades of lecturing on poetry, philosophy, and Dante specifically through the "evening institutes" scattered around London that catered to industrious working people who pursued learning and culture in the off hours.[17] Nonetheless, *The Figure of Beatrice*'s composition was a great strain. When he sent the completed manuscript to his publisher, Faber & Faber, he lamented how far it had fallen short of his hopes. "It has slid from being what it ought to be," he confided to his devotee Anne Renwick, "down to what I could make it."[18] The author feared the judgment of one editor at Faber above all, T. S. Eliot. Eliot hoped to make the book accessible to a general audience, and so he complained that Williams's writing was too "obscure" (an amusing instance of the pot calling the kettle black) and demanded that Williams rewrite the introduction. Meanwhile, Lewis, who rarely

---

[16]Grevel Lindop, *Charles Williams: The Third Inkling* (Oxford University Press, 2015), 259.
[17]For more on Williams's lecturing, see Lindop, *Charles Williams*, 89-91, 184-266.
[18]Lindop, *Charles Williams*, 357.

aligned with Eliot on questions of style, judged the book "the clearest thing" Williams had written. Lewis "forbids me to touch it," Williams informed the poet Anne Ridler, "He even told my wife that the whole book was extraordinarily clear, 'which has not always been, Mrs. Williams, a virtue of your husband's work.'"[19]

Although Lewis would always harbor some reservations about Williams's romantic theology, he respected *The Figure of Beatrice*. In the preface to the memorial collection that Lewis edited after Williams's premature death the following year, published in 1947, for example, he claims to have "learned much" from Williams's literary criticism, "particularly from *The Figure of Beatrice*."[20] His most revealing remarks on *The Figure of Beatrice*, though, appear in a 1959 letter to Barbara Reynolds, scholar of Italian literature and Sayers's friend, biographer, and accidental collaborator:

> His view of Dante was . . . highly idiosyncratic. But my own opinion, for what it's worth, is that the Figure of B[eatrice] is a book every student of Dante must reckon with—the sort of book which may offend narrow experts as much by its merits as by its faults. If he knows less than they about Florentine politics and the history of the language, he knew a good deal more about poetry and love—possibly about Heaven and Hell.[21]

Lewis goes on to observe that sometimes "a scholar, dealing with work by an amateur of genius, can present its real strength freed from the flaws his imperfect knowledge imposed on it." He hoped that Reynolds would do exactly that. As we will see below, the very qualities Lewis names here—Williams's superior grasp of poetry and love, heaven and hell, and his relative lack of interest in medieval Florentine politics—were attractive to Sayers as she plotted her translation of the *Comedy* with ordinary readers in view.

---

[19]Quoted in in Lindop, *Charles Williams*, 358.
[20]Lewis, preface, in *Essays Presented to Charles Williams* (Oxford University Press, 1947), vii.
[21]C. S. Lewis to Barbara Reynolds, March 19, 1959, in *CLCSL*, 3:1031.

## 3. SAYERS READS WILLIAMS (AND THEN DANTE)

Williams's fears about *The Figure of Beatrice* turned out to be unfounded. Within a few months of publication, the book received applause in prominent places, and a year later he was elected to the Oxford Dante Society (joining Lewis among its members) on the strength of the book. On August 29, 1943, *The Figure of Beatrice* earned a positive review from Desmond MacCarthy, the well-regarded literary critic at the *Sunday Times*. MacCarthy's praise piqued the interest of Sayers, who promptly bought a copy and then quickly consumed it. In her first piece of Dante criticism to reach print, the 1947 essay ". . . And Telling You a Story," she shares that she had been attracted to *The Figure of Beatrice* "not because [the book] was about Dante, but because it was *by Charles Williams*."[22]

Though the book delighted her, she was not yet moved to "tackle Dante in person." That would require the additional push of the moment of embarrassed self-honesty discussed in chapter one. Dante's reputation for being "obscure" didn't help, nor did the poem's length: "After all, fourteen thousand lines are fourteen thousand lines, especially if they are full of Guelfs and Ghibellines and Thomas Aquinas."[23] But on August 11, 1944, she accepted an air-raid siren as the signal to begin. As she and her husband headed to the bomb shelter in the back garden of their house in Witham, she grabbed the *Inferno* volume of an inherited Temple Classics edition of the *Comedy* off the shelf.[24]

In *An Experiment in Criticism*, Lewis writes of how "the first reading of some literary work is often, to the literary, an experience so momentous that only experiences of love, religion,

---

[22]ATYS, 1. As we saw in chapter 1, there is no reason to doubt her claim: she indeed knew Williams better of the two authors.

[23]ATYS, 1.

[24]That is the same edition—in which the Italian is printed opposite and English crib—Lewis had used to read *Purgatorio* in 1918.

or bereavement can furnish a standard of comparison. Their whole consciousness is changed. They have become what they were not before."[25] This was such a juncture in the life of Dorothy Sayers. Here's how she explains it in the 1947 essay:

> Coming to him as I did, for the first time, rather late in life, the impact of Dante upon my unprepared mind was not in the least what I had expected, and I can remember nothing like it since I first read *The Three Musketeers* at the age of thirteen. . . . I bolted my meals, neglected my sleep, work, and correspondence, drove my friends crazy, and paid only distracted attention to the doodle-bugs which happened to be infesting the neighborhood at the time, until I had panted my way through the Three Realms of the Dead from top to bottom and from bottom to top; and that, having finished, I found the rest of the world's literature so lacking in pep and incident that I pushed it all peevishly aside and started from the Dark Wood all over again.[26]

Our other two authors had their own "surprised by Dante" moments.[27] But Sayers's is the most remarkable of all because it caused the immediate reorientation of her professional energies. As the introduction already suggested, Sayers worked tirelessly on Dante's behalf from this point on—giving lectures, writing essays, and, most importantly of all, translating eighty-seven of the *Comedy*'s one hundred cantos for a recently launched publishing initiative designed to bring the classics to common readers known as Penguin Books. The last project began, astonishingly enough, only three months after Sayers had completed her circuit through the *Comedy*, and in acknowledgment of her Dantean debts to him, she endeavored to bring Williams along for the ride.

---

[25]C. S. Lewis, *An Experiment in Criticism* (Cambridge University Press, 1961), 3.

[26]ATYS, 2.

[27]I wish that I could claim credit for coining that phrase, but Sayers used it first in her correspondence with Williams: Dorothy L. Sayers to Charles Williams, September 14, 1944, in *LDS*, 3:76.

## 4. WILLIAMS READS SAYERS (READING
## AND RENDERING DANTE)

Less than a week after she headed to the bomb shelter with *Inferno* in hand, Sayers began to bombard William with reports on her progress. Several were written over multiple days; nearly all measured in the thousands of words; one was thirty-six handwritten pages long. She offered detailed commentary on Dante's storytelling techniques, language, allegory, theology, even his "bedworthiness."[28] Williams was charmed, if overwhelmed. He apologized for his inability to match the velocity and length of Sayers's letter campaign. Within a few weeks, he was sharing them with others, as he related in mock-Arthurian style on September 1, 1944:

> The King's Majesty heard with great joy the news contained in the dispatches received this morning from the distinguished commander of the Expeditionary Force. The King has caused these dispatches to be published throughout Logres, and has proclaimed a public holiday in His capital city at Camelot. He awaits with serene impatience the fuller information promised. The achievement of the City by all coheres in His complete intention. The Lord Taliessin permits himself to add his private congratulations, and so all the Lords of the Table.[29]

As Reynolds relates, Williams was speaking in code: He is Taliessin (central character of his own Arthurian verse), Lewis is the king, and the other Inklings are the lords of the table. (Reynolds also glosses the bit about the king's impatience and "the achievement of the City" as Lewis's wish that Sayers would "read triumphantly to the end of *Paradiso*."[30]) Williams, then, has a rightful claim

---

[28]Dorothy L. Sayers to Charles Williams, October 18, 1944, in *LDS*, 3:100.

[29]Quoted in Barbara Reynolds, *The Passionate Intellect: Dorothy L. Sayers' Encounter with Dante* (Kent State University Press, 1989), 34.

[30]Reynolds, *Passionate Intellect*, 34.

to being the first publisher of Sayers's Dante criticism. He was convinced, though, that Sayers's thoughts deserved a far wider hearing than the court assembled at the Eagle and Child. Less than a week later, he made the proposal noted in the introduction that the letters or "something like them" be printed by his employer so that the general public would benefit from "all you say about the laughter and lightness and fun—even—of Dante."[31]

In response to her concerns that it would be presumptuous for a novice to do so, Williams made a humble appeal: "Many more people will read a pamphlet by you than a book by me, as we both very well know."[32] He believed that "something like that would really be of the greatest use among all sorts of darlings who will otherwise . . . not read him? Yes, but they *may* read him, and without precisely the eyesight you bring." Williams perceived that Sayers could grow and inform Dante's contemporary readership to a far greater extent than *The Figure of Beatrice*, and subsequent events proved him right on a far greater scale than he imagined. The vehicle, though, would not be a lightweight pamphlet; it was the massive undertaking of rendering of Dante's masterpiece in English.

Williams was among that translation's first readers—perhaps the very first. On December 7, 1944, Sayers alerted him that she had "fallen into the clutches of a monster" and hinted that she might one day "lay before you the web it has spun."[33] A week later she advertised that she was "preparing a slice of my Arachne's web to send you for a Christmas present," which duly arrived a few days before the holiday: the first five cantos of *Inferno*. She blamed Dante's devilishly intricate rhyme scheme, *terza rima*: Once you get started, she told him, you keep making adjustments to what

---

[31]Quoted in *LDS*, 3:77.
[32]Charles Williams to Dorothy L. Sayers, [September 1944], DSP, folder 115a.
[33]Dorothy L. Sayers to Charles Williams, December 7, 1944, in *LDS*, 3:115.

you've already done until an entire canto has been worked out.[34] Williams exhorted her to keep going: "Do! Now; in the first rush. Consider that you have done five out of the 100 and the very little extra work that finishes it. . . . I wait with thrilling expectation for the next batch."[35]

When that batch arrived (*Inferno* VI–IX) on January 28, 1945, Sayers added—after a lengthy exposé on choices she had made in her rendering—a request: "Charles, if ever this preposterous effort of mine sees the light of publication. . . . Do you think sufficiently well of it to do the necessary arguments and notes?"[36] The audience she had in mind, she went on to explain, would be the sort of people who attended Williams's lectures at the evening institutes:

> Those intelligent London students of yours—people, anyhow, who didn't know any Italian, or want to; and were not interested in Catholic culture; and hadn't any Latin or astronomy or theories of symbolism; but who might be got to take an interest in Dante if they could be persuaded that [the *Comedy*] was an exciting kind of story with some sort of "spiritual aspect" in it.[37]

Simply stated, she wanted the project to speak to the "common reader," and despite the eccentricates of Williams's style, she believed he was uniquely equipped to help her.

She was, of course, speaking from experience. Immediately after completing her dash through the *Comedy* in August the previous year, she informed Williams how grateful she was *not* to have read the epic until "I had your book as a guide." She didn't find "the usual sort of notes and comments"—that is, the ones she found in the Temple Classics edition—very helpful at

[34]Dorothy L. Sayers to Charles Williams, before December 21, 1944, in *LDS*, 3:115.
[35]Quoted in Barbara Reynolds, *Passionate Intellect*, 42.
[36]Dorothy L. Sayers to Charles Williams, January 28, 1945, in *LDS*, 3:128.
[37]Sayers to Williams, January 28, 1945, in *LDS*, 3:128-29.

getting at the spiritual core of the *Comedy*. They point readers to the pertinent passages in Thomas Aquinas, she granted, and they give "tedious" accounts of the dead people Dante meets, "but one would really never guess from them that the whole thing is a poem about something happening inside Dante"—as Williams had shown her.[38] He had a singular grasp of and concern for the poignancy of Dante's allegory. She sought to enlist Williams because his method set historical trivia aside. She wanted him to close the temporal gap between medieval and modern and reveal the poem's continuing *relevance* to ordinary readers' lives.

He agreed.

On May 9, 1945, Sayers wrote to announce that she had convinced E. V. Rieu, Penguin's founder and the translator of its first title, *The Odyssey*, to sign on to their arrangement (despite his concerns about Williams's difficulty). She would translate the *Comedy*, releasing her *Inferno* as soon as it was ready and then *Purgatorio* and *Paradiso* in due course, and Williams would furnish each installment with an introduction, canto summaries, glossary, and notes.[39] Sayers would thereby repay the favor of Williams's tutelage by wrapping her translation in his words.

Six days later, he died.

## 5A. LEWIS READS SAYERS (THE DANTE CRITIC)

After Barbara Reynolds, C. S. Lewis has a strong claim to being the second most attentive contemporary reader of Sayers's Dantean publications. He read and annotated her first and second collections of Dante criticism, *Introductory Papers on Dante* (1954) and *Further Papers on Dante* (1957). His praise of the first, in fact, led Sayers to inquire whether he might write a preface for the second, to which he replied that he only did so for up-and-coming

---

[38]Dorothy L. Sayers to Charles Williams, August 31, 1944, in *LDS*, 3:70.
[39]Dorothy L. Sayers to Charles Williams, May 9, 1945, in *LDS*, 3:141-42.

authors and, besides, "Everybody knows I know less about D. than you do."[40] In one of his last literary acts, he wrote a review (generally positive) of Sayers's posthumously published third collection of Dante criticism—*The Poetry of Search and the Poetry of Statement* (1963)—which became a posthumous publication of his own when it ran after a few weeks after his death in November 1963. He read her *Hell* and *Purgatory* translations shortly after their debuts (as discussed below). He corresponded about Dante with her repeatedly from 1945 to 1957, the year of her death. The final words she received from him on Dante—in a June 1957 letter— were in praise of *Further Papers*: "I'd like to go through the whole thing with you," he wrote. "You've never done better work in this kind: and the scraps of translation bode well for your *Paradiso*."[41]

His first words to her on Dante, twelve years earlier, extended an invitation. As noted in the introduction, Lewis wrote a few days after Williams's passing to ask whether she would be willing to contribute to a collection of essays published in his honor.[42] A plan for a book had already been in the works: It was to be a *Festschrift* welcoming Williams back to London after he had spent the war years in Oxford (due to his employer relocating its London office there). Sayers gave an immediate yes, and her proposed topic was, once again, Dante's "incomparable" storytelling. Thus, that first published piece of Dante criticism noted earlier, ". . . And Telling You a Story," appeared in *Essays Presented to Charles Williams* under the editorial oversight of C. S. Lewis. "It is a stunning essay and will, by itself, make the book memorable," Lewis told her when he sent the proofs for her review on December 29, 1946.[43] Her contribution was placed first in the collection—ahead of Tolkien's

---

[40]C. S. Lewis to Dorothy L. Sayers, August 5, 1955, in *CLCSL*, 3:638. His annotated copies of both volumes are held in the Wade Center's C. S. Lewis Library collection.

[41]C. S. Lewis to Dorothy L. Sayers, June 25, 1957, in in *CLCSL*, 3:860.

[42]C. S. Lewis to Dorothy L. Sayers, May 17, 1945, in *CLCSL*, 3:649-50.

[43]C. S. Lewis to Dorothy L. Sayers, December 29, 1946, in *CLCSL*, 2:750.

now classic essay "On Fairy-Stories" and Lewis's own essay "On Stories"—reflecting her popularity at the time.

Yet Lewis and Sayers's exchange over the piece was not without disagreement, and that too is an important part of our story. A year earlier, after having "romped" through her submission, Lewis rattled off multiple points and passages that he admired, such as her discussion of "the mirroring of the theme" of each of canticle by its "poetic quality."[44] (Hell has an appropriate "grossness," she writes there, and "corresponding to it, . . . a certain crowded and close-grained quality in the workmanship." Yet "as the soul ascends Mount Purgatory, it strips off grossness," and the poetry does likewise.[45]) Yet he also attached a sheet of comments and suggestions that included a note in which he questioned her flat assertion in the draft that Dante's style is "lucid." "Great Gods!! Yes, I know it is in *places*," Lewis wrote, "but *lucid* just like that! Whose style would you call obscure I'd like to know?"[46]

To which she replied (on Christmas Eve 1945, no less), "*Lucid*—I think I do mean 'lucid'—just like that! I don't really think the style is obscure—indeed, what stumps the translator at every turn is its heartbreaking simplicity." She admitted that Dante's allusions to once-current events were "obscure" to *modern* readers, as might be his references to scholastic theology and astronomy, but those were not deliberate obfuscations on the poet's part.[47]

---

[44]C. S. Lewis to Dorothy L. Sayers, December 18?, 1945, in *CLCSL*, 2:685.

[45]ATYS, 28.

[46]Quoted in Reynolds, *Passionate Intellect*, 48.

[47]Dorothy L. Sayers to C. S. Lewis, December 24, 1945, in *LDS*, 3:183. Although she didn't know it at the time, Sayers was siding with T. S. Eliot. In his 1929 *Dante*, Eliot argues, "The style of Dante has a peculiar lucidity—a *poetic* as distinguished from *intellectual* lucidity. The thought may be obscure, but the word is lucid, or rather transparent." T. S. Eliot, *Dante* (Faber & Faber, 1929), 18-19. Writing to Eliot in the first days of 1948, after reporting that she had read his *Dante*, Sayers brought it up: "You use the word 'lucid,' which was precisely the word I found myself (with some astonishment) using, to the positive alarm of Mr. C. S. Lewis, who demanded 'if I called Dante lucid, what on earth did I call obscure?'" Dorothy L. Sayers to T. S. Eliot, January 8, 1948, in *LDS*, 3:349.

(To use critic George Steiner's helpful term, these are "contingent" difficulties: One can resolve the difficulty by "looking it up."[48]) Dante's "thought," she conceded, "is often difficult, but I don't think it is made any more so by the language, except perhaps just here and there." Nor in her mind was the allegory obscure: "Once one has got the hang of the central idea, it is all extraordinarily clear and consistent, and more meanings come hopping at you like rabbits."[49]

She didn't budge. In the published version of the essay, the sentence in question reads, "His [Dante's] diction was not, as I had imagined, uniformly in the grand manner, but homely, lucid, and fluent."[50]

We are now thoroughly equipped to grasp why this disagreement about Dante's language took place and why, over the ensuing decade, Dante was a source of mutual appreciation and amicable controversy between them. For Lewis, adorer of *Paradiso*, Dante's poetry presented an irreducible mystery: Its language and thought were *intensely* complex, "even crabbed," and yet the *Comedy* could soar to altitudes no other poem could touch. It was as if Thomas Aquinas's *Summa* had been fitted with angel's wings. And Lewis was a scholar of the Middle Ages, let us not forget, so issues that might have appeared as minutiae to her were of tremendous consequence to him. Sayers, meanwhile, was campaigning for the "common reader." In these comments to Lewis, she articulates the seemingly necessary articles of faith of the *Comedy*'s translator: that Dante's style *is* lucid; that the light shining through his verses

---

[48]George Steiner, "On Difficulty," in *On Difficulty and Other Essays* (Oxford University Press, 1972), 47.

[49]Sayers to Lewis, December 24, 1945, in *LDS*, 3:183. Whose style *did* she consider obscure? In the next paragraph, she answered: Robert Browning in his *Agamemnon* translation, Henry James (often), William Blake's *Prophetic Books*, and Charles Williams's *Taliessin Through Logres*, though she judged the last *less* difficult than Blake at least "because at the back of it there are Catholic and Arthurian assumptions which are traditional."

[50]ATYS, 2.

can be, however dimly, channeled into a foreign tongue; that Dante's allegory *is* "clear and consistent"; that one doesn't have to practice esoteric arts to decode it. Sayers believed that Dante wasn't just a pastime for the dons (including her correspondent); he had once been and could again be for the laity of the literary world. Lewis looked up to Dante in heaven. Sayers sought to bring Dante down to earth.

## 5B. LEWIS READS SAYERS (THE DANTE TRANSLATOR)

If we go by sales, then we must conclude that she was successful in that enterprise. Her *Inferno* translation—published as *Hell*—appeared in November 1949; within three months, fifty thousand copies—the *entire* first printing—had been sold. (And sales would remain good: Fifty years later, the number of copies sold exceeded 1.25 million.[51]) The cultural authorities who were enlisted to review the book were split, however. To her delight, Irish author Hugh de Blacam sent her the brief but glowing review he had written for *The Sunday Independent* in which he declared hers the "most faithful, most poetic, and the most readable" of "all the great English versions."[52] In her response, she lamented, however, that some of the reviewers on her own island—"knowing, I fear, but little of Dante, and hurriedly raking out [nineteenth-century Dante translator H. F.] Cary and Macaulay's 'Essay on Milton,' have been disconcerted—both by the mixed style of the translation, and also by the insistence on the allegorical interpretation."[53] Some learned reviewers were more than disconcerted. In a review she

---

[51]I take the sales figures from Barbara Reynolds, "Fifty Years On: Dorothy L. Sayers and Dante," *VII: Journal of the Marion E. Wade Center* 16 (1999): 3-6.

[52]Quoted in *LDS*, 3:480. Writing a few years later, Dante scholar and Dominican friar Kenelm Foster similarly lauded Sayers's *Hell* as "a real tour de force-five thousand lines rhyming in an intricate pattern, the *terza rima*, which I should have thought an extraordinarily difficult one to handle in English, though Miss Sayers herself speaks of the task with noticeable *sans gêne*." Foster, "Dorothy Sayers on Dante," *Blackfriars* 38 (October 1957): 426.

[53]Dorothy L. Sayers to Hugh de Blacam, January 18, 1950, in *LDS*, 3:480.

likely didn't see, Charles Singleton, eminent American Dantist, declared the translation a catastrophic failure, decrying, above all, the "padding" that resulted from Sayers's attempt to reproduce Dante's meter and rhyme scheme in English. "Time and again," Singleton groaned, "Dante is made to say things in English he would never have dreamt of saying in Italian."[54]

The anonymous reviewer for the *Times Literary Supplement*, meanwhile, offered an overwhelmingly appreciative assessment, emphasizing the necessary tradeoffs involved in translating Dante.[55] "'Swift, exciting, and topical,' is Miss Sayers's description of what Dante wished his poem to be," the reviewer points out at the start, "and so far as its merit lies in those qualities the translation is brilliantly successful." Those were *not* the qualities, however, "that our grandfathers and great-grandfathers sought in the Victorian pilgrimages into the world of Dante. They sought, and found, remote grandeur and jewelled precision." Such "majestic renderings" as the Cary translation (first issued in two volumes in 1805–1806), the reviewer perceives, encourage "reverent distance." Sayers, meanwhile, seeks to restore the vitality of the story: "It is Dante the story-teller who has gripped her, and the story told in her fluid, racy, and unanxious verse excites us." Her translation "fails," the reviewer grants, "to communicate the exceptional grandeur" of some incidents (citing the example of Ulysses's appearance in *Inferno* XXVI), but "this grandeur is the joint product of the poet and of the generations who have canonized his lines, and Miss Sayers is too much personally in love with Dante to be Dantesque." If that is a fault, the review concludes, then it "is most certainly a

---

[54]Charles Singleton, review of *The Comedy of Dante Alighieri the Florentine, I: Hell*, by Dorothy L. Sayers, *Speculum* 25, no. 3 (July 1950): 394.

[55]Writing to E. V. Rieu, Sayers called it "an excellent notice." Dorothy L. Sayers to E. V. Rieu, April 14, 1950, in *LDS*, 3:502. The review appears to have been written by Cecil Jackson Squire Sprigge, perhaps in collaboration with his wife Sylvia Sprigge. The two were journalists who had been deployed to Italy years earlier by British news agencies.

fault on the right side which is likely to win for Dante the sincere interest of fresh and exploring minds."[56]

I quote the *Times Literary Supplement* review at length because it closely resembles the line Lewis took on Sayers's translation, though his critique was sharper and his praise a few decibels short of full-throated. Writing to Sayers on November 11, 1949—a few days after receiving a copy from Penguin, which she had written to alert him was coming—he reported that he was already two-thirds of the way through the poem. The "speed" with which he had been consuming it—"resulting as it does from inclination and rather frowned on by my literary conscience"—certified that "you have got (what you most desired) the quality of an exciting story."[57] The Dante that she had discovered in her gallop through the *Comedy*, the Dante whom she had publicized in the essay he had edited, had shone through: Dante the storyteller.

Lewis's "literary conscience" was frowning, presumably, because he didn't just want the story: He wanted to steep himself in the poetry. (He rather liked, we might say, the "remote grandeur and jewelled precision" that the old translations had conveyed.) This was the man, after all, who advised his friend ten years earlier to read only a "small daily portion" of *Paradiso*, "letting the *images* and the purely intellectual conceptions sink well into the mind."[58]

Unsurprisingly, his comments on her handling of Dante's language are mixed. He found her "metrical audacities"—by which he seems to have meant something like bold but unconventional rhythmic patches—"nearly all effective in their places, i.e. as things in your poem." The Dante of these passages seemed to him "rather like" Robert Browning. That was not high praise—for Browning

---

[56]"Dante the Story-Teller," review of *The Divine Comedy: Hell*, by Dorothy L. Sayers, *Times Literary Supplement*, April 14, 1950, 224.

[57]C. S. Lewis to Dorothy L. Sayers, November 11, 1949, in *CLCSL*, 2:996.

[58]C. S. Lewis to Arthur Greeves, January 30, 1930, in *CLCSL*, 1:876.

was known for his emphatic, modern, and at times *jagged* rhythms. Yet Lewis assured her that a Browningesque Dante is "certainly better than making him like Milton"—as previous translators, Cary most influentially, had done. But how close was this to the real Dante? He warned her, too, that her use of colloquialism would bring "the largest of all hostile criticism." While he found the practice for the most part defensible, he confessed that at times, "I feel they suggest not intimacy & directness but flippancy—like Byron's *Don Juan*."[59]

We must now pause momentarily to see for ourselves the contrast between Cary and Sayers on which Lewis's analysis turns. The first ten lines of *Inferno* are sufficient to expose their glaring differences. Cary, writing in blank verse (unrhymed iambic pentameter), renders Dante's opening thus:

> In the midway of this our mortal life,
> I found me in a gloomy wood, astray
> Gone from the path direct: and e'en to tell
> It were no easy task, how savage wild
> That forest, how robust and rough its growth,
> Which to remember only, my dismay
> Renews, in bitterness not far from death.
> Yet to discourse of what there good befell,
> All else will I relate discover'd there.
> How first I enter'd it I scarce can say.[60]

In his lectures on translating Homer, Victorian critic Matthew Arnold famously argued that while Homer "says a thing, and says it to the end, and then begins another," Milton "[tries] to press a thousand things into one. . . . With Milton line runs into

---

[59]Lewis to Sayers, November 11, 1949, in *CLCSL*, 2:997. Sayers, as we will see in a moment, grasped that he was finding fault, though she likely did not understand the degree. Upon completing *Don Juan*, Lewis famously scribbled in the back of the book, "Never again."

[60]H. F. Cary, trans., *The Vision, or, Hell, Purgatory, and Paradise of Dante Alighieri* (Taylor and Hessey, 1814), 1.

line, and all is straitly bound together."[61] When Lewis (among others) spoke of translators—foremost, Cary—"making [Dante] like Milton," he was referring not only to translators' usage of a high linguistic register (the *Times Literary Supplement* reviewer's "remote grandeur"). He was also talking about Cary's imitation of Milton's habit of inverting word order and love of subordinate clauses, the resulting sentences coiling themselves in knots as they snake over numerous lines. In Italian, Dante's first sentence ends in line 3. In Cary's Miltonic English, it ends in line 7.

Sayers, meanwhile, uses (roughly) the same meter but adds the challenge of Dante's triple rhyme scheme, *terza rima*, mentioned above:

Midway this way of life we're bound upon,
   I woke to find myself in a dark wood,
   Where the right road was wholly lost and gone.
Ay me! how hard to speak of it—that rude
   And rough and stubborn forest! the mere breath
   Of memory stirs the old fear in the blood;
It is so bitter, it goes nigh to death;
   Yet there I gained such good, that, to convey
   The tale, I'll write what else I found therewith.
How I got into it I cannot say.[62]

We can now grasp why—whatever this translation's deficiencies—ordinary readers found it easier to digest than Cary's. But the passage also displays the quirks noted by the reviewers and Lewis. She is undeniably guilty of Singleton's charge of adding details to Dante's text to maintain the rhyme scheme. Where Dante had written *che nel pensier rinova la paura* ("the thought of which renews my fear"), Sayers writes, "Mere breath / Of memory stirs the old

[61]Matthew Arnold, *On Translating Homer* (Longman, Green, Longman, and Roberts, 1861), 72.
[62]Dorothy L. Sayers, trans., *The Divine Comedy 1: Hell* (Penguin, 1949), 71.

fear in the blood."[63] Lewis's concerns about replacing Milton with Browning, moreover, find support in the choppy sequence "Yet there I gained such good, that, to convey / The tale, I'll write the other things I found therewith." Dante's lines are better represented by Robert Hollander and Jean Hollander's translation: "But to set forth the good I found / I will recount the other things I saw."[64] Finally, Lewis's worries about colloquialism stem from phrases such as "how I got into it," where Dante says simply "how I entered."

Despite his reservations, Lewis could see that Sayers was drawing out aspects of Dante that the nineteenth-century versions had hidden. Whereas her predecessors had striven to "get in the *altissimo poeta* at *all* costs," she had rendered "Dante the lively 'scientifictionist' at all (reasonable) costs," and in that way made a notable contribution. He told her that it would be an aid to him in the future in making sense of difficult passages.[65] Four days later, having reached the end, he pronounced it "a stunning work" and told her that the translation had passed the "real test": "However I set out with the idea of attending to your translation, before I've read a page I've forgotten all about you and am thinking only of Dante, and two pages later I've forgotten about Dante and am thinking only about Hell. *Brava, bravissima.*"[66]

Three days after that, Sayers replied. She had received "a lot of nice letters about the *Inferno*," she began, but counted his "the very nicest" because he had a mature understanding of the project

---

[63]John D. Sinclair, trans., *The Divine Comedy of Dante Alighieri: Inferno* (Oxford University Press, 1939), 23.

[64]Robert Hollander and Jean Hollander, trans., *Inferno* (Vintage, 2000), 4.

[65]Lewis to Sayers, November 11, 1949, in *CLCSL*, 2:996.

[66]C. S. Lewis to Dorothy L. Sayers, November 15, 1949, in *CLCSL*, 2:997. In his 1956 review of her *Purgatory*, Lewis's fellow Inkling Colin Hardie made the same point in an altogether glowing assessment: "The translation as a whole is more than an accomplished tour-de-force; it conveys a great deal of Dante's poetry style, and for long stretches reaches such a marriage of two minds and two languages as no longer to seem a translation." Hardie, review of *The Divine Comedy II: Purgatory*, by Dorothy L. Sayers, *The Modern Language Review* 51, no. 2 (1956): 286.

and translation in general. She granted that what she had done would not be to everyone's taste but expressed gratitude to hear that *on the whole* Lewis's evaluation was positive. Sayers being Sayers, though, she could not let Lewis's remark about "metrical audacities" pass without comment. "About the metre—that does greatly interest me" begins her multiparagraph justification of her approach. The upshot was that Sayers believed that previous translators didn't sufficiently vary the texture of their lines; she was trying a new thing. She owned Browning's influence, defended his underappreciated powers as a "metrist," and argued that because Browning lived in Italy for decades and was "steeped in" Dante, the poet "might not be a bad model" for her project. Lord Byron was too, she adds: "It's interesting that my faults should remind you of two of our most Italianate poets."[67] His critique, she was showing him, might contain a deeper insight than he realized.

A week later, he made a partial concession, granting that she had a point about Byron and Browning being "our most Italianate poets."[68] "But," he then asked, "is Dante?" There is no need to go point by point through the ensuing letters, in which they debated questions of pronunciation and rhythm (which in his case included scanned lines for her edification at one point). You get the drift. The last issue he raises in his first reply to her reply, though, is telling: "There were several passages when you 'rose', thus answering one's anxious question 'This is all very fine, but what'll she do with the Paradiso?'"[69]

---

[67]Dorothy L. Sayers to C. S. Lewis, November 18, 1949, in *LDS*, 3:465, 467.

[68]C. S. Lewis to Dorothy L. Sayers, November 21, 1949, in *CLCSL*, 2:999-1000.

[69]He points to the same passage that the *Times Literary Supplement* mentioned as a failure: her rendering of Ulysses's famous speech in *Inferno* XXVI. He takes parts of it as an encouraging sign ("'the uninhabited world behind the sun,' good" [XXVI.117]), though he tut-tuts over the fact that the Greek captain then refers to his oration as "my little speech" (XXVI.121)—"It does conjure up vicars and bazaars!" Of course, he acknowledges to close, *C'est facile aux speculatifs d'être sevères*—"It's easy for theorizers to be severe." C. S. Lewis to Dorothy L. Sayers, November 15, 1949, in *CLCSL*, 2:784.

The issue would rise again with the delivery of her *Purgatorio* translation in 1955. Writing on July 31, Lewis applauded her performance: "Your *Inferno* was good, but this is even better. One w[oul]d say the same to Dante about the originals, no doubt."[70] He thought that the "metrical licenses" were employed to better effect this time. Her *Purgatory* made him "hungry for [her] *Paradiso*." Less than a week later, though, he playfully remarked that she was facing certain defeat in that contest: "Of course you and everyone else marches to certain death in translating the *Paradiso*: the best you can hope is to die swan-like." There was simply nothing like Dante's poetry in the third canticle:

> In trying to give pupils an idea of D's final style I've often said "You must imagine something wh[ich] is at the v[ery] same moment as massive as Milton and as airy as Shelley." But even then it is better than either, beats each at his own game. And even then (again) I still haven't got the grave processional movement—that devout *canzone*-ish, demure stateliness,—nor the factual, first-person science-fiction narrative quality—oh, I wouldn't be in your shoes for anything![71]

The critical insights on offer here will be our concern in chapter seven. I quote them now because these "pregnant words on Dante's style," as she called them, so pleased Sayers that she warned Lewis that she might quote them in her *Paradiso*.[72] She thought that "by confronting us with a sort of implacable 'be ye perfect,'" Lewis "[made] a powerful plea *ad misericordium* for all translators' frailties." In other words, Lewis was setting the bar so impossibly high that the reader could only feel mercy for the poor translator. Once again, she turned his words around to her own purposes. Invoking the carts that bore the condemned to the guillotine in

---

[70]C. S. Lewis to Dorothy L. Sayers, July 31, 1955, in *CLCSL*, 3:634.
[71]C. S. Lewis to Dorothy L. Sayers, August 5, 1955, in *CLCSL*, 3:638.
[72]Dorothy L. Sayers to C. S. Lewis, August 8, 1955, in *LDS*, 3:638.

the days of the French Revolution, she promised Lewis, "When the tumbril calls I will do my best to make a swanlike end."

Alas, he never had the chance to judge the form of her celestial swan dive because she died two years later, her *Paradiso* unfinished. She left behind complete renderings of the first twenty cantos, which Reynolds supplemented with the last thirteen (following minimal guidance from Sayers's papers) as well as the introduction and notes. Penguin published the combined effort in 1962. While Lewis's riff on Dante's "final style" would not appear therein, Reynolds's introduction in fact begins with him: "It has been said"—by C. S. Lewis, a footnote at the bottom of the page reveals—"that the joys of Heaven would be for most of us, in our present condition, an acquired taste."[73]

Lewis thus got the last word (on this side of the grave at least) in their Dantean debate. Commissioned by Sayers's son to write a panegyric to be shared at her funeral in January 1958, Lewis stressed the range of her exploits—first as a writer of detective fiction, then as a dramatist, and finally as a translator of medieval literature.[74] ("The variety of Dorothy Sayers' work makes it almost impossible to find anyone who can deal properly with it all," he remarked. "Charles Williams might have done so; I certainly can't.") Regarding her adventures as translator, Lewis of course dwelled on Dante. He recommended the essay whose publication he had overseen to all future readers of her version: "There you get the first impact of Dante on a mature, a scholarly, and an extremely independent mind. That impact determined the whole character of her translation." He recalled how she had been surprised by Dante: "his sheer narrative impetus, his frequent homeliness,

---

[73]Barbara Reynolds, introduction, in *The Divine Comedy 3: Paradise* (Penguin, 1962), 17.
[74]Walter Hooper explains that as "Lewis was unable to attend the service"—held at St. Margaret's Church, London—"his composition was read by the Lord Bishop of Chicester." Hooper, preface, in *On Stories: And Other Essays on Literature*, by C. S. Lewis (HarperCollins, 1982), xxviii.

his high comedy, his grotesque buffoonery." (Notice that he did not mention lucidity.) He acknowledged the "audacities in both language and rhythm" that resulted from her approach—as well as the potential loss of "sublimity and sweetness"—yet he stressed that "what Dorothy was trying to represent by her audacities is quite certainly there in Dante."[75]

To close, he raised the question of her unfinished *Paradiso*— the publication of which, at that hour, would have seemed highly unlikely. Between *Inferno* and *Purgatorio*, "She had risen," he argued, "just as Dante himself rose in his second part: growing richer, more liquid, more elevated."[76] Observing that, he had begun to wonder, "Would she go on rising?" It's not clear whether Lewis ever opened the Sayers-Reynolds *Paradise*. Thus far, no verdict on it has been found among his papers.[77] In the parting words of his panegyric, though, he set all questions of translation aside. He told the mourners that she had moved past the Florentine master's poem to what it signified: "She died instead; went, as one may in all humility hope, to learn more of Heaven than even the *Paradiso* could tell her."

## 6. SAYERS READS LEWIS (AND WRITES HIM AND WILLIAMS INTO HER TRANSLATION)

The panegyric betrays that Lewis had been a loyal Sayers reader for years; had she played that same role at his funeral, she would have been as capable of recounting the arc of his writing career. In

[75]C. S. Lewis, "A Panegyric on Dorothy Sayers," in *On Stories*, 94.

[76]Lewis, "Panegyric on Dorothy Sayers," 95.

[77]C. S. Lewis, "Rhyme and Reason," review of *The Poetry of Statement and the Poetry of Search*, by Dorothy Sayers, in *Image and Imagination* (Cambridge University Press, 2013), 239. He makes no mention of it in the review of *The Poetry of Search and the Poetry of Statement* (1963). When the translation comes up, he cites an example from *Hell* to illustrate her use of "colloquialism and comically violent rhythm." His overarching stance is the same as we have heard above: she went "to one extreme" in attempting to correct earlier translations that put Milton's voice in Dante's mouth.

chapter one, we saw evidence of this in her remark to Williams in mid-August 1944 that prior to plunging into the *Comedy*, she read his *The Figure of Beatrice* as well as Lewis's *Preface to Paradise Lost* (published October 8, 1942), the latter likely for the same reason that she read *The Figure of Beatrice*: because she was interested in what *the critic* had to say. (Of Milton, meanwhile, Sayers the Dante maniac would go on asserting what her pre-Dante self had told her friend a few weeks before reading the *Comedy*: "Milton was a thunderingly great writer of religious epic, provided it did not occur to you to compare him with Dante."[78]) She had at that point read *The Screwtape Letters* as well, and praised it in her first-ever letter to Lewis in April 1942.[79] In her Dante-themed correspondence with Williams, Lewis's name comes up repeatedly, and Sayers displays a wide acquaintance with Lewis's writing, fictional and nonfictional, including *The Allegory of Love* (a response I will discuss in chapter four). To close this chapter, though, I want to consider a book Sayers read in the midst of her back-and-forth with Lewis regarding ". . . And Telling You a Story": *The Great Divorce*.

Having previously been serialized in the *Guardian* newspaper as "Who Goes Home? or The Grand Divorce," the novel appeared as a single volume under the new title *The Great Divorce: A Dream* on January 14, 1946. Sayers immediately acquired a copy and read it with pencil in hand. Being then engaged in translating *Inferno*, she was understandably on alert for debts to Dante. Twice the connection was so strong that she registered three letters in the margin: "Inf."[80] She wrote to Lewis to praise the book and ask

---

[78]See Dorothy L. Sayers's lecture "Dante and Milton" (1952) in *FPD*, 148-81.

[79]Sayers "was the first person of importance who ever wrote me a fan-letter," Lewis wrote in 1963. "I liked her, originally, because she liked me; later, for the extraordinary zest and edge of her conversation—as I like a high wind."

[80]Marginal note by Sayers in *The Great Divorce*, by C. S. Lewis, 1946, pp. 15, 81. Dorothy L. Sayers Library collection, Marion E. Wade Center, Wheaton College, Wheaton, IL.

about Dante's influence. On January 22, Lewis thanked her for kind words about the novel and then replied, "It owes more to the *Purgatorio* than to the *Inferno*. It all grew out of the Tragedian and the Lady: specimen of a meeting like that of Beatrice and Dante in the Earthly Paradise and what happens when one side won't play."[81] Notice, though, that he claims that it owes *more*—not *only*—to *Purgatorio*. He was not telling her that she was wrong, just that the work's origins lay in reimagining a famous episode from *Purgatorio*—"the same predicament, only going wrong," as he wrote to William Kinter, an American academic, a few years later.[82]

The first of the two annotations—"Inf IX"—can be quickly dispensed with since we have it on Lewis's authority that she was right. The moment in question appears when the narrator queues up for the bus at the start of *The Great Divorce*. After noting the vehicle's decoration—"blazing with golden light, heraldically coloured"—he describes its operator: "The Driver himself seemed full of light and he used only one hand to drive with. The other he waved before his face as if to fan away the greasy steam of the rain."[83] His appearance elicits a "growl" from the passengers. Having translated *Inferno* IX a little more than a year earlier, Sayers would have immediately recognized the driver's waving hand. In that canto, an angel comes to the aid of Dante and Virgil, who are locked out of the gates of Dis. They watch hellions scatter at his approach like frogs at the sight of a snake. In Sayers's version, the rescuer is described as follows:

> His left hand, moving, fanned away the gross
> > Air from his face, nor elsewise did he seem
> > At all to find the way laborious. (lines 82-84)[84]

---

[81]C. S. Lewis to Dorothy L. Sayers, January 22, 1946, in *CLCSL*, 2:700.

[82]C. S. Lewis to William Kinter, in *CLCSL*, 3:314.

[83]C. S. Lewis, *The Great Divorce: A Dream* (Geoffrey Bles, 1946), 15.

[84]Sayers, *Divine Comedy 1: Hell*, 125.

In the letter to Kinter, Lewis verifies that the bus driver is "certainly, and consciously, modeled on the angel at the gates of Dis."[85] Score one for Dorothy.

The second case is more subtle yet also more significant to our story. It appears immediately after the episode that Lewis told Sayers was modeled on Dante's reunion with Beatrice in the Earthly Paradise in *Purgatorio*. That scene reunites Frank, an emotionally manipulative husband who has come up from the "grey town" on the bus, with his wife Sarah, blissful resident of the heavenly realm. The former attempts to engage in emotional blackmail, projecting an "image" of his pain, the "Tragedian," in order to rob Sarah of her joy (as he had done in their married life on earth). But Sarah is not moved. That is what struck Sayers.

Sayers keyed in on the narrator's admission to his guide, the George MacDonald figure, that he was made uneasy by Sarah's apparent lack of sympathy for her husband: "'And yet . . . and yet . . . ' said I to my Teacher . . . , 'even now I am not quite sure. Is it really tolerable that she should be *untouched by his misery*, even his self-made misery?'"[86] Next to these words Sayers wrote "Inf II" in the margin. She was remembering the moment in *Inferno* II when Virgil tells Dante that Beatrice, citizen of paradise, had visited him in limbo to commission him to serve as Dante's guide. Virgil relates that he asked how she could stand to visit hell. She replied:

> Of hurtful things we ought to be afraid,
> > But of no others, truly, inasmuch
> > As these have nothing to give cause for dread;

---

[85]Lewis to Kinter, in *CLCSL*, 3:313-14. He also notes in his "Dante's Similes" paper (1940) that this is "surely the best angel ever made by a poet." C. S. Lewis, "Dante's Similes," in *Studies in Medieval and Renaissance Literature*, ed. Walter Hooper (Cambridge University Press, 1966), 69.

[86]Lewis, *Great Divorce*, 81, italics added.

My nature, by God's mercy, is made such
  As your calamities can nowise shake,
  Nor these dark fires have any power to touch. (lines 88-93)[87]

In the Italian, Beatrice says, *la vostra miseria non mi tange*—literally, "Your misery cannot touch me." Score two for Dorothy.

Sayers wasn't done with *The Great Divorce*, however. To understand what she did next requires a little context.

Writing to Wilfred Scott-Giles, the heraldry expert and artist behind her edition's famous maps, a month after Lewis's reply, Sayers remarked that Penguin's plan to release *Hell* in July was unrealistic: "There's such a devil of a lot of commentary and annotation to do."[88] Williams's death had thrown the full weight of the project on her. The translation—including a bevy of front, back, and interstitial materials by Dorothy Sayers—wouldn't appear until November 1949. But on May 22, 1946, with the original timelines still in mind, she delivered her completed canto-level notes to Rieu.[89]

In keeping with her instructions to Williams as to what the Penguin reader needed from the commentary, those notes are frugal about historical details. (The biographies of minor characters, for example, are banished to the glossary, "where the reader may look them up or not as he likes."[90]) Yet they are also (again, as Sayers charged Williams) strikingly *forthright* about the spiritual stakes of Dante's actions, architectures, and images—especially when compared to the standard-issue *Comedy* commentary.

---

[87]Sayers, *Divine Comedy 1: Hell*, 80.

[88]Dorothy L. Sayers to W. R. Scott-Giles, February 25, 1946, in *LDS*, 3:201. Sayers solicits Scott-Giles's help with the maps in this letter.

[89]Dorothy L. Sayers to E. V. Rieu, May 22, 1946, in *LDS*, 3:236.

[90]Sayers, introduction, in *Divine Comedy 1: Hell*, 66. she gives the example of *Inferno* V. It's enough to know that the characters *mentioned* are "famous lovers," she observes, but to understand Dante's conversation with Francesca, one needs additional information about Paolo and Francesca's illicit relationship and death.

Her note on Beatrice's lines from *Inferno* II cited above offers a perfect illustration of her commentary's spiritual side: "The souls of the blessed can still pity the self-inflicted misery of the wicked, but they can no longer be hurt or infected by it." She then quotes Lewis—"actions of pity will live for ever; the passion of pity will not," provides the page number where the reader can find it in *The Great Divorce*, and recommends the novel for "[handling]" "the subject . . . in a very illuminating way."[91]

As hardly needs saying, this move is highly unconventional. Directing the reader of a classic to a recently published work of fiction simply wasn't done in notes at the time—and would still be unusual today. If a contemporary book were referenced, it would almost certainly be (then as now) a nonfictional study of the author or the author's genre or time period. Coming off her reading of *The Great Divorce* only a few months (or perhaps weeks) before she wrote this note, however, Sayers felt no such inhibitions. Williams had shown her that Dante's conversation partners were not only to be found among the dead. She was convinced that Lewis had done first-rate Dante criticism in the passage I have quoted. Since she had no prejudice against modern fiction in this regard, she urged the reader troubled by Beatrice's apparent frigidity to consult Dr. Lewis's dream vision.

It gets better. In a preceding note on the same page, she calls on our third traveler to offer an overarching assessment of Virgil's meeting with Beatrice:

> Of all this passage, Charles Williams says: "Beatrice has to ask [Virgil] to go: she cannot command him, though she puts her trust in his 'fair speech.' Religion itself cannot order poetry about; the grand art is wholly autonomous. . . . We should have been fortunate if the ministers of religion and poetry had always spoken

---

[91] Sayers, notes on *Inferno* II, in *Divine Comedy 1: Hell*, 83.

to each other with such courtesy as these." (*The Figure of Beatrice,* p. 112)[92]

This has the look of the conventional pivot to a learned commentator. But notice that Williams is not cited to explicate Dante's language or context (the standard business of commentary). He is called in for his enduring wisdom about the relationship between religion and poetry that he believed to be embodied in the episode.[93] He is doing what Sayers so treasured in his Dante criticism—refusing to see the past as a foreign country. In both cases, she was enlisting her friends to break down the historical barrier between then and now, Dante and us.

These two notes present in microcosm the story I've been telling across this chapter. Reading Williams led Sayers to read Dante, and she then told him *all* about it. He encouraged her to join him in sharing Dante with everyone else. She began to translate the *Comedy,* and while doing so she read Lewis, who was also overseeing her first published essay on Dante. She then weaves Williams's and Lewis's voices into her commentary. In the letter to Kinter on Dante references in *The Great Divorce,* Lewis revealed that he "intended readers to spot these resemblances: so you may go to the top of the class!"[94] Williams and Sayers clearly also belong at the top of the class. Indeed, we might say that the three authors were team-teaching.

Across this chapter, we have seen a *cohort* of Dante critics coalesce. Sayers, Williams, and Lewis played leading roles in launching each other's Dantean expeditions. They built on each

---

[92]Sayers, notes on *Inferno* II, in *Divine Comedy 1: Hell,* 83.

[93]The passage is also notable because a few months later Lewis and Sayers engaged in an epistolary debate regarding the relationship between faith and writing, he at one point rebuking her for putting her "artistic conscience" before her duty as a Christian to edify readers, and she replying that good workmanship—without the need to be preachy—was sufficient fulfillment of one's calling as a Christian writer. See, in particular, C. S. Lewis to Dorothy L. Sayers, *CLCSL,* 2:728-29, and Sayers to Lewis, July 31, 1946, in *LDS,* 3:252-54.

[94]Lewis to Kinter, in *CLCSL,* 3:314.

other's ideas. At times, they critiqued each other's efforts. Their readings of and writings on Dante comprise a network of allusions, quotations, and citations. As a result, we cannot understand how one approached Dante without consulting the work of the other two.

They followed the way of Dante together.

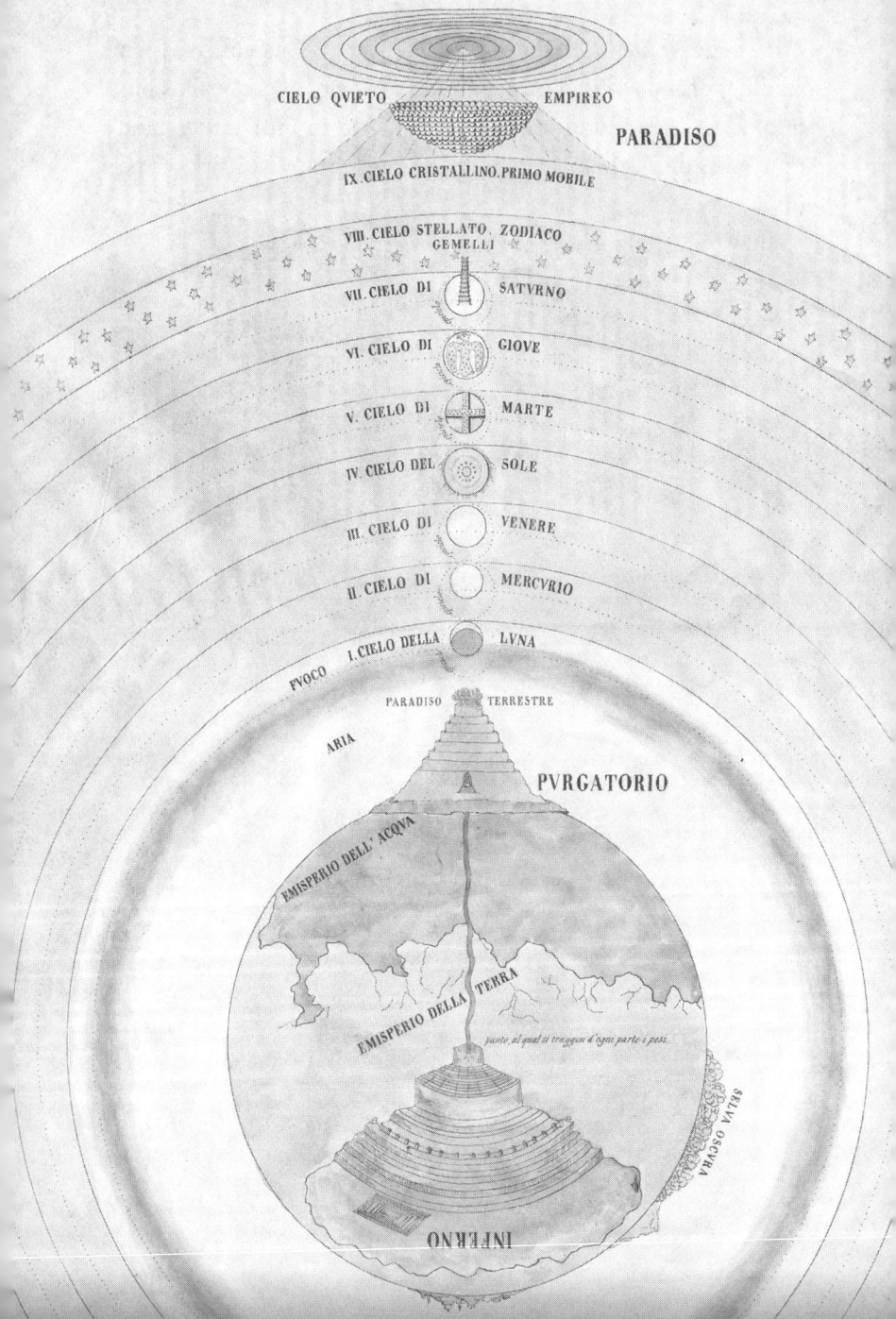

**Figure 3.1.** Michelangelo Caetani, *Figura Universale della Divina Commedia* (Rome, 1855)

# 3

# HELL WITHIN AND WITHOUT

*It's not a question of God "sending" us to Hell. In*
*each of us there is something growing up which will*
*of itself be Hell unless it is nipped in the bud.*

C. S. Lewis, "The Trouble with 'X'" (1948)

*That is Dante's vision of a corrupted society. Whether it is borrowed or*
*original matters little. The question is rather: is it rational? is it true?*
*Can we recognize the steps of that inexorable progression? Have we*
*seen anything at all like it?*

Dorothy L. Sayers, "The City of Dis" (1947)

WE HAVE HEARD LEWIS INFORM SAYERS that her *Inferno*
translation passed the "real test": Within a few lines, the reader had
forgotten about the translator, and within a few pages, the reader
had forgotten about Dante and was "thinking only about Hell."[1]
He may have been remembering a sentence from her ". . . And
Telling You a Story" that he had read a few years earlier, in which
Sayers argues that Dante "conceives that 'his whole business is to
show us Hell,' and that is precisely what he shows us—not 'the

---

[1]C. S. Lewis to Dorothy L. Sayers, November 15, 1949, in *CLCSL*, 2:997.

poetry of Hell,' but simply Hell."[2] Sayers took Lewis's report as the compliment it was intended to be, replying a few days later that if people could be moved by her translation she would be well pleased and "best of all, as your second note says, they can forget me for Dante and Dante for Hell." She continued, "I think *Inferno* is really frightening. It has the quality of Hell—the infinite dreary malice and the infinite vicious monotony."[3] In the last statement, she was elaborating on Williams's observation on *Inferno* in *The Figure of Beatrice* that "In hell there is no progress, only insignificant monotony."[4]

Hell is a topic that most people would prefer *not* to think about, of course, and even among the faithful, showing a keen personal interest in hell may make one's fellow parishioners anxious. So why would Lewis be grateful to Sayers for carrying his thoughts there? And why, in turn, would she be glad to learn that her translation had that effect? And why would any of my three pilgrim readers be engaged by images of "monotony"—infinite, vicious, meaningless? Not being lovers of *Inferno*'s "dramatic horrors" (to borrow a phrase from Sayers) for their own sake, what did my authors find in Dante's hell that led them to make repeated visits? Why—and, just as importantly, *how*—did they want others to undertake Dante's journey through hell?

One reason is obvious: because they didn't want readers to become its permanent residents. In this wish, they were following Dante's lead. In the same passage of ". . . And Telling You a Story" cited above, Sayers explains that Dante "desires that his Hell should evoke an emotional repulsion, issuing in a vigorous rejection by the will, just as he desires that his Purgatory and Paradise should be embraced with equal vigour, by the undivided

---

[2]ATYS, 12.
[3]Dorothy L. Sayers to C. S. Lewis, November 18, 1949, in *LDS*, 3:467.
[4]FB, 227.

personality." A short while later she argues that *Inferno* shows us "evil stripped of its last shred of glitter; and the deeper we go the more suffocating does the atmosphere become, and the meaner grows the aspect of the evil selfhood thus stripped naked."[5] Hell, in short, tears away the charming facades that cloak evil in this world. Beginning with her first thorough reading of *Inferno* in August 1944 and in numerous subsequent dispatches, Sayers urged others to read *Inferno* because it was an exciting story. But she kept coming back to *Inferno*, as did Williams and Lewis, because the story, the shocking images, the memorable characters and their speeches—the whole poetic performance—were in the service of something greater. In *Inferno*, my cohort received an education in evil.

That education betrays itself in numerous incidents and declarations that appear across my trio's writings. For instance, in the new preface that Lewis wrote for *The Screwtape Letters* when it was reissued in 1961, he argues that Dante's devils are "the best" that literature has to offer: "His devils, as Ruskin rightly remarked, in their rage, spite and obscenity, are far more like what the reality must be than anything in Milton," the Miltonic devils being too full of "grandeur and high poetry." While Lewis's devils work at desks, under the veneer of official politeness they are spiritually Dantean (*not* Miltonic): "Every now and then it"—the "thin crust" of workplace manners—"gets punctured, and the scalding lava of their hatred spurts out."[6] In *Descent into Hell* (1937), to cite another fictional example, Williams likens the "gabbling" of his Lilith character to Dante's Lucifer: "The old woman stirred and tried to speak; there issued from her lips a meaningless gabble, such gabble as Dante, inspired, attributes to the guardian of all

---

[5] ATYS, 13.
[6] C. S. Lewis, preface, in *The Screwtape Letters and Screwtape Proposes a Toast* (Geoffrey Bles, 1961), ix-x.

the circles of hell."[7] In *The Figure of Beatrice*, he emphasizes
the passivity of Dante's Satan (in contrast to Milton's), his form
"fixed in ice from the mid-breast down," the traitor against God
"gnawing" on infamous human traitors with his monstrous three
mouths. No high poetry flows from those maws.[8]

Yet among the members of my cohort, Sayers not only had the
most to say about *Inferno* but also developed at greatest length
three key ideas about the *Comedy*'s first canticle that Williams
and Lewis shared. Thus, Sayers will be the lead voice in this
chapter, with Williams and Lewis chiming in regularly. In what
follows, I examine those three ideas: first, that heaven clarifies
hell (and hell heaven); second, that reading *Inferno* ought to be an
exercise in spiritual introspection; and third, that *Inferno* extends
a chilling but nonetheless profitable account of the breakdown
of communal life (what Sayers and Williams call "the Way of the
City") under the weight of our vices. Again and again we will hear
my trio saying: Don't look away, don't close the book, and, most
importantly of all, don't mistake what you hear in *Inferno* for the
message of the *Comedy* as a whole.

## HEAVEN COMES FIRST

In "The Meaning of Heaven and Hell," originally delivered as a
lecture to the Summer School of Italian Studies at Cambridge
in 1948, Sayers acknowledges right off the bat that the order of
Dante's three canticles presents a problem in the modern context.
In plot terms, she notes, hell makes perfect sense as a starting line
for the journey. The very premise of the story is that Dante needs
to see where he is headed if he persists in his wandering ways
before he may mingle with the penitents on Mount Purgatory
and the blessed in the Empyrean. Hell, moreover, makes no sense

---

[7]Charles Williams, *Descent into Hell* (Faber & Faber, 1937), 207.
[8]*FB*, 144.

as the terminus for a poem called *The Comedy*. Yet hell represents an awkward starting point for many contemporary readers,
Sayers admits, because they lack the intellectual background that
Dante could count on *his* contemporaries to possess. For the
modern reader, "with his often very inadequate theology and
his inherited tradition of vague and kindly humanism," *Inferno* is
likely to appear "this huge block" of outmoded, offensive ideas
that are "irreconcilable with the religion of love."[9] Some readers,
she anticipated, would try to get around the block by trying to
concentrate on "the poetry"—irrespective of its meaning—
while others would "write Dante down as a spiteful politician or
a vindictive sadist" before moving on to another book—almost
certainly not *Purgatorio* or *Paradiso*.[10]

What a pity, Sayers sighs. For while "experientially" the canticles appear in the right order, from an *intellectual* standpoint, the
poem's arrangement is backwards. This is true, she contends, in
two respects. The first is specific to Dante's biography, in which
"Heaven preceded Hell."[11] As the poet records in *Vita Nuova*, that
early collection of love poems that made Dante's name in Florence,
he was called to poetry after "[glimpsing] the vision of eternity"
through the figure of Beatrice. His career began not with sin and
judgment and death but a love that gestured to greater glory.

The second reason is anchored in the theology of the Middle
Ages (among other ages). In keeping with the church's teaching,
Sayers observes, Dante held that "Heaven—or rather God in
Heaven—is the only unconditioned reality." Another way to put
this is to say that everything starts with and depends on God.
Even if Dante's plot starts elsewhere, his *thinking* begins with the
beginning—with the God of Genesis 1, who created everything.

---

[9]Dorothy L. Sayers, "The Meaning of Heaven and Hell," in *IPD*, 45.
[10]Sayers, "Meaning of Heaven and Hell," 45-46.
[11]Sayers, "Meaning of Heaven and Hell," 46.

The universe raises the question, in turn, why God did it. Why create? As Sayers points out, Dante tells us in *Purgatorio* that to ask such questions is to venture into depths where we are liable to drown: God's "primal *why* / Lies so deep hid, no wit can wade so far" (VIII.67-68).[12]

Nonetheless, Sayers argues, we may hazard a few thoughts. One line of traditional Christian thinking, she found "nobly summed up" in *Paradiso* XXIX:[13]

> Not to increase His good, which cannot be,
>> But that His splendour, shining back, might say:
>> *Behold, I am*, in His eternity,
> Beyond the measurement of night and day,
>> Beyond all boundary, as He did please,
>> New loves Eternal Love shed from His ray. (lines 13-18)[14]

From her inherited Temple Classics edition of *Paradiso*, Sayers had learned that "Dante is careful in the use of 'splendor' [*splendore* in Italian] for reflected, not direct light," meaning the "splendour" here is the reflection of God's glory in creation. While the "new loves" mentioned at the end of the second stanza are the angels, the Temple Classics editors (like many other commentators) read in these stanzas a general statement regarding God's motive for creation: "Therefore we must not understand this passage as declaring the manifestation of his own glory to be God's motive in creation, but rather the conferring of conscious being, the sense of existence, upon his creatures."[15]

In her lecture, Sayers boils the motive down to one word: "The reason, says Dante, was *generosity*." God, she continues, "wanted, and

---

[12]Dorothy L. Sayers, trans., *The Divine Comedy 2: Purgatory* (Penguin, 1955), 128.

[13]Sayers, "Meaning of Heaven and Hell," 47.

[14]Dorothy L. Sayers and Barbara Reynolds, trans., *The Divine Comedy 3: Paradise* (Penguin, 1962), 309.

[15]Editor's note, in *The Paradiso of Dante Alighieri* (J. M. Dent, 1904), 360.

wants, to share His reality." It is pure generosity, Sayers stresses; God
does not do it for "gain": "that is impossible; for all things come from
Him, and He could no more *add* anything to Himself by making a
universe than a poet can add anything to *him*self by writing a poem."[16]
(Beside this passage, Lewis wrote in his copy, "Much less."[17]) She
goes further: God "desired that there should be others, derived from
Himself but distinguishable from Him, and with a dependent but
genuine reality of their own, having each a true selfhood, which
should reflect back to Him the joy and beauty and goodness that
they received from Him."[18] Rational beings, she adds later in the
lecture, engage in this reflection freely: "They say, 'I am;' and with
the whole power of their selves they eagerly mean what they say."[19]

Yet that assent, Sayers stresses, must be to *reality*. And what is
the creature's reality? She highlights three defining "facts of the
situation" (a.k.a. the human condition): that we are created beings,
that our purpose is to reflect God's glory to the "utmost" that our
powers allow, and that "true selfhood" can be reached *only* if we do
as Dante does in *Paradiso*: allow our "will and desire" (XXXIII.144)
to turn, starlike, around God. Yet in the gift of selfhood there also
lies a grave danger: that the creation may reject the "facts" and,
rather than revolving around the source of its light and life, seek
the point of its existence *in itself*. "This," Sayers declares, "is the fall
into illusion, which is Hell."[20]

## HEAVEN IN REVERSE

Through this careful chain of thought, Sayers was striving to bring
her audience into the distorted mental world of *Inferno*. She

---

[16]Sayers, "Meaning of Heaven and Hell," 47, italics original.
[17]Marginal note by Lewis in *IPD*, 47. C. S. Lewis Library collection, Marion E. Wade Center,
Wheaton College, Wheaton, IL.
[18]Sayers, "Meaning of Heaven and Hell," 47.
[19]Sayers, "Meaning of Heaven and Hell," 62.
[20]Sayers, "Meaning of Heaven and Hell," 62.

was not relying on Dante alone to explain the hellish condition, though. In characterizing hell as the refusal of "assent" to reality and the "fall into illusion," Sayers drew on the works of the other two travelers on the way of Dante. In *The Figure of Beatrice*, for example, Sayers had read the following compact comparison of Dante's three realms: "Heaven is the absolute thing; Purgatory, the approach to it, is in proper relation to it; but the improper relation of Hell is twisted." Williams continues: "It was said of God that 'his necessity is in Himself,' and this is the only necessity. Hell is the place of those spirits who wish to have their necessity in themselves. . . . The only illusion is that there is in us a necessity to demand something other than He; the only disillusion is to find it is not so, and that our only necessity is love."[21]

Williams had thus mulled two of the essential truths that Sayers reported in the 1948 lecture, though we can see (and not for the last time in this book) that Sayers's manner of unpacking the argument is much more accessible. When Williams names heaven "the absolute thing," he is invoking the sense in which philosophers speak of something being "absolute"—that it is unconditioned, complete, free, perfect. As such, the other two realms exist in relation to heaven—one proper, one twisted—not the other way around. The second truth is that hell gathers those who "wish to have their necessity in themselves." The operative word is *wish*. Creatures may wish to belong wholly to themselves; but that is contrary to fact, Williams likewise held. *Inferno*, Williams would have us see, is the record of the myriad ways that souls suffer if they cling to such self-deception.

Recall, too, that less than two years before she delivered her lecture, Sayers had read, rapidly and approvingly, *The Great Divorce*. The very same episode in the novel that made its way into

---

[21]FB, 147.

Sayers's notes for *Inferno* II—George MacDonald's remarks on the "action of pity" enduring forever while the "passion" does not—is cited in the lecture. Sayers's insistence that heaven and hell are, respectively, matters of assenting to or refusing "reality" suggests a further debt to a line of thought running through Lewis's novel. It is brought to the surface in this exchange between the narrator and MacDonald:

> "Ah, the Saved . . . what happens to them is best described as the opposite of a mirage. What seemed, when they entered it, to be the vale of misery turns out, when they look back, to have been a well; and where present experience saw only salt deserts memory truthfully records that the pools were full of water."
>
> "Then those people are right who say that Heaven and Hell are only states of mind?"
>
> "Hush," said he sternly. "Do not blaspheme. Hell is a state of mind—ye never said a truer word. And every state of mind, left to itself, every shutting up of the creature within the dungeon of its own mind—is, in the end, Hell. But Heaven is not a state of mind. Heaven is reality itself. All that is fully real is Heavenly."[22]

The phrase "Heaven is reality itself" is often glossed by commentators on Platonic lines, and Lewis would surely have acknowledged Plato's influence on his portrayal of heaven as solid reality compared to the shadowy denizens of the gray town.[23] But Sayers, steeped as she was in Dante when she read *The Great Divorce*, would have seen more going on here. Lewis is exploring the same set of concerns circling around the priority of heaven that Williams raised in the passage just quoted. Heaven is *fully* real; all else is real to the extent that it participates in that reality. In *Miracles* (1947), Lewis in the

---

[22]C. S. Lewis, *The Great Divorce: A Dream* (Geoffrey Bles, 1946), 62-63.

[23]Louis Markos, for example, calls *The Great Divorce*'s suggestion that "heaven is not only more real than hell but also more real than the earth" "the supreme Christianizing of Plato's distinction between the World of Being and the World of Becoming." Markos, *From Plato to Christ: How Platonic Thought Shaped the Christian Faith* (IVP Academic, 2021), 210.

same vein calls God the "basic Fact or Actuality, the source of all
other facthood," and "the opaque centre of all existences, the thing
that simply and entirely *is*, the fountain of facthood."[24] To make
anything else the center of one's existence is to fall into illusion.
To be true to one's self—as the "ghosts" do in *The Great Divorce*—
therefore, is not the noble course we take it to be but the gravest
of errors.[25] With Dante, Sayers and Lewis depict hell as the choice
to remain forever in the "dungeon" of one's own mind. Hell is the
fierce embrace of *un*reality.[26]

In one of the most penetrating passages of her 1948 lecture,
Sayers cites Williams directly and, we may suspect, Lewis
indirectly when she draws out the consequences of "[refusing]
assent to reality":

> If we rebel against the nature of things and choose to think that
> what we at the moment want is the center of the universe to which
> everything else ought to accommodate itself, the first effect on
> us will be that the whole universe will seem to be filled with an
> implacable and inexplicable hostility. We shall begin to feel that
> everything has a down on us, and that, being so badly treated,
> we have a just grievance against things in general. That is the
> *knowledge of good as evil* and the fall into illusion.[27]

If we persist in that illusion—if we coddle our resentments and
inflame our outrage—then, Sayers warns, we are choosing, and
receiving a "foretaste" of, the corrosion of life in hell.

---

[24]C. S. Lewis, *Miracles* (Geoffrey Bles, 1947), 107, 111.

[25]In the same exchange, MacDonald parrots the ghost's self-justifications as follows: "In the
actual language of the Lost, the words will be different, no doubt. One will say he has always served his country right or wrong; and another that he has sacrificed everything to his
Art; and some that they've never been taken in, and some that, thank God, they've always
looked after Number One, and nearly all, that, at least they've been true to themselves."

[26]We will see in chapter 5 that Sayers then developed the illusion/reality dichotomy to describe the action of purgation: the penitents on Mount Purgatory move from the one to
the other, from the self to God.

[27]Sayers, "Meaning of Heaven and Hell," 64, italics added.

The phrase "the knowledge of good as evil" Sayers borrowed from Williams. He first characterized sin this way in *He Came Down from Heaven* (1938), and Sayers was soon taken with the idea, citing it in print the following year.[28] The phrase expresses the core of Williams's account of human fallenness: "Man at the time of the Fall, and continuously and voluntarily since, insisted on knowing good and evil; that is, good *as* evil (since there was nothing but the good to know, the evil could only lie in the manner of knowing)." Williams sums up the lesson in a tight phrase: "All is in the end a question of how we choose to know."[29]

As theologian Charles Hefling explains, Williams's interpretation of Genesis 3 hinges on the contrast between two modes of knowing: God's and humankind's. Knowing by "sheer intelligence," the former may "know good not only in itself but in its deprivation—possible, that is, to know evil—without thereby bringing the deprivation into existence." Humanity (whom Williams called "the Adam"), by contrast, knows experientially—in time and space. The first humans thus knew evil "in the only way they could know it, which was the same as the way they already knew the good—by experience."[30] Into a world of good things, they introduced rupture, deception, confusion, enmity, shame—in a word, evil.

Sayers then illustrates the lesson not by dialing up villains from *Inferno* but conjuring incidents from domestic life.[31] Her

---

[28]Dorothy L. Sayers to the editor of *The Church Times*, August 1, 1939, in *LDS*, 2:132.
[29]*HCDH*, 150.
[30]Charles Hefling, introduction, in *Charles Williams: Essential Writings in Spirituality and Theology* (Cowley, 1993), 22-23.
[31]In this lecture, she recycles a scenario that she had proposed a few years earlier to explain Williams's ideas about evil to a mystified correspondent: You board the train to Watford when you mean to go to Stanmore and then, upon discovering you error, denounce it as the "wrong train," as if the train were somehow unjust, when you are the cause of all the trouble *to yourself.* In the earlier version, Sayers had been the errant traveler: "My ignorance, carelessness, or perversity, has caused me to know the perfectly good train as an evil

most sinister example is a jealous husband who, in his attempt to possess his spouse "body and soul," practices the hermeneutics of suspicion at home. If his spouse enjoys the company of friends and pursues interests other than him, he lodges accusations on the grounds of infidelity at not deeming him all-sufficient. If she forgoes other company and "waits on him hand and foot," he accuses her of "making a martyr of herself."[32] In his evil eyes, she can, in short, do no good. The man could walk right into *The Great Divorce* and be perfectly at home (indeed, he has more than a passing resemblance to the Tragedian mentioned in the last chapter), and that should not surprise us. Sayers, Williams, Lewis, and Dante were of one mind about evil: that it is for humans utterly and devastatingly commonplace. All four authors believed that we fool ourselves if we think evil is not an *everyday* affair and a constant temptation for each and every one of us.

"What is Hell?" Sayers asked in her 1948 lecture. Following Dante, and in concert with Williams and Lewis, she taught her listeners that hell is the closing of our hands to God's generosity, the rebellion against our natures as dependent beings, the shuttering of our minds to the true order of creation.[33] She distilled her answer thus: "Hell, in a manner, is Heaven in reverse."[34]

---

train, and that is to create positive evil in the world." Dorothy L. Sayers to K. C. Harrison, March 4, 1940, in *LDS*, 2:152.

[32]Sayers, "Meaning of Heaven and Hell," 65.

[33]As Sayers well understood, the fearful structural symmetries of the three realms of the Dantean afterlife declare heaven's precedence as well: *Inferno* begins in a dark wood at the bottom of a hill and then passes through nine circles; *Purgatorio* encompasses two "preparatory zones" and seven terraces, and culminates in an Edenic forest on the top of the mountain; *Paradiso* passes through nine celestial spheres on the way to the Empyrean, where the blessed, a heavenly rose, resides with God. Against the background of heavenly reality, the true nature of Mount Purgatory becomes clear: There the penitents labor to live entirely in God's reality. Through rigorous practices of self-renunciation, they strive to become free to serve God, to see God, and to love God *fully*.

[34]Sayers, "Meaning of Heaven and Hell," 68.

## IS IT TRUE?

Throughout this book, I seek to reveal my cohort's significance as readers of Dante. I recommend their works to anyone (not just newcomers) who wants to understand Dante's place in literary history, his techniques (including the thorny business of his allegory; see chapter four), his picture of the cosmos, his fullness (as I'm calling that special sort of satisfaction the *Comedy* provides). But in my view, my authors' truly outstanding contribution in the wartime and postwar contexts in which they were publishing was to argue that the *Comedy* is *true*.

Unsurprisingly, they did so in differing fashions, and even less surprisingly, Sayers was the most forthright in this regard, especially regarding *Inferno*. As she began to lecture on Dante and assembled the front and back matter of *Hell*, she was frustrated to find little help from the *dantisti* in addressing the kinds of questions that mattered to ordinary readers and she believed ought to matter to all readers. While she respected learned studies of the linguistic, historical, and theological features of the *Comedy*, she believed that the academics were in danger of missing the point of the exercise. What about life? What about the soul? The attraction of Williams's approach therefore only grew as she read other volumes of Dante criticism.

In her 1947 lecture "The City of Dis," Sayers began by telling her audience exactly that. She quoted from the opening and closing words *of The Figure of Beatrice* to illustrate that for Williams the *Comedy* was the outgrowth of the poet's lived experience and may speak to ours: The "whole of [Dante's] work," Williams declared in the latter case, "is the image of a Way not confined to poets."[35] In the two passages, Sayers saw "a guide to the first principles of literary criticism" that could be summarized as two questions:

---

[35]*FB*, 233.

"What did this poem mean in the experience of the poet? And what does it mean in our own experience?"[36]

In the lecture, and throughout her commentary on *Hell*, Sayers endeavored to apply these "first principles." When Sayers gazed on the master plan of *Inferno*, she observed its likeness to what she knew lurked in own self and to stories recounted in the newspaper. Dante, she had come to see, was a profound spiritual psychologist and sociologist who peered more deeply into the psyche "than the psycho-analyst's plummet ever sounded," as she said in another lecture in 1947.[37] In the midst of many labors assembling the *Hell* volume, she told her audience of "The City of Dis" lecture, she had experienced a deathly epiphany in which she beheld a "vision of the whole depth of the Abyss." Dante's hell did not seem some far-off historical ruin, the vestige of an ignorant bygone era—it was "something actual and contemporary." It stood before her "a judgment of fact" that could not be historicized away.[38] It begged the question that the professionals seemed allergic to asking: Had Dante written truly of evil?

In an inspired passage, she contends that gauging Dante's accuracy is not an archival problem for PhDs, anyway. It is a personal one for each reader who takes up the poem: "The map of Hell is the map of the black heart; if we want to verify it, we cannot do so from books. At most, we may profit by the title of a little household handbook very popular in my childhood . . . : it was called *Enquire Within*." Her next words condense the moral of *Inferno* with a riff on Jesus' words in Luke 17:21: "The Kingdom of Hell, like the Kingdom of Heaven, is within you."[39]

---

[36]Dorothy L. Sayers, "The City of Dis," in *IPD*, 127.
[37]Dorothy L. Sayers, "Dante's Imagery: I—Symbolic," in *IPD*, 11.
[38]Sayers, "City of Dis," 128.
[39]Sayers, "City of Dis," 130.

# SECTION OF THE HELL.

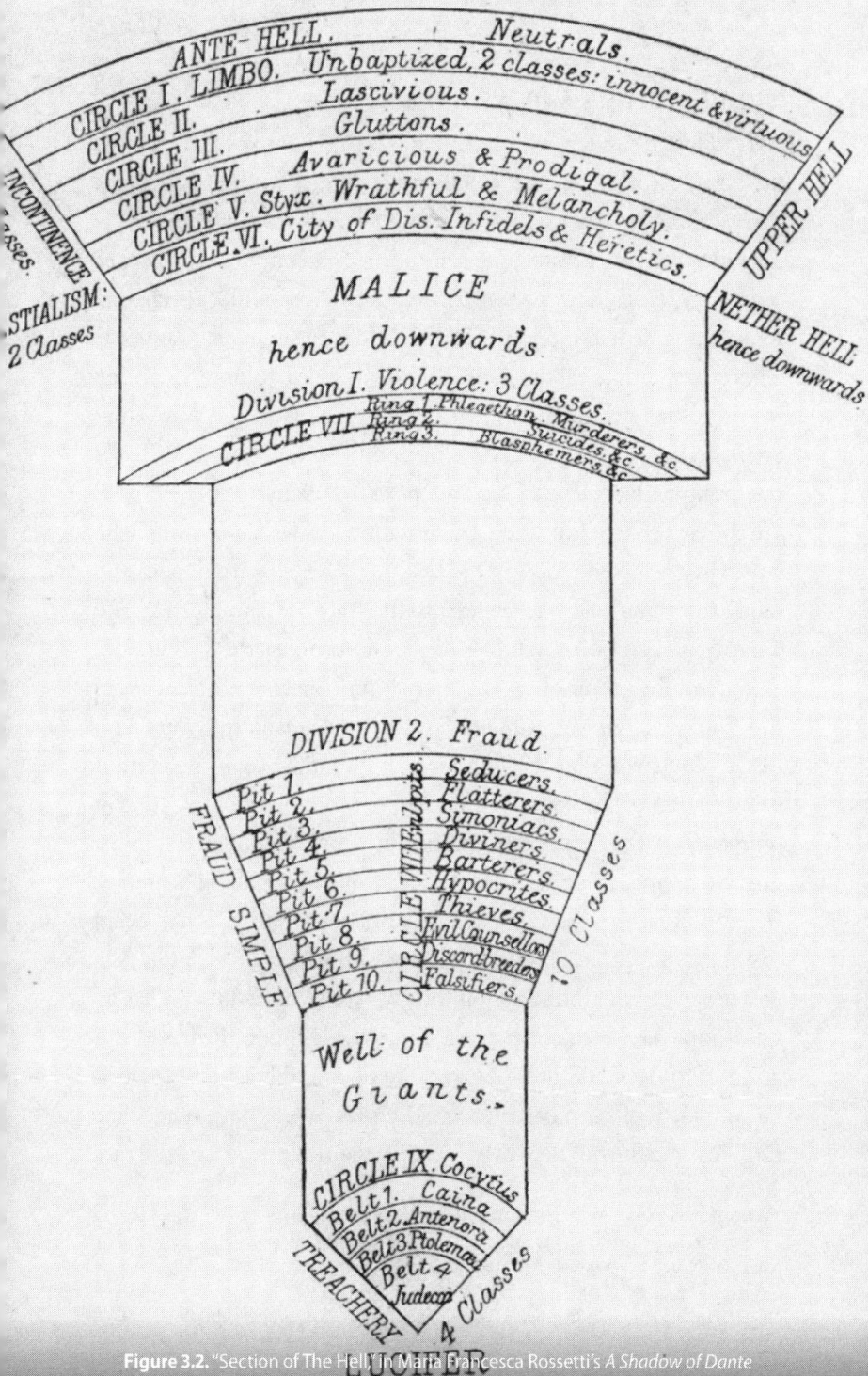

ANTE-HELL.     Neutrals.
CIRCLE I. LIMBO. Unbaptized, 2 classes: innocent & virtuous
CIRCLE II.    Lascivious.
CIRCLE III.    Gluttons.
CIRCLE IV.   Avaricious & Prodigal.
CIRCLE V. Styx. Wrathful & Melancholy.
CIRCLE VI. City of Dis. Infidels & Heretics.

INCONTINENCE ...ses.

...STIALISM: 2 Classes

UPPER HELL

NETHER HELL hence downwards.

MALICE

hence downwards

Division I. Violence: 3 Classes.

CIRCLE VII   Ring 1 Phlegethon. Murderers &c
    Ring 2.     Suicides. &c
    Ring 3.     Blasphemers &c

DIVISION 2. Fraud.

FRAUD SIMPLE

Pit 1.   Seducers.
Pit 2.   Flatterers.
Pit 3.   Simoniacs.
Pit 4.   Diviners.
Pit 5.   Barterers.
Pit 6.   Hypocrites.
Pit 7.   Thieves.
Pit 8.   Evil Counsellors
Pit 9.   Discord-breeders
Pit 10.   Falsifiers.

CIRCLE VIII Malebolge

10 Classes

Well of the Giants.

CIRCLE IX. Cocytus
Belt 1. Caina
Belt 2. Antenora
Belt 3. Ptolemæa
Belt 4. Judecca

TREACHERY

4 Classes

LUCIFER

**Figure 3.2.** "Section of The Hell" in Maria Francesca Rossetti's *A Shadow of Dante* (Longmans & Green, 1894 edition)

...ace Chap. V.)

## ENQUIRE WITHIN AND WITHOUT

To read *Inferno* under Sayers's guidance is thus not to be ferried off to the distant world of medieval Italy, where Guelphs and Ghibellines carry on their petty quarrels at a safe remove from us; it is to be invited to read oneself and one's city *against the background of Dante's increasingly bleak pictures of evil in its true form.* As we will see in chapter four, Williams had offered Sayers freedom to interpret Dante's allegory in multiple dimensions. But for her *Hell* volume, as she explains in the introduction, she had focused on two: the Way of the Soul and the Way of the City.[40] The poem, Sayers stresses, is *always* operating on both levels (and still more simultaneously), and both are concerned with salvation. "Civilizations, as well as persons," she writes in the introduction, "need to know the Hell within them and purge their sins before entering into the state of Grace, Justice, and Charity and so becoming the City of God on earth."[41] Therefore, along with her counsel to "enquire within," Sayers urges readers of the *Comedy* to *enquire without.* Publicly and privately, Sayers wondered aloud whether the first level of investigation—the serious examination of the soul—would be the more difficult for her contemporaries, the degeneration of society obviously being a familiar literary theme. (George Orwell's *1984*, for example, appeared in the same year as Sayers's *Hell*, 1949.) But she suspected that recent history had created an opening. "If we know how to read it," she writes early in the introduction to *Hell*, "we shall find that it has an enormous relevance both to us as individuals and to the world situation of to-day." Not too long ago, the poet and his world seemed backward, fossils of a barbaric age. But those who "have so recently rediscovered the problem of evil, the problem of power, and the ease

---

[40]As explained elsewhere in this book, these terms represent Sayers's reformulations of the moral (or tropological) and typological (or "allegorical" in the narrower sense) levels of the fourfold medieval approach to the interpretation of Scripture and, depending on whom you ask, the *Comedy* too.

[41]Sayers, introduction, in *The Divine Comedy 1: Hell*, trans. Sayers (Penguin, 1949), 69.

with which our most God-like imaginings are 'betrayed by what is fake within,'" she wagered, would be ready to give Dante a hearing.[42]

As a result of these beliefs, Sayers's commentary on *Inferno* in her *Hell* volume never holds the vices it describes at arm's length. Just the opposite! Her notes build bridges between each of the circles of hell, and many of their subdivisions, to modern concerns. Her account of the "vestibule" of hell described in *Inferno* III is a case in point. Here Dante and Virgil observe the company traditionally known as the "Neutrals," a pack that includes humans who never picked between good and evil ("whose lives knew neither praise nor infamy," in Dante's phrasing) and angels who stayed out of the war in heaven between Lucifer and God. The note begins with the details that one would expect, noting Dante's likely debt to the *Aeneid* here and the zone's novelty among Christian thinkers about the afterlife. In these details Sayers discharges the first office of the critic named above: to provide the details we need to catch the poet's meaning.

But Sayers also wants the reader to ask what the poem "means in our experience," so she continues, naming the vestibule as "the abode of the weather-cock mind, the vague tolerance which will neither approve nor condemn, the cautious cowardice for which no decision is ever final." She then vividly recasts the canto's central image: "The spirits rush aimlessly after the aimlessly whirling banner, stung and goaded, as of old, by the thought that, in doing something definite whatsoever, they are missing doing something else."[43] The clever addition is "as of old" to this present-tense narration, which implies that they are *still* running—and so still accepting new members to their deplorable fitness club. Seven decades earlier, John Ruskin had expressed a fear "that few modern readers of Dante understand the dreadful meaning of this hellish outer district, or suburb, full of the

---

[42]Sayers, introduction, 9-10.
[43]Sayers, note on canto II, in *Divine Comedy 1: Hell*, 89.

refuse or worthless scum of Humanity."[44] Sayers sought to express that her understanding of that meaning in the recognizably modern terms of "vague tolerance" and the fear of missing out.

Remarkably enough, Sayers keeps up this moral commentary—interwoven with necessary historical and literary references—all the way down to the bottom of the pit.[45] Her portrayal of the downward spiral is deeply indebted to Williams, whose commentary on *Inferno* in *The Figure of Beatrice* stresses that the movement from the lustful in the second circle to the traitors in the ninth shows the gradual siphoning off of all human goods from the act of sinning. The lustful, at least, had something lovable in view; their problem was to put a "secondary" good (the lover) above the primary good that is God (in whom *only*, as discussed above, Dante believed we could find peace and ultimate fulfillment). Thus, as Sayers writes, following Williams, in lust there is still a degree of "mutuality in it and exchange," whereas at the bottom of the hell all connection to others is lost.[46] Her diagnosis of the lustful is also notable because Sayers says directly there what her other notes on the vices suggest: "We need not confine the *allegory* to the sin of unchastity." Note the phrase "we need not confine"—that is her ruling principle of

---

[44]John Ruskin, note on Letter LXI, *Fors Clavigera* (George Allen, 1876), 41.

[45]Generally speaking, early readers described Sayers's paratextual materials as a strength of the translation. Reviewing *Divine Comedy 1: Hell* in 1951, for example, Edward Williamson of Johns Hopkins University says so in the first sentence: "The value of this book lies in its critical apparatus" (he was less enthusiastic about the translation). In his 1963 review of Sayers's *The Poetry of Search and the Poetry of Statement*, Lewis calls the apparatus "eminently laudable" and "a model of judicious popularisation which has already proved useful to thousands." Even some approving readers found Sayers's shifts in the notes from facts to values jarring, however. Poet Dudley Fitts, reviewing Sayers's *Divine Comedy 1: Hell* and *Divine Comedy 2: Purgatory* together for *The New York Times* in 1955, for one, reported, "I find her most effective when she is simply informative; her philosophical and theological reflections are too unfocused for taste, too sentimentally patronizing in the homiletic manner of Mr. C. S. Lewis." Edward Williamson, review of *Dante: The Divine Comedy, I: Hell*, by Dorothy L. Sayers, *Modern Language Notes* 66, no. 3 (1951): 200; Dudley Fitts, "An Urge to Make Dante Known," review of *Dante: The Divine Comedy, I: Hell*, by Dorothy L. Sayers, *New York Times*, November 6, 1955.

[46]Sayers, note on canto II, in *Divine Comedy 1: Hell*, 101.

interpretation: She burrows into Dante's circles, discerns their psychological insights, and then strikes out from there.

To read Sayers's notes, then, is to receive one tutorial after another on the evils that *remain* with us and in us. Accordingly, in her remarks on the virtuous pagans residing in the first circle (a.k.a. limbo), Sayers quickly bypasses the traditional problem commentators wrestle with: Why weren't the virtuous pagans saved? Instead, Sayers zeroes in on what she sees as their spiritual deficiency, a shortfall of imagination: "The souls 'have what they chose;' they enjoy that kind of after-life which they themselves imagined for the virtuous dead; their failure lay in not imagining better."[47] Then she pivots from antiquity to modernity, aligning the ancient *limbicoli* to the this-worldly humanism bequeathed to us by the Renaissance and the Enlightenment: "It is the weakness of Humanism to fall short of the imagination of ecstasy; at its best it is noble, reasonable, and cold, and however optimistic about a balanced happiness in this world, pessimistic about a rapturous eternity."[48] Now, Sayers is unquestionably open to the charge at this moment (and others in her *Hell* commentary) that she is reading the contemporary scene back into the medieval poem. But I suspect that if given the opportunity to plead her case, Sayers would argue that she was moving in the other direction—bringing the spiritual lesson of the poem to bear on the modern world to discern the vice in question's current instantiation. For that was what she took Dante to be doing: digging down to the very roots of humanity's persistent vices. The specific costume that the vice wears may be subject to changing fashions, but the essence endures. To engage in this sort of spiritual archaeology was the invitation of Dante's

---

[47]Sayers, note on canto III, in *Divine Comedy 1: Hell*, 95. She was echoing Williams, who called the first circle the "Limbo of the suspended Imagination."

[48]For more on the concept of humanism and Christian responses thereto in the war years, see Alan Jacobs's superb book *The Year of Our Lord 1943: Christian Humanism in an Age of Crisis* (Oxford University Press, 2018).

allegory as she understood it. The *Comedy*'s story is fictional (even if it asks us to play along with the idea that Dante really made the trip), but its spiritual subject matter is *real*. She says so flatly in the introduction to *Hell*: "The real environment within which all the events take place is the human soul."[49]

What about the City? Williams had argued that the third circle—home of the stuck-in-the-mud gluttonous—marks the transition from mutual indulgence into "separateness." Sayers follows her friend in her commentary—calling gluttony "solitary self-indulgence"—but emphasizes its communal significance to a greater degree: "Here is no reciprocity and no communication; each soul grovels alone in the mud, without heeding his neighbours." Conditions worsen with each successive drop in elevation. The avaricious and prodigals (fourth circle)—who spend eternity rolling rocks together—reveal how our "selfish appetites" make us antagonistic to those of others. The wrathful (fifth circle) actively resist community, whether by venting their ire "in sheer lust for inflicting pain and destruction," or withdrawing into "a black sulkiness which can find no joy in God or man or the universe."[50] The heretics (sixth circle) are at once intellectually obdurate and duplicitous. Again, the commentary transmits Williams's wisdom, Sayers's note on heresy largely consisting of a long quotation from *The Figure of Beatrice* that ends, "A heretic, strictly, was a man who knew what he was doing; he accepted the Church, but at the same time he preferred his own judgment to that of the Church. This would seem impossible to imagine, except it is apt to happen in all of us after our manner."[51]

When she reaches the seventh circle, whose theme is violence, Sayers's diagnosis of contemporary social ills becomes even more pointed. Her take on the usurers is representative: They are "types of

---

[49] Sayers, introduction, 14.
[50] Sayers, notes on cantos IV, VII, in *Divine Comedy 1: Hell*, 107, 114.
[51] *FB*, 127.

all economic and mechanical civilizations which multiply material luxuries at the expense of vital necessities and have no roots in the earth or in humanity."[52] Usury, on Sayers's telling, is not *just* a personal sin; it is a sign of corruption within the wider social order. The City sins: that too, Sayers shows her reader, is Dante's teaching.

Nowhere is the political character of the "city of desolation" (as Sayers renders the *città dolente* of *Inferno* III.1) clearer than the eighth circle, whose theme is fraud. Its citizenry includes pimps, flatterers, seducers, sorcerers, false counselors, sowers of discord, thieves, hypocrites, and sellers of church and state offices. Reading Sayers's notes here becomes increasingly painful; she no doubt meant them to be disturbing. The sowers of discord are "the fanatics of party, seeing the world in a false perspective, and ready to rip up the whole fabric of society to gratify a sectional egotism." Of the sorcerers, she writes, "Magic to-day takes many forms, ranging from actual Satanism to attempts at 'conditioning' other people by manipulating their psyches." The falsifiers, she contends, "may be taken to figure every kind of deceiver who tampers with the basic commodities by which society lives—the adulterers of food and drugs, jerry-builders, manufacturers of the shoddy."[53]

The *Inferno* is not a safe classic, on Sayers's telling, but dystopian literature whose portrait of communal disintegration remains shocking.[54] In the eighth circle, she argues in her notes, we behold "the image of the City in corruption: the progressive disintegration of every social relationship, personal and public. Sexuality, ecclesiastical and civil office, language, ownership, counsel, authority, psychic influence, and material interdependence—all the media

---

[52]Sayers, note on canto XVII, in *Divine Comedy 1: Hell*, 178.

[53]Sayers, notes on cantos XXVIII, XX, XXIX, in *Divine Comedy 1: Hell*, 250, 199, 256.

[54]At this stage, the natural companion piece to her translation from Lewis's works may not be *The Great Divorce* but *That Hideous Strength* (1945). See David Downing's *Planets in Peril: A Critical Study of C. S. Lewis's Ransom Trilogy* (University of Massachusetts Press, 2008), where he argues that Lewis uses *Inferno* as his "structural subtext" in *That Hideous Strength*.

of the community's exchange are perverted and falsified."[55] Merci-
fully, Sayers observes in "The City of Dis" lecture, we will never
see this social nightmare *fully* realized on earth, for in this present
life the City of Dis mingles with the City of God. In *Inferno*, Dante
grants us a gruesome vision of "the City as it would be if the
good were, through the gaps, as it were in time and space, wholly
drawn away."[56]

What could be worse than the dystopia of circle 8? Only, Sayers
writes, "the final abyss where faith and trust are wholly and for
ever extinguished," so no basis for community remains.[57] The last
stage of hell is the abandonment of the City. In a brilliant reversal
of our expectations, the poet stations here a lake not of fire but ice.

Trapped in the ice are traitors—to kin, to country, to guests, to
lords and benefactors—who make no meaningful contact with
their neighbors, with the exception of a handful of souls whose
lot is to chew on their neighbors forever. Williams called it a
"dreadful monastery."[58] Sayers names the lake of ice "perhaps the
greatest image in the whole *Inferno*." In her notes to canto XXXII,
she instructs her reader that the image displays: "A cold and cruel
egotism, gradually striking inward till even the lingering passions
of hatred and destruction are frozen into immobility." That, she
continued, "is the final state of sin."[59] As Williams grasped, the
deeper into hell Dante travels, the "more and more clearly" the
punishments are "simply the sin itself."[60] This depiction of hell as a
place, ultimately, of solitary self-confinement brings us back to *The
Great Divorce*. There hell's residents move progressively away from
the town center so that, as the man on the bus with the bowler hat
reports, the oldest ones now live "millions of miles away from us

---

[55]Sayers, note on canto XVIII, in *Divine Comedy 1: Hell*, 185.
[56]Sayers, "City of Dis," 149.
[57]Sayers, note on canto XVIII, in *Divine Comedy 1: Hell*, 185.
[58]*FB*, 141.
[59]Sayers, note on canto XXXII, in *Divine Comedy 1: Hell*, 275.
[60]*FB*, 138.

and from one another."[61] To Lewis's heaven's rallying cry, "Further up and further in," his hell replies, "Further out and further apart."

In Dante's *Inferno*, Sayers, Williams, and Lewis did not find the torture chamber of a vindictive God. Instead, they beheld the sins we coddle within ourselves bearing their poison fruit. In *Screwtape Letters*, Lewis imagines that the devils counter the beatific vision of God enjoyed by the blessed with a "Miserific Vision" of their own.[62] That phrase seemed to Sayers an apt characterization of the bleak prospect the reader faces in *Inferno*. "At the bottom of Hell," she argues in "The Meaning of Heaven and Hell" lecture, "is the Miserific Vision, as the Beatific Vision is at the height of Heaven: and as the Beatific Vision is the knowing of God in His Essence, so Hell is the knowing of Sin in its essence."[63]

The damned cannot profit from this knowledge, cannot profit by gazing on their own distorted images; that is Dante's scheme. Yet Sayers, Williams, and Lewis grasped that *the reader* may benefit from their inspection, increasingly difficult though it may be to look, for in studying *Inferno*'s portraits of corruption we may recognize those in ourselves and our cities. Dante's hell is not remedial, my trio saw, but Dante's *vision of hell* is. Through the vision, the soul may gain "self-knowledge" of "all its evil potentialities."[64] By contemplating the kingdom of hell and recognizing that it is within and around us, we may yearn for another kingdom. We may seek another way.

"I do not think that all who choose wrong roads perish," Lewis writes in the preface to *The Great Divorce*, "but their rescue consists in being put back on the right road."[65] He could declare this with confidence because he had read Dante. Following the poet, and in the company of our three pilgrim readers, we will seek the right road in the chapters ahead.

---

[61]Lewis, *Great Divorce*, 20.
[62]C. S. Lewis, *The Screwtape Letters and Screwtape Proposes a Toast* (Geoffrey Bles, 1961), 77.
[63]Sayers, "Meaning of Heaven and Hell," 68.
[64]Sayers, introduction, 68.
[65]Lewis, *Great Divorce*, 8.

**Figure 4.1.** Illustration for *Purgatorio* XXIX [the Allegorical Procession] by Amos Nattini, in Dante's *Divina commedia: imagini di Amos Nattini* (Milano: Istituto nazionale dantesco, 1923)

# 4

# MUCH ADO ABOUT ALLEGORY

*The allegory of [Beatrice] is (Dante said)*
*at least fourfold, perhaps multifold.*

CHARLES WILLIAMS, *THE FIGURE OF BEATRICE*

*It is this strain which makes me uncertain of the growing belief that*
*if a Dante speaks of a professedly allegorical lady in terms of violent*
*passion we may conclude that she was not wholly allegorical. That*
*would be so with most of us: with Dante, perhaps less.*

C. S. LEWIS, "IMAGERY IN THE LAST ELEVEN
CANTOS OF DANTE'S COMEDY"

ADDRESSING THE STUDENTS at the Training College, Darlington, a school for teachers, in 1954, Sayers took as her theme "The Writing and Reading of Allegory." "Allegory, of late years," the lecture begins, "has been suffering from what is popularly known as 'a bad Press.'"[1] In literary circles, the term had become an epithet—often accompanied by *cold, frigid,* or other subzero adjectives—inflicted on books the critic found too abstract, too didactic, lifeless. Worse still, it was applied, "quite at random," to works that were not formally allegories at all "but which [happen] to contain

---

[1]Dorothy L. Sayers, "The Writing and Reading of Allegory," in *PSPS*, 201.

some religious or moral teaching that the critic dislikes or fails to understand." She cites the example of Lewis's *Perelandra* (1943), "a fantasy of the kind we now call 'space fiction,' recounting quite straightforwardly the beginnings of rational life on that planet, and how a new fall of man was prevented by the intervention of a voyager from our own earth." Lewis had foreseen the possible misunderstanding and explicitly stated in a two-sentence preface that "All the human characters in this book are purely fictitious and none of them is allegorical."[2] Nonetheless, a critic had, after recounting the space travel portion, curtly closed out his review, "Then the allegory begins." Thus, Sayers sighs, "Having . . . deliberately filed away the book in the wrong pigeonhole, he took it for granted that about a work of that kind there was nothing useful to be said."[3] Sayers's lecture seeks to set the record straight—not just to help readers file titles in the correct pigeonholes but, more importantly, to restore the appreciation of a venerable literary game (her metaphor) that moderns have forgotten how to play.

Although she cites Lewis only once directly after mentioning *Perelandra* (when she borrows his translation of a few verses by Ovid), her lecture's account of allegory's rules, origins, and delights is deeply indebted to her friend. Lewis stressed that allegory, at its best, is not a mere dressing up of abstractions but a mode of reflecting on and memorably relating experience. Early on in her lecture, Sayers defines allegory in exactly those terms as "a distinct literary form, whose aim and method is to dramatize a psychological experience, so as to make it more vivid and more comprehensible."[4] The history of allegory that follows offers a compact summary of the arc traced in *The Allegory of Love*.

---

[2] C. S. Lewis, *Perelandra* (Bodley Head, 1943), 6. The next year Lewis lamented, "Despite the preface they all will take it as an 'allegory' and then blame me for not making it clear." C. S. Lewis to Delmar Banner, January 7, 1944, in *CLCSL*, 2:504.

[3] Sayers, "Writing and Reading of Allegory," 201.

[4] Sayers, "Writing and Reading of Allegory," 202.

Dante, unsurprisingly, cuts a dashing figure in Sayers's version of that history. He is initially summoned to clear up a potential source of confusion. Citing a passage in *Vita Nuova* in which Dante emphasizes that his personification of Amor (Love) corresponds only to an idea—not a real "corporeal substance"—Sayers offers two instructions on the right use of allegory: first, that we should not "attribute to abstractions the kind of reality that belongs to actual persons," and second, that we must treat the literal and figurative meanings as independent stories—"each coherent and complete in itself."[5] Thus, when Formalist and Hypocrisy wander off to certain death in *Pilgrim's Progress*, we should not weep for those two gentlemen from Vain-Glory but worry about the spiritual dispositions that they represent. Sound advice, right?

And yet immediately after quoting Dante, Sayers pivots and points out that Dante, "the greatest of all allegorists," also presents "a special case" in which we *should* acknowledge the characters in the allegory as actual persons—who, moreover, represent "qualities in a person!" The special case is, of course, the *Comedy*. The epic is held up as the exception to the rule that Sayers had taken from *Vita Nuova*:

> In *The Divine Comedy* he invented a method so individual that no one has ever really succeeded in using it on the grand scale again. All his characters do, indeed, represent "qualities in a person;" but he has used, instead of personified abstractions, actual historical or mythical personages who are fitted to serve as natural symbols of those qualities. Thus the various kinds of Pride are represented not by a lady called "Superbia," or a giant called "Orgoglio," but by such people as Capaneus, Farinata, Umberto, Aldobrandesco, Oderisi the Painter, and Provenzan Salvani. Thus at one stroke Dante abolishes the limitations that fetter the conversation and behavior of abstractions and regains something of the freedom

---

[5]Sayers, "Writing and Reading of Allegory," 213.

that belonged to the mythological treatment of the gods. Yet, although so penetrated with symbolism, and set in a great symbolic framework, *The Comedy* can be interpreted allegorically at no fewer than three levels, without any encroachment of the figure upon the thing figured, or vice versa.[6]

In this passage, Sayers steers into some of the choppiest waters in Dante criticism (past, present, and future), and her claims about the mechanics of Dante's allegory, the number of levels on which the poem can be interpreted, even terms such as *symbolism*, were hotly contested at the time. One of the parties whom she was disputing, this chapter shows, was C. S. Lewis. Taking issue with Lewis's approach to Dantean allegory, she sided with Williams's manner of handling the *Comedy*'s allegorical dimensions, although (as we will see) she also put her own touch on the matter.

Admittedly, in focusing this chapter on controversies surrounding allegory, I may seem to be committing exactly the scholarly sin Sayers denounced in the last chapter: retreating to one of the ivory tower's innermost chambers to debate the *Comedy* on purely intellectual terms. Yet we must not let the "bad Press" on allegory deter us. The topic, this chapter shows, leads us into some of my trio's most fascinating claims about Dante's artistic prowess, the salvific function of the imagination, and the poet's place in the history of Christianity. That said, if you find while reading this chapter that in the battle between Boredom and Patience, Boredom gets the upper hand, feel free to cut your losses and skip ahead to chapter five. The air of Mount Purgatory will clear your head.

---

[6]Sayers, "Writing and Reading of Allegory," 213-14.

## ALLEGORY VERSUS SYMBOLISM

Among the members of my cohort, Lewis was unquestionably the best equipped to write a book-length study on the ins and outs of Dantean allegory. He had been reading Dante in Italian since he was a teenager. He was a medievalist with a one of the world's great research libraries at his disposal. As I have just noted, he truly wrote *the* book on allegory for his generation, so he knew all about Dante's predecessors, contemporaries, and successors in the tradition. That we have no such book or even an essay on the topic, that the four-hundred-page study of medieval allegory he did write includes no chapter on the *Comedy*'s uniqueness (all the while naming Dante over forty times over the course of the book), speaks, as we say, volumes.[7]

Sayers's 1954 lecture is likewise striking because, once again, it tracks closely with *The Allegory of Love* for long stretches and yet her notes on Dante's "special case" have no correlative in Lewis's book—even as she alludes to one of Lewis's claims within the paragraph cited above. Her point about "the freedom that belonged to the mythological treatment of the gods" derives from Lewis's argument that as Roman poets turned to allegory, their portrayals of the gods became increasingly one-dimensional. Bacchus, for one, devolved into drunkenness. Sayers's astute observation is that by using "actual" people as his vehicle to exemplify vices, Dante expanded the range of what, say, pride can look like, sound like, act like. Lewis had memorably declared that "the twilight of the gods is the mid-morning of the personifications"; Sayers saw a new day dawning in the *Comedy*.[8] Lewis, the evidence suggests, saw more of the same.

---

[7] Lewis *does* portray Dante as exceptional in *The Allegory of Love* for his approach to the other noun in the book's title—to Williams's delight. C. S. Lewis, *The Allegory of Love: A Study of Medieval Tradition* (Oxford University Press, 1936).

[8] Lewis, *Allegory of Love*, 52.

In 1936, Lewis in fact enlisted Dante not as an outlier but as an authority on how the game was normally played among poets, as we will see in a moment. In his late essay "The Vision of John Bunyan" (1962), Lewis boils that game down to its essential move: "Allegory gives you one thing in terms of another."[9] Notice the one-to-one ratio: Allegory, on Lewis's consistent telling, deals in exact concepts and, at its best, strong images that tighten our grasp of those concepts.[10] That stands in opposition to what Lewis called "symbolism," as he explains in "A Sacred Poem," his 1939 review of Williams's *Taliesson Through Logres* mentioned in the introduction: "In Allegory the images stand for concepts (giant Despair, Mr. Legality), in Symbolism for something the poet has experienced but which he has not reduced, perhaps cannot reduce, to a concept. Allegory can always be translated back into the concepts: the 'meaning' of a symbolical work cannot be stated in conceptual language because it is too concrete."[11] Allegory, for Lewis, brings the known into sharper focus, while symbolism was Lewis's way of talking about objects or events with more diffuse significations—things often hard to isolate imaginatively and so fix in familiar phrases. Lewis also spoke of myth in this way. Allegories had one meaning, and that meaning was a matter of public record; symbols and myths were open to multiple and variable meanings, including distinct personal ones to different onlookers.[12]

---

[9] C. S. Lewis, "The Vision of John Bunyan," in *C. S. Lewis: Selected Literary Essays*, ed. Walter Hooper (Cambridge University Press, 1969), 148.

[10] There are no levels to navigate. The challenge allegory poses to the writer is to produce a vivid image, while that to the reader is to dive in (not to decode): "We ought not to be thinking 'This green valley, where the shepherd boy is singing, represents humility;' we ought to be discovering, as we read, that humility is like that green valley. That way, moving always into the book, not out of it, from the concept to the image, enriches the concept" (Lewis, "Vision of John Bunyan," 149).

[11] C. S. Lewis, "A Sacred Poem," review of *Taliessin Through Logres*, by Charles Williams, *Theology* 38 (1939): 270.

[12] Writing to Peter Milward, SJ, in 1956, Lewis argues, for example, that "a good myth (i.e. a story out of which ever varying meanings will grow for different readers and in different ages) is a higher thing than an allegory (into which one meaning has been put). Into an

The major evidence from *The Allegory of Love* clusters in a few pages of an early chapter on the nature and history of allegory as a poetic form. The chapter notably begins with an epigraph from Dante's *Convivio* that hints at the role Lewis asks Dante to play: *Veramente li teologi questo senso prendono altrimenti che li poeti,* meaning "Certainly the theologians take this sense differently than do the poets." To grasp what Lewis meant by hanging these words atop the chapter, we need to read what immediately follows the quoted text: "but since my intention here is to follow the way of the poets, I apply the allegorical sense according to how it used by the poets." Poetic allegory is Lewis's target—the kind in which, as Dante writes in the same passage, a truth is "hidden under the mantle" of fiction—not the multilayered sort that medieval commentators mined in the texts of Scripture.[13]

In the opening pages of the chapter, Lewis then divides allegory and symbolism. The division, we must acknowledge, was already well established. A generation earlier, Irish poet Aubrey de Vere, to cite a representative example, had declared, "Symbols have a real, and allegories but an arbitrary existence. All things beautiful and excellent are symbols of an excellence analogous to them, but ranged higher in Nature's scale. Allegories are abstractions of the understanding and fancy."[14] Symbols, in other words, tap into some deeper identity between things, while allegories are clever connections. One is discovered; the other "made up." On Lewis's telling in 1936, the two mental actions are alike insofar as both "represent what is immaterial in picturable terms," yet they move

---

allegory a man can put only what he already knows: in a myth he puts what he does not yet know and cd. not come to know in any other way." C. S. Lewis to Peter Milward, September 22, 1956, in *CLCSL*, 2:550.

[13] Andrew Frisardi, trans., *Dante: Convivio: A Dual Language Critical Edition*, by Dante (Cambridge University Press, 2018), 59.

[14] Aubrey de Vere, "Characteristics of Spenser's Poetry," in *Essays Chiefly on Poetry* (Macmillan, 1887), 17.

in different directions. The "allegorist" (Lewis's term) "[starts] with an immaterial fact, such as the passions which you actually experience," and then "[invents] *visibilia* to express them." Lewis offers the example of "hesitating between an angry retort and a soft answer": "You can express your state of mind by inventing a person called *Ira* with a torch and letting her contend with another invented person called *Patientia*" (as Roman poet Prudentius does in the *Psychomachia*). The "symbolist," by contrast, strives to "read . . . something else through its sensible imitations, to see the archtype in the copy," to reach (Lewis adds) the immaterial world through the material. He then suggests that while alike to a degree, the two imaginative acts have distinct genealogies. Allegory he traces to ancient Roman epic, symbolism to the Platonic dialogues, though he argues that the latter's "greatest expression" would come much later—with Romanticism.[15]

Given that de Vere could make the same distinction in two sentences, we may wonder why Lewis goes into so much detail. He tells us, "I labour the antithesis because ardent but uncorrected lovers of medieval poetry are easily tempted to forget it." Living in the wake of the Romantic revolution in taste, modern readers favor symbolism over allegory and so are apt to treat a pleasing allegory as if it were a symbol. Here Lewis provides his own translation of the passage in *Vita Nuova* cited above: "'You may be surprised,' says Dante, 'that I speak of love as if it were a thing that could exist by itself; and not only as if it were an intelligent substance, but even as if it were a corporeal substance. Now this, according to the truth, is false. For love has not, like a substance, an existence of its own, but is only an accident occurring in a substance.'"[16]

Lewis comments: "However the personification is to be defended, it is clear that Dante has no thought of pretending that

---

[15]Lewis, *Allegory of Love*, 44-45.
[16]Lewis, *Allegory of Love*, 46-47.

it is more than a personification. It is, as he says himself a moment later, *figura o colore rettorico*, a piece of technique, a weapon in the armoury of ῥητορική."[17] Lewis's point is that we want Amor to be *more* than a personification; we want the poet to be "reaching after some transcendental reality which the forms of discursive thought cannot contain."[18] In short, we moderns want Dante to be a symbolist. Yet the poet is, by his own telling, an allegorist, someone deliberately employing a falsehood to illustrate a psychological truth—in the case of Amor, fabricating a "lordly figure, frightening to behold, yet seemingly filled with wondrous joy" (*Vita Nuova* I).[19]

Based on Dante's authority, Lewis makes a sweeping declaration about the character of medieval allegorical poetry: "The great allegorist's firm thinking leaves no room for misunderstanding. There is nothing 'mystical' or mysterious about medieval allegory; the poets know quite clearly what they are about and are well aware that the figures that they represent to us are fictions." He summarizes the lesson thus: "Symbolism is a mode of thought, but allegory is a mode of expression."[20]

What about the *Comedy*? Lewis does not answer that question directly in *The Allegory of Love* (or anywhere else), but a footnote

---

[17]Lewis, *Allegory of Love*, 47. Lewis's interpretation of this passage was not uncontroversial among medievalists. See, for example, Dantist and fellow Inkling Colin Hardie's "Dante and the Tradition of Courtly Love," in *Patterns of Love and Courtesy: Essays in Memory of C. S. Lewis* (Northwestern University Press, 1966), 26-44. Hardie takes an extreme position, arguing that there is less "allegory" (as Lewis conceives of it) in the *Vita Nuova* and "hardly any allegory or deliberate personification" in the *Comedy*.

[18]Lewis, *Allegory of Love*, 47.

[19]Andrew Frisardi, trans., *Vita Nuova: A Dual-Langauge Edition*, by Dante (Penguin, 2022), 7.

[20]Lewis, *Allegory of Love*, 48. Lewis would come to regret this phrasing. Writing to Professor Eliza Marian Butler, an English scholar of German literature, in 1940, he admitted that if he "had it now to do again," he would make a distinction not between allegory and symbol but between allegory and "symbolical narrative or myth." He explains that he would now define allegory as follows: "Each symbol, in isolation, has a meaning and the total meaning is built up out of these." C. S. Lewis to Marian Butler, August 18, 1940, in *CLCSL*, 2:438.

below the sentences I have just quoted hints at his view in 1936. "The experienced reader may be surprised to find no mention here, and little mention below, of Philo, Origen, and the multiple senses of scripture," the note begins. Lewis was anticipating that his scholarly peers would ask why he had not discussed the aforementioned "allegory of the theologians" as an influence on medieval allegorical love poetry. The absence is deliberate, Lewis now announces, for in his view the evidence is scant that the imitation of the multiple senses of Scripture "played any part in the original intention of any erotic allegory." That was a charged claim because Dante—or someone many medievalists took to be Dante—claimed to be doing exactly that in the Epistle to Cangrande.[21] Lewis closes the note by replying to that potential objection: "Dante himself, while parading four senses (*Conv.* II.i, and *Ep.* xiii = x in some editions), makes singularly little use of them to explain his own work."[22] The arresting phrase is "parading." Lewis is casting doubt on the familiar evidence—found in the *Convivio* and the Epistle—that Dante was seriously expecting his allegory to be interpreted in the same multidimensional fashion as Scripture. Whatever Dante claimed, in practice he was an allegorist like the rest.

## BUZZING SIMILES

Before we dismiss Lewis from this examination, we should note that even while advocating this more constrained notion of allegory, he shared—only a few years later—one of the most vivid testimonies to the pluripotency of Dante's language ever written. The setting was the Oxford Dante Society, where on February 13,

---

[21]Lewis seems to accept Dante's authorship of the epistle here. Later on he would reject the notion, calling the author of the epistle "Pseudo-Dante." See C. S. Lewis to Eugene Vinaver, August 22, 1959, in *CLCSL*, 3:730.

[22]Lewis, *Allegory of Love*, 48n.

1940, Lewis read a paper titled "Dante's Similes." The paper's objective is to identify the different kinds of similes used in the *Comedy*, the last of which Lewis deems uniquely "Dantesque."

Ordinarily, poetic similes are brief transactions, poetic analogies of only situational interest, as when in *Iliad* XI Homer likens Ajax charging the Trojans to a river, "swelled with wintry rains," crashing down on the plain.[23] Released from that violent scene, the analogy quickly evaporates. In Lewis's special Dantean case, by contrast, the analogy is not fleeting because the paired objects—the simile's target and source—are "bound by a profound philosophical analogy or even identity. *Like*, in these similes, is always tending to turn into *same*."[24]

As an illustration, Lewis cites *Paradiso* I.46-54. In these lines, Beatrice trains her eyes on the sun in a manner hazardous to mortal vision, and Dante, who had been eyeing her, does likewise. In recounting those upward glances, Dante-the-poet employs two similes—the first compares the Dante-the-character's shifting gaze to light reflected off a horizontal surface flashing back toward its source, and the second compares that reflected light to a pilgrim longing to return home. The first simile—the reflected light—performs the basic function of a simile in Homer or Virgil, Lewis notes: It highlights the causal relation between Beatrice's action and Dante's imitation. Yet there is more going on here. The target (Beatrice and Dante staring at the sun) and the source (light reflected upward) are also alike, Lewis observes; both constitute "responses to light."[25] Light is being likened unto light; *likeness* is sliding into *sameness*. The convergence of target and source is then hastened by the second simile—the comparison of reflected light

---

[23]Alexander Pope, trans., *The Iliad of Homer*, ed. Steven Shankman (Penguin, 1996), 530.
[24]C. S. Lewis, "Dante's Similes," in *Studies in Medieval and Renaissance Literature*, ed. Walter Hooper (Cambridge University Press, 1966), 71.
[25]Lewis, "Dante's Similes," 73.

to a pilgrim—since Dante and Beatrice are on a pilgrimage to their eternal home with God.

Target thus reflects source, and source reflects target, but Dante is not casting us into a funhouse hall of mirrors. All these images are anchored in—and thereby amplify—larger structures of thought and feeling that Dante has assembled from the open-source materials of the Middle Ages, including the traditional iconography of the church (e.g., life is a pilgrimage to the eternal Jerusalem) and the Aristotelian-Christian conception of the universe (what Lewis calls "the Medieval Model" in *The Discarded Image*). Against that background, Lewis then reads the *Comedy* allegorically, one of the rare instances where we can see him doing so. He makes three observations. First, as they gaze upward, Dante and Beatrice, are "*literaliter* to the sun (and *allegorice* to God) what all reflected beams are to the original source of light." Second, Dante is *literaliter* to Beatrice here what "the human understanding" is *allegorice* to Wisdom.[26] And, third, the relationship between beams of light and their sources mirrors the relationship between the universe and *its* source, the first cause, the Unmoved Mover.

The allegorical dynamics are entirely traditional—God is light, Beatrice is the representative of divine wisdom—and that speaks to Lewis's larger point in the piece that Dante's metaphysics, physics, and "scheme of the ascent to Heaven" are derived from the standard sources (such as Ptolemy and Cicero). Dante is not gesturing to unnamable mysteries or occult knowledge (as the symbolist poet might); he is activating his tradition, revealing complex linkages within the great chain of being. The literal and allegorical levels draw on, and feed back into, a cosmic network of meaning: "The whole of Christian-Aristotelian theology is

---

[26]Lewis, "Dante's Similes," 73.

thus brought together." The result is enormously satisfying to the intellect (like Lewis's) steeped in the medieval model: "Every idea presented to the mind, as in a figure, repeats the subject in a slightly different way, and suggests further and further applications of it. It reverberates from that one imagined moment over all space and time, and further."[27]

Lewis, a master hand at analogy, strains to find an apposite image to describe the effect. It's the positive equivalent of a "man stirring up a hornet's nest," he suggests. He tries bees—if they "were associated only with honey and not with stings, I should say that Dante every now and then wakes up a whole beehive." He switches to light focused through a glass—such an image "seems to focus all the rays of his universe at single point"—and then again to a network—"or touching some wire that sets the whole system vibrating in unison." Toward the close of the paper, he contends that Dante reanimates even the most shopworn words: "The very nature of his universe seems to fill his key words—words such as *love, light, up, down, high, low, sun, star* and *earth*—with such a wealth of significance that their mere mention becomes solid poetry 'more gold than gold' without more ado."[28]

Even though Lewis stays within the conventional allegorical schema in his analysis, his words reveal that the Dante of the *Comedy* goes light years beyond the normal procedures of medieval allegory. The *Comedy*, on Lewis's telling in 1940, *is* a special case. Indeed, Lewis goes on to suggest that the "great passages" of the *Comedy* have such a "reality" that they follow one right back into one's own: "They don't fade as you come awake. They can stand daylight. We are made to dream while keeping awake at the same time."[29]

---

[27]Lewis, "Dante's Similes," 76, 74.
[28]Lewis, "Dante's Similes," 73, 76.
[29]Lewis, "Dante's Similes," 77.

## THE FIGURE OF BEATRICE

In "A Sacred Poem," Lewis argues that one might be tempted to read Williams's Arthurian poems as allegories. Lewis uses the poet's "central symbol," Byzantium, as a test case. If handled (mistakenly) as an allegory, it could be taken as having at least four referents: the "actual" city of Byzantium; the "total Man or Person as opposed to his members"; "order, discipline, civilization"; and the "Divine Order." Yet it is *not* an allegory, Lewis underscores. Williams did not start with "concepts like 'Man' or 'Order'" and then build Byzantium around them. Rather, Williams, being a symbolist, "started with something in his experience, characterized by glory, but also by a strict mathematical quality," and then discerned whiffs of that something in numerous other experiences as he lived and moved and had his being in the world. So a symbol such as Byzantium, Lewis argues, is "not a communal fancy-dress for half a dozen concepts: it is an imaginative net to catch that single, utterly concrete constituent of experience which has no name and which we come to know by using the symbol."[30] That account bears a striking resemblance to how Williams came to describe Dante's imagination, except that Dante's symbol had a name—Beatrice.

Before Williams set Dante among the symbolists, though, he had to overcome *The Allegory of Love*. He apparently found Lewis's distinction between allegory and symbolism a challenge to his previous thinking about Dante, and in assorted unpublished writings we see him wrestling with the possibility of bringing the two together. In "Courtly Love," a lecture delivered on January 29, 1937, for example, Williams acknowledged that "we tend to mix [allegory] up with symbolism. I realise here, Mr. Lewis does check my own tendency to introduce symbolism into Dante."[31] And yet

---

[30]Lewis, "Sacred Poem," 272.

[31]Charles Williams, lecture, in Raymond Hunt Papers, Marion E. Wade Center, notebooks, vol. 12, p. 2154. See also Paul Fiddes's superb discussion of this lecture in the first chapter

in *He Came Down from Heaven,* published the next year, Williams implies that Lewis's manner of talking about allegory comes up short when faced with Dante's complexity.

In the passage in question, Williams examines an episode in *Vita Nuova* in which Dante encounters a young woman named Giovanna, whose nickname is Primavera (Spring). Amor uses wordplay on Giovanna's two names to springboard into biblical typology, telling the poet that Giovanna (= feminine version of John) is a John the Baptist figure who "will come first" (= *prima verra*), thereby equating Beatrice's arrival to the advent of Jesus. The seemingly blasphemous typology is valid, Williams suggests, within Dante's story line because Giovanna and Beatrice *are* precursors to the coming of the "true light" (Jn 1:9). Thus, Williams argues that allegory, and here we must suspect that he means *Lewis's* notion of allegory, doesn't seem quite adequate: "The allegory is almost a symbolism; that is, it has almost not a likeness but an identity."[32]

Five years later, in *The Figure of Beatrice,* Williams moved Dante fully into the realm of symbolism *as he defined it.*[33] In the book's first paragraph, nearly its first words, Williams introduces Dante as "one of those poets who begin their work with what is declared to be an intense personal experience"—the vision of Beatrice on a street in Florence in the ninth year of his life. Dante's early poetry, Williams then suggests, is the record of that experience, and his later poetry its recollection: "The image of Beatrice existed in his thought; it remained there and was deliberately renewed."[34]

---

of *Charles Williams and C. S. Lewis: Friends in Co-Inherence* (Oxford University Press, 2021). See also a notebook entry on *The Allegory of Love* in Charles Williams Papers, CW-MS-320 and CW MS-363, especially "Lecture on the Philosophical Journey in Dante III," Charles Williams Papers, Marion E. Wade Center, Wheaton College, Wheaton, IL.
[32]*HCDH,* 73.
[33]There are other available critical formulations, such as "insight symbolism," "mystical analogy," and "symbol-allegory."
[34]*FB,* 7.

In calling her an "image," Williams was choosing a loaded phrase for multiple reasons. He was, in the first place, echoing the book's editor, T. S. Eliot. In his 1929 *Dante* monograph, Eliot had argued that "for a competent poet allegory means *clear visual images*. And clear visual images are given much more intensity by having a meaning"—though, he then notes, the reader doesn't need to know "what that meaning is" to enjoy the heightened "intensity."[35] Williams agreed that allegory trades in intense images (as did Lewis, as we have seen), but he was not content to leave the question of meaning dangling.

In his view, the power of the "image of Beatrice" for Dante was the innumerable needs that it answered in his heart and mind. The image didn't have a single meaning; it was more like a funnel or a net (to borrow Lewis's image) that captured, and helped Dante to comprehend, other experiences, thoughts, beliefs, and, yes, images. To explain these dynamics, Williams reached into the reservoir of ideas that Lewis had tried to keep out of discussions of medieval allegory—the Romantic tradition. He cites the authority of one of that tradition's leading lights, Samuel Taylor Coleridge: "Coleridge said that a symbol must have three characteristics (i) it must exist in itself, (ii) it must derive from something greater than itself, (iii) it must represent in itself that greatness from which it derives." He goes on to explain that he has chosen *image* over *symbol* because he questioned whether the word *symbol* still "sufficiently expresses the vivid individual existence of the lesser thing."[36] *Image* was the favored word, then, in order to make crystal clear that Beatrice was to Dante a matter of his sensory, not merely imaginative, experience. She was a "fact."[37] "Dante's

---

[35]T. S. Eliot, *Dante* (Faber & Faber, 1929), 29.

[36]A few pages later, his rebellion from Lewis's paradigm is complete when he argues that the Dantean way is illuminated by William Wordsworth's argument that "the Imagination . . . is the faculty by which images, actual or poetic, are understood."

[37]See chapter 6's discussion of how Williams used the word *fact*.

whole assertion," Williams writes, "was that he could not have invented Beatrice."[38]

On Williams's telling, Beatrice operated in Dante's imagination on multiple planes simultaneously—an allegorical figure encountered in real life and ever deepened in mature recollection. "Beatrice was, in her degree," Williams observes in the same passage, "an image of nobility, of virtue, of the Redeemed Life, and in some sense of Almighty God himself. But she also remained Beatrice right to the end." To put it another way, Williams's notion of the image sought to capture the coexistence in Dante's imagination of the poetic image and the theological *imago*, the immanent signifier serving the transcendent signified but never subsumed by it. Accordingly, Williams took issue with two camps among Dante's commentators, whom he dubbed the "allegorists" and the "spiritualizers." The former "deny altogether the mortal identity of Beatrice, and turn her wholly into Theology or Divine Grace or what not. Her smiles are, for them, always metaphorical; her anger is abstract and not feminine; her teasing—but for them she does not tease."[39] Under the scrutiny of the spritualizers, meanwhile, Beatrice "becomes so dim that she is, in fact, nothing but a kind of vapour of the soul, a mist that goes up out of the ground of the heart." Both parties refuse to undertake the more complicated balancing act that Dante's allegory demands. Beatrice is always *at*

---

[38]*FB*, 7. Williams's embrace of symbolism may also have been influenced by a passage from philosopher George Santayana's 1910 book *Three Philosophical Poets: Lucretius, Dante, and Goethe*, which Williams copied into a notebook at some point in the 1930s. After noting that for Dante, "moral distinctions . . . are displayed in the order of creation," and thus available for the poet's inspiration and imitation, Santayana writes, "The Creator himself was a poet producing allegories. The material world was a parable which he had built out in space, and ordered to be enacted. History was a great charade. The symbols of earthly poets are words or images; the symbols of the divine poet were natural things and the fortunes of men. . . . The poet's method repeated the magic of Genesis. His symbolical imagination mirrored this symbolical world; it was a sincere anticipation of fact, no mere labored and willful allegory."

[39]*FB*, 101.

*once* the "objective Beatrice" and the medium of "the Power which is expressed through her." This duality was encapsulated for Williams in a "maxim" that he believed he'd read somewhere but almost certainly invented: "This also is Thou, neither is this Thou."[40]

## A NOTE ON CRITICAL POSITIONING

Who was Williams thinking of when he spoke of the "allegorists" and "spiritualizers"? Of the latter, I suspect he had the pervasive depiction of Beatrice as a pale spirit in nineteenth-century art in mind, though there is also a strong tendency in Victorian writing on the *Comedy* to portray Beatrice as a being of pure spirit in life and death. Of the former, the popular Temple Classics edition that Sayers took to the bunker is representative. A few pages in, Sayers was told, for example, that "Virgil stands for Wordly Wisdom," and a short while later that Beatrice stands for Divine Wisdom and St. Lucy for "Illuminating Grace."[41]

Could Williams have been referring to Lewis as well? As the second of this chapter's epigraphs suggests, Lewis voiced misgivings about strong assertions of the "objective reality" of Beatrice in a paper he read to the Oxford Dante Society in 1948, "Imagery in the Last Eleven Cantos of Dante's *Comedy*." Lewis readily granted that Dante was passionate about Beatrice (no bloodless spiritualizer he), but he wondered aloud whether Dante had the sort of mind that made a *wholly* allegorical lady an object of intense reverence. In that same piece, moreover, Lewis defines Dante's imagery not on Williams's terms but as "every appeal to the imagined exercise of the five senses, always excepting those images which are directly represented as parts of Dante's story."[42]

---

[40]*FB*, 8.

[41]Note on canto I, *Inferno of Dante Alighieri* (London: J. M. Dent, 1906), 11.

[42]He meant, in other words, images summoned by Dante's imagination (as in a simile). C. S. Lewis, "Imagery in the Last Eleven Cantos of Dante's *Comedy*," in *Studies in Medieval and Renaissance Literature*, 78.

Given that Williams had been voted a member of the Society on the strength of *The Figure of Beatrice*, Lewis's audience would have likely marked his practical dissent from Williams's conception of the Dantean "image" (which Lewis does not mention in the talk).

Meanwhile, by virtue of his insistence on Beatrice's objective reality in the *Comedy*, Williams would seem to be moving in harmony with the two critical heavies inaugurating what some have called a revolution in Dante studies (a new *dantismo*) around this time—German émigré Erich Auerbach and American Charles Singleton. Each critic, albeit for different reasons, contended that we must jettison the traditional allegorical affiliations of Dante's characters and restart the interpretive process by taking their historical reality seriously.[43] "Virgil is not an allegory of an attribute, virtue, capacity, power, or historical institution," Auerbach writes in his landmark study "*Figura*" (1938). "He is neither reason nor poetry nor the Empire. He is Virgil himself."[44] Singleton championed the interpretation of the *Comedy* under the banner of the allegory of the theologians (in which, once again, the "literal" sense should be taken as historical reality just as theologians treated the texts of the Bible). To him we owe the witticism, "The fiction of the *Comedy* is that it is not a fiction."[45]

Auerbach, however, likely never read Williams, and Williams almost certainly had not read Auerbach, whose writings on Dante had not yet been translated into English. Singleton, by contrast,

---

[43]For an illuminating comparison of their positions, see David Thompson, "Figure and Allegory in the *Commedia*," *Dante Studies* 90 (1972): 1-11.

[44]Erich Auerbach, "Figura," trans. Ralph Manheim, in *Scenes from the Drama of European Literature* (Meridian Books, 1959), 70. Auerbach, it is important to note, goes on to argue that Virgil's "historical" reality is not the same as that of, say, Shakespeare's historical personages, where we meet them *in life*: "Virgil in the Divine Comedy is the historical Virgil himself, but then again he is not; for the historical Virgil is only a *figura* of the fulfilled truth that the poem reveals, and this fulfillment is more real, more significant than the *figura*. With Dante, unlike modern poets, the more fully the figure is interpreted and the more closely it is integrated with the eternal plan of salvation, the more real it becomes" (71).

[45]Charles S. Singleton, "The Irreducible Dove," *Comparative Literature* 9 (1957): 129.

did know Williams's work and did not like what he found. In his 1950 review of Sayers's *Hell*, he lamented Williams's influence on the translator, arguing, "Williams' views, with their arbitrary categories and special jargon, have done more to obscure than to illumine Dante's poetry."[46] Reviewing Sayers's *Introductory Papers on Dante* a few years later, Singleton balked at her claim that *The Figure of Beatrice* "initiated what is likely to prove the next great movement in Dantism," remarking that he had "serious doubts about that likelihood" and "[took] hope from the fact that there is so far no sign of the movement getting under way." He was glad, though, to find evidence in the book that Sayers "has broadened her own views of Dante's poetry and has ventured down paths of speculation never attempted by the Master. Thus, even though the Images and the Ways are still here, there is much more."[47] In that last sentence, Singleton was decrying the theological and aesthetic superstructure that Williams erected around Dante and Beatrice. Yet what was a distraction in his view was an attraction to Sayers, and so a few further words on Ways and Images are necessary before I can reintroduce my third traveler.

## THE WAY OF THE AFFIRMATION OF IMAGES

When Williams submitted his book on Dante to Faber, he called it *The Way of the Affirmation of Images* and proclaimed the study's unity by putting the word *image* in the title of every chapter. Responding on September 2, 1942, Eliot complained about the saturation of the book with these images, which he found not only overdone but confusing. "What puzzled me to begin with," Eliot wrote, "was that practically everything except God appears to be

---

[46]Charles S. Singleton, review of *The Comedy of Dante Alighieri the Florentine, I: Hell,* by Dorothy L. Sayers, *Speculum* 25, no. 3 (July 1950): 395.

[47]Charles S. Singleton, "Dark Wood of Allegory," review of *Introductory Papers on Dante,* by Dorothy L. Sayers, *Kenyon Review* 17, no. 4 (1955): 656-57.

an image and if it is an image one is tempted to say, 'An image of what?' It seems to belong to a kind of personal language of your own."[48] In the coming weeks, the images were stripped from all the title places and the work rechristened *The Figure of Beatrice*.

Eliot had spoken more truly than he knew. Williams had for decades been meditating on the avenues by which God tempts humans to heaven. Practically everything is indeed an image of God in Williams's thinking, and far from a "personal language," he considered images the divine idiom uttered throughout creation. In his glowing review of *The Figure of Beatrice* for *Blackfriars* in 1943, Dantist and Dominican friar Kenelm Foster outlines Williams's "doctrine" (as Foster rightly calls it) as follows:

> The world we know is a crowd of images of the divine being, each a focus, a prevailing preponderant image to a particular person at a particular time. We move forward by affirming as well as by rejecting. . . . And the pattern runs through all the world making a universal community, a City. A City made up of cities, of which one was Florence; a community of foci, of which one was Beatrice.[49]

As Foster goes on to explain, Williams's book doesn't just lay out the doctrine. It recapitulates Dante's career—from *Vita Nuova* to *Paradiso*—as the poet's gradual advancement in his apprehension of images, beginning with Beatrice's *salute* on the Florentine street ("[She] greeted me with such a virtuous manner that I seemed to see to the very bounds of beatitude") to the Godhead, with many other figures aiding or hindering his progress along the way.[50]

Williams was thus doing far more than literary criticism in the book. He was developing a theological program—one in which the artist gets to play one of the leading parts—that had been previewed

---

[48]T. S. Eliot to Charles Williams, September 2, 1942, Charles Williams Papers, folder 244, Marion E. Wade Center, Wheaton College, Wheaton, IL.

[49]Kenelm Foster, review of *The Figure of Beatrice*, *Blackfriars* 284 (November 1943): 421-22.

[50]Frisardi, *Vita Nuova*, 7.

in his idiosyncratic history of the church, *The Descent of the Dove* (1939). That book proposes that there are two movements within the history of Christianity, which Williams names the "Way of the Rejection of Images" and the "Way of the Affirmation of Images." The Negative Way belongs to asceticism and the sort of mysticism found in Pseudo-Dionysius and *The Cloud of Unknowing*. It treats the world as a distraction from the serious business of pursuing God. The Affirmative Way, by contrast, discovers the world to be a blessing on the same holy errand.[51] It's a maddening book, especially for those of us who like sentences and paragraphs to connect.[52] But the division of the two ways is evocative, as this balanced formula attests: "The one Way was to affirm all things orderly until the universe throbbed with vitality; the other to reject all things until there was nothing anywhere but He."[53]

Less difficult to discern is Dante's role in the matter. Again and again, Williams points to Dante as the great exemplar of the Affirmative Way, and he names the "image of Beatrice" as Dante's central image—yet without, at any point in the book, pausing to offer a thorough definition of this all-important concept. Williams also presents the sequence of Dante's writings as "an exhibition of a process" whereby the soul comes to understand and undertake its true "function," to know God. That process "begins when a boy and a girl meet in the streets of Florence; it ends when the whole web of interchanging creation pour themselves towards the *Deivirilis* ["Divine-Human" = Christ] (to borrow a word from

---

[51]Williams suggests that the Affirmative Way finds a doctrinal warrant in the Athanasian Creed, specifically its confession that Jesus Christ "Who, although He is God and man, yet He is not two, but one Christ. / One, not by conversion of the Godhead into flesh, but by taking of that manhood into God."

[52]A contemporary reviewer wrote, with justice, that Williams "experiences as much difficulty in getting his thoughts across to more pedestrian minds as did the mystics to whom he devotes such a generous amount of space." P. V. Norwood, review of *The Descent of the Dove*, by Charles Williams, *The Journal of Religion* 20, no. 4 (1940): 423.

[53]Charles Williams, *The Descent of the Dove* (Religious Book Club, London, 1939), 132.

the Areopagite) within the point of Godhead."[54] Over eight pages, Williams then quickly reviews Dante's "whole work" from *Vita Nuova* to *Paradiso*, but one can tell that Williams has much more to say about both Dante's oeuvre and its exhibition of the Affirmative Way.

As its original title mentioned above was to make plain, *The Figure of Beatrice: A Study in Dante* is Williams's guide to the Way of the Affirmation of Images. Williams really meant the book's subtitle. *The Figure of Beatrice* is not a study of the art of Dante's poetry (Williams engages in little extended close reading) but a study of the growth of the poet's imagination in relation to its central symbol. His overarching argument, as already hinted above, is that the figure of Beatrice served that imagination as a master symbol akin to nature in Wordsworth's poetry; Dante refers all the "other shapes" that came into his mind—"of people and places, of philosophies and poems"—to the one image. His daring was to "[bring] that figure as near as he could to the final image, so far as he could express it, of Almighty God."[55]

Although romantic love was Dante's line on the Affirmative Way, his was not, Williams observes early on, the *only* path. Nature was another, the City (always capitalized) another yet, and art could be one too. *The Figure of Beatrice* multiplies, in turn, Images and Ways. Williams knew all about the allegory of the theologians with its four senses—the literal, typological (also known, confusingly enough, as allegorical), moral (a.k.a. tropological), and anagogical (or mystical). He had lectured on them, and these too are discussed, sporadically, in the book.[56] But he also freely adapted the old

---

[54]Williams, *Descent of the Dove*, 132.

[55]*FB*, 8.

[56]He dares at one point to suggest that "Dante's four headings" ("granted that their implicit content would be less rigid in our day than in his") could be applied to nearly any "great poetry." He could make that proposal because he saw allegory as an expression of the Way of the Affirmation of Images, not the other way around (*FB*, 104).

scheme, as when he argues early in his tour of *Inferno* "that the literal meaning of the poem here covers four 'allegorical' meanings, (i) the Way of Romantic love, (ii) the Way of Romanticism in general, (iii) the Way of the City, (iv) the Way of the soul at all times."[57] As the words of this chapter's epigraph make clear, Williams considered the traditional fourfold division a starting point, not the limit of the levels of Dante's allegory. In his own way, Williams also bore witness to the *Comedy*'s overflowing polysemy. To gaze upon Beatrice was to see everything else transformed; one couldn't attend closely enough.

One can see why, for an academic like Singleton, all of this was a bit much. If one's approach (like Singleton's) was principally concerned with the explication of the text, if one would only compare Dante to his predecessors and contemporaries (*never* his successors centuries hence), if one was concerned with the soul's journey to God as the *medieval* mind conceived it (not the Christians of all eras)—then *The Figure of Beatrice* must have seemed a scandal indeed. But Sayers warned us in chapter two: For Williams, "*time*, in a sense, did not exist." Dante had not invented the Affirmative Way; he was simply the most eloquent of its chroniclers. The Way had already been in place before he received Beatrice's greeting, and it remained it place in after Dante's death. It was open now.

## SAYERS RESPONDS

At this point, our third reader demands readmission to the discussion. For Sayers deserves as much credit as Williams for developing this notion of the Dantean image, and far more for publicizing it. While admiring Lewis's scholarship on allegory (as witnessed above), she too found his hard division between allegory

---

[57]FB, 117.

and symbolism frustrating. In her copy of *The Allegory of Love*, she wrote a rebuttal on the bottom of the page following Lewis's remarks on *Vita Nuova*. She chides Lewis for not discriminating between the *two* modes of representation evident in the *Comedy*:

> True—but this applies only to D's use of "conventional" allegorical figures (personified abstractions) within the body of the work (cf. the Beasts the persons of the 2 pageants). It does not apply to the "natural symbols" (real persons) of the *Comedy*—Virgil is not merely "an accident in a substance," nor is Beatrice. What D. is explaining in the V. N. is the apparition of a conventional symbol among the "real" characters of a literal story (not an allegory).[58]

Sayers reiterated the distinctions she is making here, albeit with slightly varying terminology, multiple times in the years ahead—as the quotation from her 1954 lecture noted at the start of this chapter has already shown. The key distinction is the ancient one—known in Dante's day—between symbols whose meanings derive purely from convention, which is to say by common agreement, and those that share some quality with the thing they represent. The sort of allegory Lewis has in mind—the Bunyan kind—deploys conventional symbols in the form of "personified abstractions" (e.g., Despair, an emotion, is personified as a Giant). Amor in *Vita Nuova* is such a "conventional" symbol, she admits, yet is also a peculiar one, being the lone personification in a story world otherwise populated by real people.

Dante's technique in the *Comedy* is comparatively "natural." Here the real people are mobilized as symbols of vices, virtues, and higher realities because of their earthly exploits. In her *Inferno* introduction, Sayers cites the example of Virgil: "[Dante] is accompanied through Hell, not by a personified abstraction called

---

[58]Marginal note by Sayers in *The Allegory of Love* by C. S. Lewis, 1936, p. 48, Dorothy L. Sayers Library collection, Marion E. Wade Center, Wheaton College, Wheaton, IL.

Reason, or Wisdom, or Science, or Art or Statecraft, but by Virgil the Poet, a real person, who is, by his own nature, qualified to symbolize all these abstractions."[59] When she wrote the note in her copy of *The Allegory of Love*, Sayers could already see, moreover, that we don't need to choose irrevocably between allegory and symbol in Dante's "special case." The poet employs "conventional" "allegorical figures" such as the three beasts Dante encounters at the beginning of *Inferno* as well as "natural" "symbolic images" like Virgil and Beatrice. The latter sort, moreover, don't have to operate in the one-to-one fashion of Bunyan's Formalist, Hypocrisy, and Giant Despair.

The marginal note was likely deposited just before she wrote to Williams on September 14, 1944—one month after she'd had her life-changing encounter with Dante in the backyard bunker. Toward the end of a lengthy report on her progress through the *Comedy*, she complained that Lewis "rather does suggest that Dante is all allegory, but if you go on to say that Beatrice herself is an 'allegorical figure,' you get into difficulties." She thought it "misleading" "to call the whole thing 'an allegory.'" She then told Williams that the deficiency of Lewis's account demonstrates why "your whole system of the interpretation of images is so enormously important."[60] A few years later, she solemnized her debt to his teaching in the dedications to her *Hell* and *Purgatory* volumes. They begin:

> To the Dead Master
> of the Affirmations
> Charles Williams[61]

---

[59]Dorothy L. Sayers, introduction, in *The Divine Comedy 1: Hell*, trans. Sayers (Penguin, 1949), 13.

[60]Dorothy L. Sayers to Charles Williams, September 14, 1944, in *LDS*, 3:77-78.

[61]In each case, she followed the dedication with words from the canticle in question in which Dante expresses his gratitude to fellow poets.

Williams haunts the two volumes. She quotes him directly on numerous occasions, some of which have already been cited in this book. But his legacy is even more significant in her adoption of his notion of the image in Dante. Now, in the introduction to her *Hell* translation, she pitches her choice of the word *image* on pragmatic terms. In order to steer clear of the potential confusion raised by the word *symbol* (she had just shown that a symbol could be conventional or arbitrary), she explains that she will "follow the example of Charles Williams and others and refer to Dante's natural symbols as his 'images.'"[62] Yet this is more than a convenience, for along with Williams's image she also imported his manner of freely handling Dante's allegory.

In the last section of introduction to *Hell*, for instance, she gives the reader capsule summaries of seven "Greater Images" (language she borrows from Williams but uses more scrupulously): Dante, Virgil, Beatrice, hell, purgatory, paradise, and "The Empire and City." Each of these images, the reader here learns, has at least a double function in the poem and sometimes more. Beatrice, for instance, is "in the *story* what she was in real life: the Florentine girl whom Dante loved . . . and in whom he seemed (as is sometimes the case with lovers) to see Heaven's glory walking the earth bodily." Because she had been to Dante "the vehicle of Glory," Sayers continues, she is "in the *allegory*, from time to time likened to, or equated with, those other, 'God-bearers': the Church, and Divine Grace in the Church, the Blessed Virgin, even Christ Himself."[63] Her notes on nearly every canto of *Inferno* and *Purgatorio* then follow this model, explaining the significance of the most salient local images—whether people, places, objects, or activities such as the punishments in hell (as discussed in chapter three)—to the story and the allegory.

---

[62] Sayers, introduction, 13.
[63] Sayers, introduction, 67, italics original.

Allegory, allegory, allegory—we cannot escape that much-contested word. Thankfully, our previous travails can help us to understand Sayers's positions. Lewis had gotten allegory wrong as it applied to the micro-level of the *Comedy*'s characters and so needed correction. Williams had gotten the allegory right at the macro-level by insisting on its "multifolded" interpretation, but his explanation was insufficient. In her writings on Dante, she sought to put Williams's thinking on firmer ground and rephrase it in layperson's terms. Across her lectures in particular, Sayers tested different ways of explaining what Williams had achieved. In her 1948 lecture "The Fourfold Interpretation of *The Comedy*," for example, Sayers argues—for clever but not entirely convincing reasons—that the three traditional levels of allegorical interpretation in the Middle Ages (once again, typological, moral, and anagogical) can be translated into three Williams-eque ways: the Way of the City, the Way of the Soul, and the Way of Contemplation, the last of which she subdivides into the Negative and Affirmative Ways.[64] In her *Hell* volume, Sayers wisely simplifies things, emphasizing that the *Comedy* as a whole is an "allegory of the Way to God" and, as noted in chapter three, focusing her commentary on the Ways of the City and of the Soul. Yet even there she cannot help adding that the poem may also be interpreted as "the way of the artist, or the way of the lover," as Williams had suggested.[65]

Like Lewis and Williams, Sayers often seems delightfully overwhelmed by the task of relating how much and how exactly the *Comedy* means. Natural symbol, personified abstraction, symbolic framework, allegory, image, sense, way: No terminology was sufficient to measure the fullness of Dante's achievement. "The landscape, as well as the poetry and the 'feel' of the first eight cantos

---

[64]Dorothy L. Sayers, "The Fourfold Interpretation of the *Comedy*," in *IPD*, 101-26.
[65]Sayers, introduction, 19.

of the *Purgatorio*," Sayers writes in ". . . And Telling You a Story," "is of a quality so rare and strange that criticism has invented no suitable language to describe it."[66] And in the last analysis, the exact nomenclature didn't matter. Sayers was assembling equipment so that others could set off on the Way of Dante, and she was far more anxious that her audience would read *too little* into the *Comedy* than too much. Dante's "great images" seemed to her so lavishly endowed with meaning, as she argues in the first of this study's epigraphs, that wayfarers need not fear reading overmuch into one of them—as long as one's interpretation does not "degrade" the image or work at cross purposes to the allegory's main line (i.e., the Way to God).[67] The *Comedy* is not the exclusive property of the scholars but the "freehold" of all its readers. The urgent problem is not to solve Dante's allegory but to launch more readers upon it.

---

[66]ATYS, 28.
[67]Dorothy L. Sayers, "Dante's Imagery: I—Symbolic," in *IPD*, 19.

**Figure 5.1.** Illustration for *Purgatorio* II, in Dante's *La Commedia, col commento di Cristoforo Landino* (Venice, 1493)

$\boxed{5}$

# THE PURGATORIAL ASCENT OF LOVE

*Now from the grave wake poetry again.*

DOROTHY L. SAYERS, TRANSLATOR, *PURGATORY* I.7

*The psalms sung in Purgatory are part of the Church's ritual, but here*
*it is better to say that the ritual is part of them. Dante is not in an*
*open-air church; the roofed churches of earth are so roofed, as it were,*
*to preserve in them something of this vernal air.*

CHARLES WILLIAMS, *THE FIGURE OF BEATRICE*

ALL THREE MEMBERS OF MY COHORT preferred the *Comedy*'s second canticle to its first. Sayers judged *Purgatorio* "better written than *Inferno*—more easily, more competently, and with a more sustained poetic power."[1] Lewis, as noted in chapter two, told Sayers that what was true of her translations was true of "the originals": *Purgatorio* was better than *Inferno*.[2] Williams, meanwhile, found in *Purgatorio* a major step on the Way of the Affirmation of Images (what, after all, is there to affirm in hell?). Yet the reading public didn't share their esteem of *Purgatorio* because,

---

[1]Dorothy L. Sayers, "The Meaning of Purgatory," in *IPD*, 74.
[2]C. S. Lewis to Dorothy L. Sayers, July 31, 1955, in *CLCSL*, 3:634. Lewis also told her in a 1953 letter that *Purgatorio* was "perhaps my favorite part of the Comedy," but it clearly faced stiff competition from *Paradiso*.

for the most part, the common reader hadn't read it. Thus, the paradox related in the opening sentence of Sayers's introduction to the *Purgatory* volume: "Of the three books of the *Commedia*, the *Purgatorio* is, for English readers, the least known, the least quoted—and the most beloved."[3]

While allegory suffered from "bad Press," *Purgatorio* seemed to Sayers the victim of the "popular superstition" that Dante is the "Poet of Hell."[4] "Credulous" readers have assumed, in turn, that "a Dante out of Hell is a Dante poetically out of his element," and so never cracked the cover of *Purgatorio*. If they laid eyes on the first page, though, they might be pleasantly surprised by what they found:

> Colour unclouded, orient-sapphirine,
>> Softly suffusing from meridian height
>> Down the still sky to the horizon-line,
> Brought to mine eyes renewal of delight
>> So soon as I came forth from that dead air
>> Which had oppressed my bosom and my sight.
> The lovely planet [Venus], love's own quickener,
>> Now lit to laughter all the eastern sky,
>> Veiling the Fishes [Pisces] that attended her.
> Right-hand I turned, and, setting me to spy
>> That alien pole, beheld four stars, the same
>> The first men saw, and since, no living eye:
> Meseemed the heaven exulted in their flame— (I.13-25)[5]

Upon summiting *Purgatorio* for the first time in late August 1944, Sayers told Williams that she found the "colour" of these cantos a "sort of miracle." Amid "all that smoke and gloom" in *Inferno*, she

---

[3]Dorothy L. Sayers, introduction, in *The Divine Comedy 2: Purgatory*, trans. Sayers (Penguin, 1955), 9.

[4]Sayers, introduction, 9-10. Sayers traced the "superstition" to the "vogue for Gothick gloom and Tales of Horror" in the eighteenth century.

[5]Sayers, *Divine Comedy 2: Purgatory*, 73.

realized, Dante hadn't been able to show "what he could do in that way," but now "here it is—limpid and lovely and clean and enchanting." She marveled that Dante could produce such a powerful impression with just a handful of words and "practically no paint-box adjectives at all."[6]

A few years later, in ". . . And Telling You a Story," she again expressed wonder at the changeover from *Inferno* to *Purgatorio*:

> If the interior of Hell is like a painting by Michael Angelo, the wind-swept and sea-swept exterior of Mount Purgatory is like a painting by Perugino. The loveliness of the sky, passing from the *"dolce color d'oriental zaffiro"* to the shifting hues of the dawn, the dew-drenched grass and swaying reeds, the faint shimmering of the sea . . . —the whole picture is of a translucent and tender and unearthly beauty so utterly unlike anything in the *Inferno* that the sense of relief and escape is almost physical.[7]

This is where Sayers makes the remark (heard at the end of the last chapter) that the landscape—"as well as the poetry and the 'feel' of the first eight cantos of *Purgatorio*"—"is of a quality so rare and strange that criticism has invented no suitable language to describe it." And, even more wonderfully, Dante's new terrain and aesthetic directly "mirror" the "process of purgation."[8] It is all of a piece and of peace; *Purgatorio* is the more mature work.

The question the second canticle poses is whether we wish to become the more mature readers it demands. If we do, then Sayers promises us that we will find much to love in *Purgatorio*, for it exercises faculties and cultivates emotions that *Inferno* may cause us to forget we possess. If *Inferno* furnishes an education in evil, *Purgatorio* offers a corresponding open-air schoolroom in such salutary themes as repentance, holiness, and community.

---

[6] Dorothy L. Sayers to Charles Williams, August 25-26, 1944, in *LDS*, 3:56.
[7] ATYS, 28.
[8] As noted in chapter 2, Lewis liked this point.

Mount Purgatory is where souls labor to enter God's reality in all its goodness. And, as Sayers would remind us, since this poem is an allegory, its "real environment" is not the mountain Dante planted in the southern sea but souls—his and ours. My trio invited readers, in turn, to scale Mount Purgatory with heart and mind open to the possibility of translating its moving pictures of penance, testimonies to the abundance of divine mercy, and gestures of neighborly goodwill back into their own lives. Sayers, Williams, and Lewis felt their imaginations renewed by their journeys through *Purgatorio* and beckoned others to follow "Where human spirts purge themselves, and train / To leap up into joy celestial" (I.5-6).[9]

## WHERE SERMONS MAY BEGIN

Even though *Purgatorio* shows Dante in command of his material—even though "the poet is doing exactly what he chooses, as he chooses, and when he chooses"—Sayers acknowledges that readers may not (at first, at least) *like* what he is doing.[10] If we are only skimming the poem for bits of intense lyricism, for example, then *Inferno* will likely be more to our taste (even though, Sayers notes, "that only means that we do not really like great narrative poems as such"). More troublesome is the modern aversion to "didactic" poetry, which Sayers finds concisely expressed in one critic's prickly recap of *Purgatorio*: "Then the sermons begin."[11] Sayers acknowledges a grain of truth in the charge: *Purgatorio* does contain "long passages which can only be classed as didactic poetry—versified statements of plain theological or scientific fact"; and there are undoubtedly more of such passages in the second canticle than the first (and still more in the third), thereby

---

[9]Sayers, *Divine Comedy 2: Purgatory*, 73.
[10]Sayers, introduction, 10.
[11]Sayers, introduction, 11.

making them harder to skip over without losing the thread of the story.[12]

However, the number of such passages, their range of subject matter, and their intellectual depth, Sayers argues, reveal two important points about Dante's overarching project. The first is that hell is no place for Dante to engage in deep thought; the absence of sermons in the pit is one of *Inferno*'s gauges of how far humanity has sunk from its potential. (As Dante warns us in *Inferno* III.18, hell's inhabitants "have lost the good of the intellect.") Thus, the hellions "have no use for thinking," Sayers observes; they "pass their eternity in a bustle of purposeless activity." The sermons of *Purgatorio* mark a change in the mental atmosphere of the poem and so should be a welcome sign (finally, some adult conversation!). "Only when one has squeezed out from Hell's suffocating bottle-neck," Sayers writes, "to 'look once more upon the stars' can the mind resume its discursive and contemplative functions."[13]

The second point is that Dante isn't constrained by our highly stratified universe of genres. Nowadays, poetry occupies itself with "the personal, the emotional, and the introspective." To the physical and social sciences, we turn for facts. When we look for instruction in history, metaphysics, and ethics, we consult prose sources. Yet it has not always been so. From Lucretius in the first century BC to Wordsworth in the nineteenth century AD, and even as recently as the Victorians Robert Browning and

---

[12]Sayers, introduction, 10.

[13]Sayers, introduction, 10. In his *Dante* monograph, Eliot also endeavored to help his readers navigate the "sermons," which he correctly portrays as essential to Dante's project in the second canticle. He acknowledges that "the narrative of the ascent of the Mount, with meetings, visions, and philosophical expositions, all important," will be "difficult for the uninstructed reader who finds it less exciting than the continuous phantasmagoria of the *Inferno*." He urges the reader to approach "the philosophical passages of Dante with the humility of a person visiting a new world, who admits that every part is essential to the whole," and treat Dante's beliefs as "possible" ones. T. S. Eliot, *Dante* (Faber & Faber, 1929), 41, 44.

Robert Bridges, Sayers observes, "a writer was free if he chose
to use verse as the medium for instruction, demonstration, and
argument, and in that medium to handle morals, philosophy,
science, or any other material belonging to human experience."
Dante took full advantage of that freedom and could do so
trusting that his audience would not view "the mixture of
passion, mysticism, and science in one and the same poem" as
illegitimate. "It would never occur to [the medieval reader],"
Sayers argues, "that he ought to keep his head, his heart, and
his religious experience in water-tight compartments, or that
a poem might not properly appeal to all of them in turn." To
reckon with what Dante is doing, we must tear down the walls
moderns have thrown up between the narrow matter of poetry
and wide field of prose. She suggests that readers approach
the *Comedy* like a "serious and intelligent" novel: "For in the
fourteenth century the allegorical poem was precisely what the
novel is to-day—the dominant literary form, into which a writer
could pour, without incongruity, everything that he had to say
about life and the universe."[14]

This line of thinking had been laid down for her by Lewis.
Recall that she had read *Preface to Paradise Lost* before taking
up the *Comedy* in August 1944. There Lewis argues that
Milton viewed verse as a suitable vehicle for science just as
Dante had. The *Comedy*, Lewis argues, unites "two literary
undertakings which have long since been separated:" first, the
"high, imaginative interpretation of spiritual life" and, second,
"realistic" travel writing "about wanderings in places which no
one had reached, but which every one believed to have a literal
and local existence."[15] That makes Dante, on the one side, "the
companion of Homer, Virgil, and Wordsworth," and on the

---

[14]Sayers, introduction, 11-14.
[15]C. S. Lewis, *A Preface to Paradise Lost* (Oxford University Press, 1942), 111.

other, "the father of Jules Verne and H. G. Wells." In "Dante's Similes" (which Lewis had written a year or so before delivering the lectures that became the *Preface*), he argues that the *Comedy* performs four functions subsequently "split up and distributed among several different kinds of book": (1) a traveler's account of unreachable regions, (2) "a poetic expression of the current philosophy of the age," (3) a religious allegory, and (4) "a history of the poet."[16] It thus bears resemblances, Lewis suggests, to Verne's and Wells's lunar expeditions, Alexander Pope's *The Essay on Man*, Bunyan's *Pilgrim's Progress*, Wordsworth's *The Prelude*, and, in light of its political and historical concerns, "the memoirs of some retired statesman."[17]

Sayers was raising these issues in her *Purgatory* volume because Dante could play all of these parts *more fully* now that he was no longer confined by hell's closemindedness. With the restoration of humanity as his theme, Dante could indeed "pour, without incongruity, everything that he had to say about life and the universe" into his cantos. Not jumping ship after *Inferno* may have a beneficent effect on us, Sayers proposes. Under the influence of Dante's grand synthesis, the modern reader's "partitioned-off personality may flow together again."[18]

---

[16]C. S. Lewis, "Dante's Similes," in *Studies in Medieval and Renaissance Literature*, ed. Walter Hooper (Cambridge University Press, 1966), 68.

[17]Lewis's examples of the uniquely "Dantesque" simile—in which the connection between the two parts of the simile is "real, ontological, intelligible"—all notably appear in *Purgatorio* and *Paradiso*. Commenting on a simile in Virgil's first discourse on love in *Purgatorio* XV.64-75, Lewis offers further testimony to the increasing depth of thought and mixing of now separated genres in the second canticle when he argues that "though excellent poetry, it is the sort of simile that could equally well occur in philosophical prose" (Lewis, "Dante's Similes," 71).

[18]Sayers, introduction, 14.

# THE PURGATORY

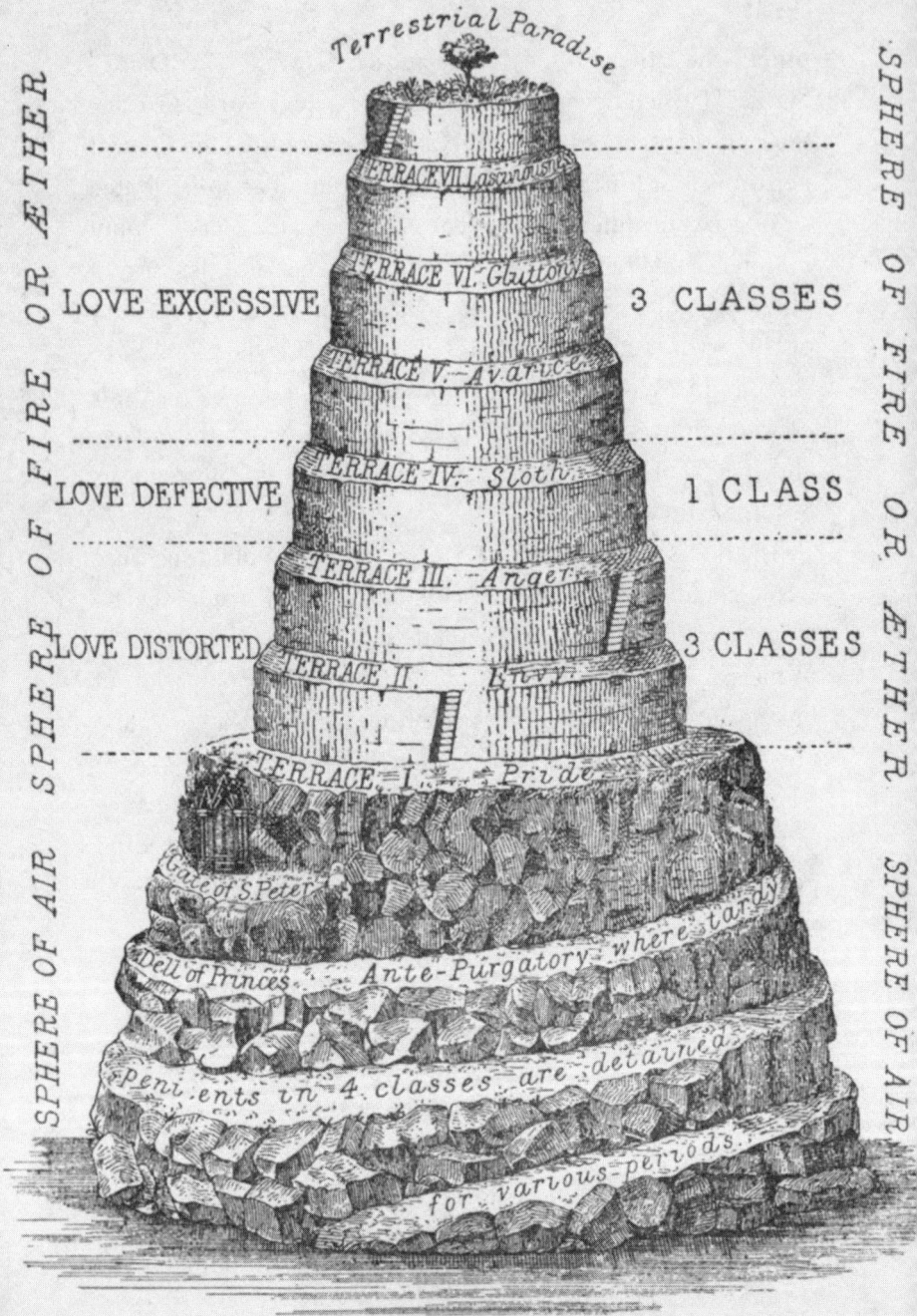

*Terrestrial Paradise*

SPHERE OF FIRE OR ÆTHER

SPHERE OF FIRE OR ÆTHER

SPHERE OF AIR

SPHERE OF AIR

TERRACE VII *Lasciousness*

TERRACE VI. *Gluttony*

LOVE EXCESSIVE          3 CLASSES

TERRACE V.—*Avarice*

TERRACE IV. *Sloth*

LOVE DEFECTIVE          1 CLASS

TERRACE III. *Anger*

LOVE DISTORTED          3 CLASSES

TERRACE II. *Envy*

TERRACE I. *Pride*

*Gate of S.Peter*

*Dell of Princes*   *Ante-Purgatory where tardy*

*Penitents in 4 classes are detained*

*for various periods*

**Figure 5.2.** "The Purgatory," in Maria Francesca Rossetti's *A Shadow of Dante* (Longmans & Green, 1894 edition)

(*To face Chap. VII.*)

## A FRESH VISION

*Purgatorio*'s "sermons," once again, aren't just longer. They also introduce new material. One of the longest discourses, delivered by Virgil at the *Comedy*'s midpoint (*Purgatorio* XVI), offers a series of love lessons that elucidate the arrangement of Mount Purgatory's seven terraces (or "cornices," as Sayers preferred to call them). While Dante's hell is organized around concepts drawn from ancient (i.e., pagan) philosophy, his purgatory is modeled on the seven capital (a.k.a. "deadly") vices—pride, envy, wrath, sloth, avarice, gluttony, and lust. "These are," Sayers explains in her introduction, "the fundamental bad habits of mind recognized and defined by the Church as the well-heads from which all sinful behaviour ultimately springs." But from what do *they* spring? Virgil here answers: love. "His argument rests upon the great Augustinian premise that evil in itself is nothing and can originate nothing positive—not even sin," Sayers explains. "It can only be a parasite upon the good which God has created."[19] Thus, Mount Purgatory is a study in love gone wrong, each of the capital sins consisting of "the love for some good, either falsely perceived, or inadequately or excessively pursued." Sayers goes to great lengths in her commentary—including charts to make the divisions easier to grasp—to clarify the rationale for the order: The lowest three terraces—pride, envy, wrath—root out perversions of love (in which the sinner directs love to a false object—such as the love of one's neighbor's *harm*); the middle one—sloth—the deficiency of love; and the upper three—avarice, gluttony, lust— excessive love (whether of money and power, pleasure, or persons).[20]

The mountain is thus richly traditional and an expression of the "medieval passion" for system and symmetry, Sayers observes. But

---

[19]Sayers, introduction, 65-66.

[20]Building on Williams's analysis of the vices in *Inferno* (see chap. 3), Sayers further observes that, as in *Inferno*, here again "warmer-hearted sins which involved exchange and reciprocity are the top, and the cold egotism which rejects community is at the bottom" (introduction, 67).

she also urges her readers to remember Dante was "not an engineer but a poet addressing a reading public, and therefore obliged both to be interesting and to satisfy his own artistic conscience."[21] Thus, the fact that hell and purgatory are not laid out on the same principles should not surprise us. Dante may have had an astonishingly tight grip on doctrine, but we should never forget that he was an artist, first and foremost. Great are his sermons, but greater are his images. In both respects, *Purgatorio* outstrips *Inferno*.

I noted above Sayers's astonishment at the imagery of *Purgatorio*'s opening cantos. She was also struck by the fact that once Dante and Virgil pass through the narrow gate in *Purgatorio* IX— once they ascend to the cornices, where capital sins are uprooted one by one—Dante sets the "living hues of nature" aside. The backdrop becomes rock, the zone of penance appropriately minimalist in its design. Yet Dante has one more surprise in store: At the summit, the imagery shifts again. Now we step into the Earthly Paradise—"Green and cool and fragrant with flowers, murmurous with bird-song and babbling brook and tree-tops rustling in the wind that moves with the turning worlds."[22] *Purgatorio* is a study in contrasts—lush here and austere there, soft grass and hard rockface, green and gray, at once commodious and toilsome.

The mountain as a whole Sayers and Williams rank among Dante's greatest images, and the former rightly stresses that Dante's vision of purgatory marked a break from earlier conceptions of it as "a region bordering Hell and rather like it." "The lowest part of [Dante's] Purgatory," she instructs her translation's reader, "is as remote from Hell as the surface of the Earth from the Centre; its summit soars beyond Earth's atmosphere to a height no eye can reach."[23] (The great historian of purgatory, Jacques Le Goff, concurs, observing that Dante

---

[21]Sayers, introduction, 14.
[22]Sayers, introduction, 14, 18.
[23]Sayers, introduction, 17.

"depicts Purgatory as a place between two extremes, but closer to one of them, straining in the direction of Paradise."[24])

Nonetheless, the penances of Mount Purgatory are often only a shade less severe than the punishments of *Inferno*: The proud bear boulders on their backs, the eyes of the envious are sewn shut, the covetous crawl along the stone floor, and the lustful run around within a raging fire. But there is a crucial difference in attitude, Sayers stresses. In hell, the impenitent cling to their vices and hate their punishments, while in purgatory the penitents hate their vices and welcome their remedies. In the introduction, Sayers explains the difference by citing one of Lewis's devilish complaints about Christians in *Screwtape Letters*: "They *embrace* those pains; they would not barter them for any earthly pleasure."[25]

Lewis, in turn, may have borrowed from Sayers on purgatory. In her 1948 lecture "The Meaning of Purgatory," Sayers posits that if "the doctrine of Purgatory [had] never been presented otherwise than it is in Dante, the Reformed Churches would have found much less reason to repudiate it; it would at any rate have offered far less opportunity for the scandal and abuse of which they complained."[26] Lewis had read Sayers's lecture, and it may have shaped or at least encouraged his claim in *Letters to Malcolm, Chiefly on Prayer* (1964) that while the Reformers were right to protest against purgatory as it was then advertised, "If you turn from Dante's *Purgatorio* to the

---

[24]Jacques Le Goff, *The Birth of Purgatory*, trans. Arthur Goldhammer (University of Chicago Press, 1981), 346. Le Goff credits Dante with "rescuing" purgatory from previous commentators' "infernalization" of the doctrine. Le Goff also clarifies that Dante had some geographical choices available thanks to prior writings on Purgatory, and his choice of a mountain was a terrific poetic one, since the mountain "points from the earth, where the future elect are when they die, to Heaven, their eternal abode." Le Goff also notes, perceptively, that the image of the mountain "expresses Purgatory's true logic, that of the climb."

[25]C. S. Lewis, *The Screwtape Letters and Screwtape Proposes a Toast* (Geoffrey Bles, 1961), 159. Eliot is also illuminating: "The souls in purgatory suffer because they wish to suffer, for purgation. And observe that they suffer more actively and keenly, being souls preparing for blessedness, than Virgil suffers in eternal limbo. In their suffering is hope, in the anaesthesia of Virgil is hopelessness; that is the difference" (*Dante*, 40).

[26]Sayers, "Meaning of Purgatory," 75.

Sixteenth Century you will be appalled by the degradation." That "degradation" lies in the movement away from Dante's emphasis on the purification of the soul. In the works of the later writers who recast purgatory as "a place not of purification but purely of retributive punishment," Lewis laments that "the very etymology of the word *purgatory* [drops] of sight. Its pains do not bring us nearer to God, but make us forget Him."[27] When Lewis then argues that "our souls *demand* Purgatory" on the grounds that they would "rather be cleaned" before entering into God's presence, he is looking back to Dante's second realm, where "the human soul is cleansed of sin / and becomes worthy to ascend to Heaven" (*dove l'umano spirito si purga / e di salire al ciel diventa degno*).[28]

Sayers thought that *Purgatorio*'s penitents embodied another keen psychological insight: that if you are not convinced of your guilt, then punishment necessarily *appears* vindictive, while if you are so convinced, "*all* punishment of whatever kind is remedial, since it lies with [the culprit] to make it so." The difference between hell and purgatory, in other words, lies in the soul's self-perception. She cites the mystic St. Catherine of Genoa: "It has been well said by a great saint that the fire of Hell is simply the light of God as experienced by those who reject it," which Sayers then translates as follows: "Those, that is, who hold fast to their darling illusion of sin, the burning reality of holiness is a thing unbearable."[29] She continues:

> To the penitent, that reality is a torment so long and only so long as any vestige of illusion remains to hamper their assent to it: they welcome torment, as a sick man welcomes the pains of surgery, in order that the last crippling illusion may be burned away. The whole operation of Purgatory is directed to the freeing of the judgement and the will. Hell is the fleeing deeper into the iron-bound prison

---

[27]C. S. Lewis, *Letters to Malcolm: Chiefly on Prayer* (Geoffrey Bles, 1964), 139-40.

[28]Lewis, *Letters to Malcolm*, 140 (author's translation).

[29]Sayers, introduction, 15-16.

of the self. . . . Purgatory is the resolute breaking-down, at whatever cost, of the prison walls, so that the soul may be able to emerge at last into liberty and endure unscathed the unveiled light of reality.[30]

The attentive reader will remember that we have seen this dichotomy between human illusion and God's reality before—back in Sayers's portrait of the hellions discussed in chapter three. Reading *He Came Down from Heaven*, once again, Sayers seized on Williams's characterization of the fall as the beginning of the "knowledge of good as evil" and the slide into illusion. In *The Great Divorce*, she heard a strong echo in Lewis's argument that while hell is a delusional "state of mind," "Heaven is reality itself." On Mount Purgatory, Sayers found pictures of souls engaged in strenuous efforts to shed their illusions and thereby tread fully in the reality of heaven. *Purgatorio*, on this understanding, presents the arduous journey to *clear-sightedness*—regarding the self, one's neighbors, creation, and the Maker of all of these. Sayers grasped this because she had read not only *He Came Down from Heaven* but also *The Figure of Beatrice*.

## THE MOUNTAIN OF AFFIRMATIONS

As noted above, Williams found in purgatory a crucial stage of the Way of the Affirmation of Images. In broad outline, Williams saw progress on the way as movement between images. It begins with the "First Image," which radiates the divine glory. In Dante's case, the medium was Beatrice; in other poets' cases, it has been Nature or the City. Then the first image fades; and it may, as in Beatrice's death, appear irretrievably lost. A second image appears, which could be an aid but also a temptation—if it numbs the lessons of the first.[31] Finally,

---

[30]Sayers, introduction, 16.

[31]In his *Arthurian Torso* commentary (see chap. 6), Lewis superbly comments on the second image as follows: "Not only does the glory fade away from one Lady: it may, more disturbingly, reappear in another. Cynics have hailed this as one more proof that the first appearance was an illusion: eulogists of romantic love have too often tried to hush it up. According to Williams we must do neither of these things. Nothing must ever be hushed up; the road to Byzantium is one of increasing awareness, vigilance, attention. If the first appearance of

after much trial, the first image is "re-asserted" (Williams's language). Yet it operates now "at a much higher and more universal level than before," as Sayers (who studied this paradigm closely—see chapter six) explains.[32] She ably carries us to the end of Williams's road:

> The glory which was once known only in the beloved creature is diffused upon all creation, and taken up into its Eternal source. This is the reunion with a Beatrice who is more than herself; and the ascent by her means to the Vision in which all the shining Images are seen "transhumanised" and summed up in the final Image—the Image of the Incarnate Christ in the very centre of the Unimaginable Godhead.[33]

Beatrice, as Sayers explains in the *Purgatory* introduction, is "a type of the Incarnate" Christ, and the "'movement of the poem as a whole' [is] towards that central Image."[34] Before the *cosmic* ascent to the final image can take place, however, Dante must be prepared for the reunion with his first one. That, Williams argues, is the business of purgatory.

In *He Came Down from Heaven*, Williams had argued that repentance "is no more than a passionate intention to know all things after the mode of Heaven."[35] Having fully seen sin in hell, Williams argues in *The Figure of Beatrice*, Dante is ready to gaze upon the "quality of eternity" through faith and repentance, that is, to know things in heavenly fashion. Practically speaking, repentance and faith require that the pilgrim of the Affirmative Way undergo "the purging

---

the glory revealed one being as all beings really and eternally are, then it ought to be expected that the glory might return to reveal similar transcendental truth about some other being." C. S. Lewis, *Arthurian Torso: Containing the Posthumous Fragment of The Figure of Arthur by Charles Williams and A Commentary on the Arthurian Poems of Charles Williams by C. S. Lewis* (Oxford University Press, 1948), 118.

[32]Dorothy L. Sayers, "The Fourfold Interpretation of the *Comedy*," in *IPD*, 123. Sayers, it is worth noting, also had the benefit of reading Lewis's account of Williams's progression in *Arthurian Torso* prior to writing this summary.

[33]Sayers, "Fourfold Interpretation of the *Comedy*," 123-24.

[34]Sayers, introduction, 36.

[35]*HCDH*, 60. Sayers concludes her 1939 essay "Strong Meat" by citing this passage.

of the Images; or, more strictly, of the mind that sees the Images."[36] We must get hellish distortions out of our heads. Williams explains:

> The mount of recollection and of reconciliation [i.e., Mount Purgatory] is on earth always before the soul that wills. It must cease to know the Images as *it* chooses; it must know them as they are; that is, as God chose them to be; that is, it must (in its degree) know them as God knows them in their union with him. Its [the soul's] duty, therefore, is to put off all evil knowledge and to put on all good; this, heavenly, it chooses here to do.[37]

Amid the muddled syntax, Williams is saying something quite profound. Remember that his image is Coleridge's symbol, and that a Coleridgean symbol "represents in itself that greatness from which it derives." The greatness in question here is God's. Purgatory, on Williams's tangled telling, is the state in which we unlearn our habits of perception that rob images of their signifying power. Purgatory is the renewal of divine symbolism, and thereby the rethickening of the penitent's reality. It is the process whereby we prepare to behold God directly by awakening to the innumerable channels through which divine glory already flows.[38] And, of course, because Williams views the *Comedy* not as a past event but the map of a present reality, because he doesn't historize, he emphasizes that what goes on in *Purgatorio*—its depiction of purgation, recollection, and reconciliation—is "on earth always before the soul that wills."[39]

---

[36]*FB*, 146.

[37]*FB*, 146.

[38]He saw, moreover, in the three steps that Dante must ascend before passing through the gate that leads to the cornices a compact image of "true affirmation." The first step, made of polished white marble, displays the "clarity and glory" of the first image. The second, rough and dark purple, recasts the image in "dark contradiction and schism." And the third, blood red, foreshadows the coming "union of the vital self" with the image. These same images Sayers names in her commentary as confession, contrition, and satisfaction, following the traditional line of interpretation.

[39]That confidence is also rooted in Williams's argument earlier in the book that the hill Dante fails to climb in *Inferno* I is the same mountain: "Dante is where he would have been at the beginning if he had come to the Mountain by the direct road" (*FB*, 145).

Now, these ideas may strike you as a bit offbeat or even downright bonkers. If so, you are in highly decorated company. As we saw in chapter four, academic critics such as Singleton—the leading American Dantist of his generation—found Williams's approach outlandish and bemoaned his sway over Sayers. Yet Williams's singular perspective has a way of bringing to life aspects of the *Comedy* that academic criticism tends to overlook or undervalue, and thus reading the poem through the defamiliarizing lens that is Williams's prose has a way of revivifying passages and images, making them strange and so fascinating again to the imagination.

Take the envious, for example. Dante and Virgil come upon them in *Purgatorio* XIII dressed in "coarse hair-cloth," "each one's shoulder [propping up] his neighbor's head, / and all of them propped against the wall" (lines 58-60). They must be so, for "their eyelids with an iron wire / Are stitched and sealed" as those of a young falcon at the outset of its training (lines 70-71).[40] In her comments on the image, Sayers observes that the envious one fears "losing something by the admission of superiority in others, and therefore looks with grudging hatred upon other men's gifts and good fortune, taking every opportunity to run them down or deprive them of their happiness." Dante's penance, in turn, addresses their vision: "The eyes which could not endure to look upon joy are sealed from the glad light of the sun, and from the sight of other men." They are made like "blind beggars," Sayers continues, "who live on alms, the Envious sit amidst the barren and stony wilderness imploring the charity of the saints, their fellow-men."[41]

All this is illuminating, of course. Yet the vice of envy takes on an added dimension when, in the same passage, Williams defines the "lowest" of the capital vices (once again, pride, envy, and wrath) as "the hurt of a neighbour," and thereby "the harming of an image or

---

[40]Sayers, *Divine Comedy 2: Purgatory*, 167-68.
[41]Sayers, note on canto XIII, *Divine Comedy 2: Purgatory*, 170.

images given to one for due love." His point is that the one whom you perceived to be a threat or rival might have been, if looked on lovingly, an image in his special sense. Simply stated, your enemy could have been a route to divine glory. On these grounds, Williams declares, "It is clearer now what that Mount is; it is the purgatorial ascent of love."[42] Purgatory, in Williams's thinking, ought to be the mix of joy and pain that we find in *Purgatorio*, and joy the far greater of the two, for it is the re-vision of reality, beginning with a hard look at oneself.

## THE ARTS OF PURGATORY

Coming at *Purgatorio* within the study of a sacred artist's career, Williams was especially alert to the roles of the arts and liturgy, two categories that overlapped extensively in Dante's world, on the mountain.[43] "The *Purgatorio* is full of the arts," he rightly observes in *The Figure of Beatrice*. "They are there for a purpose."[44] Of course, Williams acknowledges, Dante also shows the arts to be a potential distraction from the pressing work of penance.[45] For example, right after the first canto has shown us the new arrivals to purgatory singing Psalm 114 (as mentioned in this chapter's first epigraph), Dante sits down to listen to one of them, his old friend Casella, sing a secular love song. That is not what one ought to be doing on

---

[42]*FB*, 163.

[43]As Le Goff writes, "Dante had the secret of integrating into his poem the liturgy that the scholastics usually kept out of their writings." But Dante doesn't just sprinkle some liturgy here and there to make *Purgatorio* seem churchy. He weaves in liturgical gestures and performances, varying their tone and theological import. Thus, in canto V, the unshriven— meaning those who were lax about confession—are heard "singing, verse by verse / Antiphonal, the *Miserere* through." That would be Ps 51 ("Have mercy on me, O Lord"), one of the penitential psalms. The proud pray an amplified Lord's Prayer, the envious pray the litany of the saints, the wrathful are heard singing the Agnus Dei—"Lamb of God who takest away the sins of the world"—a traditional feature of the Mass—and so on. As Dantist Helena Phillips-Robins argues in a recent book, Dante may have expected that the reader would pray, sing, and chant *along with his penitents*—meaning that the *Commedia*, especially *Purgatorio*, doesn't just contain liturgy but *is* liturgy, or at least is a courteous invitation to join in.

[44]*FB*, 102.

[45]Notable too is the number of poets whom Dante meets in hell.

the holy mountain! Accordingly, purgatory's warden, the Roman statesman Cato, arrives to break up the beach party.[46]

Yet, as Williams grasped, that scene is the outlier. *Purgatorio* is permeated by rich aesthetic experiences, including on the cornices in which the penances take place. Those presences, Williams recognized, speak to the arts' proper function: "to speed the soul towards heaven." "It seems likely that Dante (with all the medievals) thought that this was what the arts were chiefly for," our critic contends in *The Figure of Beatrice*. Yet Williams also notes that the history of church censorship of the *Vita Nuova* and of ecclesial study of the *Comedy* more generally "[do] not suggest that the arts are going to be much thanked by the official ministers of heaven for their assistance."[47]

The immediate object of his attention when Williams makes these remarks is the first thing Dante and Virgil observe when they arrive on the first terrace, that of pride, in *Purgatorio* X: three white marble sculptures carved into the mountainside. They are so lifelike that Dante says that both Polyclete, the greatest classical sculptor, and nature "might blush . . . being so outdone" (lines 32-33).[48] Dante's account of the first carving is itself a gorgeous inset ekphrastic poem:

> The angel that to earth came down and bore
>> The edict of the age-long wept-for peace
>> Which broke the long ban and unbarred Heaven's door,
> Appeared to us, with a such a lively ease
>> Carved, and so gracious there in act to move,
>> It seemed not one of your dumb images;
> You'd swear an *Ave* [Hail!] from his lips breathed off,
>> For she was shown there too, who turned the key
>> To unlock the treasure of the most high love;

---

[46]Psalm 113 in the Vulgate.
[47]*FB*, 102.
[48]Sayers, *Divine Comedy 2: Purgatory*, 144.

And in her mien those words stood plain to see:
   *Ecce ancilla Dei* [Behold, the handmaiden of
      God]. (X.31-44)[49]

Thus, the first thing anyone sees when entering the rigorous part
of purgatory ("Purgatory Proper," as Sayers calls it) is not, as we
might expect, an image of *suffering*. Instead, it is a breathtaking
sculpture of the annunciation. Before we look on the penitents or
consider the vice of pride, Dante offers us the virtue the prideful
here seek: humility. The sculptures do not depict the virtue as we
normally imagine it—in dust and ashes. They reveal humility in
its radiant beauty—humility as seen from the divine point of view.
Looking down from heaven, what is more beautiful than Mary's
humble "Yes, Lord"? For it was her graceful reply that "turned the
key / to unlock" love's treasure: God coming into the world in the
humble form of the Christ child.[50]

   In Williams's view, the annunciation was a brilliant choice on
Dante's part, as it distills in an image the transformation initiated
on the mountain: "At the beginning of the way of the in-othering,
and at last of the in-Godding, is the image of the great and unique
in-Godding and the in-fleshing, '*figlia del tuo figlio*,' the great maxim
of exchange."[51] These odd locutions reference the vocabulary
that Dante invents in *Paradiso* to describe the intimacy among
the company of heaven and between the blessed and God. The
critic's argument here is that the annunciation—through Mary's
consent to be *the* unique bearer of the divine image—establishes
the conditions whereby penitents may enter into heavenly relations

---

[49]Sayers, *Divine Comedy 2: Purgatory*, 144.

[50]Tradition holds humility, as Dante knew, to be the *first* Christian virtue—in the sense that
   it is the prerequisite to the acquisition of all other virtues. Through this image and the two
   that follow, all of which depict kings in humble postures, Dante offers inspiration for the
   way up the mountain. But with the strong christological bent of all three images, he also
   previews the reward at the journey's end. Humility is the way of Christlikeness and the
   way to Christ enthroned.

[51]*FB*, 157-58.

with humanity and divinity. (The traditional theological language is "participation"; Williams calls this giving and opening of ourselves "co-inherence."[52]) On the other side of purgatory, all the images may be rightly seen, rightly known, and so loved to our utmost capacities.

The carvings suggested to Williams, moreover, the role that the arts may play in "speeding" us toward this heavenly state. The sculptures are, Williams notes, "arch-natural"—"they 'put Nature itself to shame,'" being so lifelike that the figures of Mary and Gabriel seem to be speaking.[53] He likens in turn the "intensity" of the carving to "the accuracy which Dante spoke of in his own verse," that "accuracy" being the consequence of Dante's scrupulous attention to the world. Dante's art, though, doesn't just make its subject vivid, excellent as that power may be. In the very next paragraph, Williams insists, "This intensity does not prevent complexity," and the critic then makes his case for applying the allegory of the theologians to the *Comedy*. There is no need to rehash that thinking now.[54] The key point for present purposes is that Williams portrays Dante's art as being at once realistic, even hyperrealistic, *and* densely allegorical. Art, he suggests, may enliven and thicken our intake of reality.[55]

The art of looking appeared to Williams the very essence of the *Comedy* and the Affirmative Way. Thus, when Beatrice declares in her dramatic reunion with Dante in *Purgatorio* XXX, "Look well: we are, indeed, we are, Beatrice," Williams's heart leapt up into joy celestial.[56] He deemed it "almost the greatest line in Dante and

[52]The book to read on coinherence is Paul Fiddes's *Charles Williams and C. S. Lewis: Friends in Co-Inherence* (Oxford University Press, 2022).

[53]*FB*, 102.

[54]*FB*, 102-3.

[55]Williams also sees on this terrace a warning that Dante makes to himself and his fellow artists: "It is of interest that the examples on which he here chiefly delays are those of art. There is no room on this terrace for the 'artistic temperament'; no place for the neglect of decent manners, let alone of morals (but they are one)" (*FB*, 158).

[56]*HCDH*, 75. Williams was following the precedent of editions that read her line as "*Guardaci ben! Ben sem, ben sem Beatrice*" rather than the modern preference for "*Ben son, ben son.*" Singleton is helpful: "*Guardaci*: Commentators differ in their interpretation of *ci* here.

therefore in all poetry."[57] "The general maxim of the whole way in Dante," he writes in *The Figure of Beatrice*, "is *attention*; 'look,' 'look well.'"[58] In an undated notebook entry, he wrote, "'Look well'—this is the continuous maxim of the intellect and love. It is the maxim of all poetry—both the making and the reading. . . . It [the *Comedy*] is all—the whole poem—a question of seeing, of attention; in this poetry and sanctity are one."[59]

If we look well at *Purgatorio*, what will we find? My trio would argue that we will see images worthy of diligent attention. That we will receive love lessons that, if applied in our own lives, may awaken us to the glories that already surround us. That we will discover the true and proper function of art. That we will be invited to exercise reason and imagination together. There is so very much to love on Mount Purgatory (just as Sayers promised us) that one may be tempted to linger here, as Dante was, by the friendly company, the music, the ornamentation, the breeze blowing through Edenic leaves, the unclouded colors of the sky. But we must not get too comfortable on the mountain. It is a means, not an end. To recall Sayers's apt phrase, "the unveiled light of reality" remains. Dante points us upward. As Lewis writes in *The Great Divorce*, borrowing imagery from *Paradiso*, we must go where "the Glory flows into everyone, and back from everyone: like light and mirrors."[60]

---

It could be the pronoun, in which case Beatrice, in her regal manner, would be using the plural of majesty, speaking as a monarch would, in the first person plural. This reading is often accompanied by 'ben sem, ben sem' in the rest of the verse, continuing such a plural (*sem = siamo*)." Charles S. Singleton, *Purgatorio: Commentary* (Princeton University Press, 1973), 748.

[57] *HCDH*, 75.

[58] *FB*, 16.

[59] Charles Williams, "Dante Summary," Charles Williams Papers, BR 3-128, Marion E. Wade Center, Wheaton College, Wheaton, IL.

[60] C. S. Lewis, *The Great Divorce: A Dream* (Geoffrey Bles, 1946), 82-83.

**Figure 6.1.** Gustave Doré, illustration for *Paradiso* XXXI in Dante's *The Vision; or Hell, Purgatory, and Heaven*, trans. Cary, vol. 2 (1881)

# 6

## THE PROBLEM OF GLORY

*The subject [of Paradiso] is beatitude; the*
*method is a continual variation in light.*

CHARLES WILLIAMS,
*THE FIGURE OF BEATRICE*

EVIL MAY BE A PROBLEM for philosophers and theologians, but it is no problem for artists. For many, it provides their craft's necessary working conditions. If not for evil, we would have no *Bleak House* by Charles Dickens, no *Crime and Punishment* by Fyodor Dostoevsky, no *A Good Man Is Hard to Find and Other Stories* by Flannery O'Connor. No evil, no *Last Judgment* by Michelangelo, no *Garden of Earthly Delights* by Hieronymus Bosch, no *Beheading of John the Baptist* by Caravaggio, no *Guernica* by Pablo Picasso. Take the evil—take Voldemort—out of Harry Potter, and the series would never have gotten started. Take the evil—take Sauron—out of Middle-earth, and Tolkien's *Lord of the Rings* trilogy would collapse.

As philosopher Agnes Callard has observed, apologies for the arts tend to point us to art's uplift and capacity for instilling empathy. But in Callard's reckoning, evil is the field in which art, above all narrative art, truly excels, going far beyond the staid output of those who try to reason through such matters: "My simple theory applies to narrative fiction broadly conceived, from epic poems

to Greek tragedies to Shakespearean comedies to short stories
to movies. It also applies to most pop songs, many lyric poems
and some—though far from most—paintings, photographs and
sculptures. My theory is that art is for seeing evil." Evil, on Callard's telling, "[encompasses] the whole range of negative human
experience, from being wronged, to doing wrong, to sheer bad
luck," including "hunger, fear, injury, pain, anxiety, injustice, loss,
catastrophe, misunderstanding, failure, betrayal, cruelty, boredom,
frustration, loneliness, despair, downfall, annihilation." "This list
of evils," she wryly notes, "is also a list of the essential ingredients
of narrative fiction. I can name many works of fiction in which
barely anything good happens . . . , but I can't imagine a novel in
which barely anything bad happens."[1]

Callard, let me be clear, thinks that art's eye for evil is a *good
thing*. Amid our busy lives, we look at the world with a purpose,
and our purposes become blinders, obscuring our recognition of
the "irrelevant, the unhelpful, and the downright wicked." Artists,
by contrast, "take a long hard look at what the rest of us can't bring
ourselves to examine; they are our eyes and ears."[2] They bring us
back to realities that by our diverse stratagems we keep out of
sight. To acknowledge all of this is to realize that students of the
arts—especially its storytelling wing—have enrolled themselves
in an academy of evil, presided over by some of history's greatest
investigators of the darkest passages of our psyches and our world.

Dante is, unquestionably, one of them, even one of the masters
of the art of evil. His study of evil in its myriad manifestations—
within himself and without—resulted in a taxonomy of essential
evils, which his imagination carved, circle by circle, into the
earth's crust. *Inferno* offers one canto of evidence after another for

---

[1]Agnes Callard, "Art Is for Seeing Evil," *The Point*, July 15, 2022, https://thepointmag.com
/examined-life/art-is-for-seeing-evil/.
[2]Callard, "Art Is for Seeing Evil."

Callard's thesis: It is, truly, art for "seeing evil." That was, you'll recall from chapter three, one of *Inferno*'s chief attractions for Sayers, Williams, and Lewis. And as my trio would be quick to point out that, even in *Purgatorio*, evil is still very much Dante's concern, though in this case, it's the problem of getting the evil out of those who would be made holy.

From the beginning of *Paradiso* to its end, however, Dante meets no evil. In his heavenly ascent with Beatrice, he undergoes no bad luck, no hunger, no injustice, no betrayal, no loneliness, no despair, and so on. Fears and misunderstandings, when they arise, are immediately resolved. Dante's greatest physical challenge is to endure light of ever-increasingly intensity. In *Paradiso*, I am proposing, Dante attempted something far more audacious than he had in *Inferno* and even *Purgatorio*: to write a story in which evil does not move the plot along.[3] What other story could he write? Dante's proposed solution to the narrative problem of evil (that is, doing without it as a plot driver) is already apparent in the opening lines of the canticle:

> The glory of Him who moves all things soe'er
> > Impenetrates the universe, and bright
> > The splendor burns, more here and lesser there. (lines 1-3)[4]

These lines announce Dante's new theme: He will sing of *glory*. Glory, mind you, is not an odd choice given the generic tradition in which he was working: Glory is epic's traditional theme. Yet the kind of metaphysical glory Dante describes here represents a departure from the precedents of Homer and Virgil. Dante's concern is not the glory of heroes but the glory of the cosmos's

---

[3]A careful reader of *Paradiso* may wish to dissent here: Aren't the blessed still concerned about earthly evils? Indeed they are, but those are evils to be lamented and denounced; they cannot touch the petals of the rose. Their joy is not affected. Recall that canto XXII, where Peter famously denounces Pope Boniface on the grounds that he has made a "burial ground" (Rome) a "sewer of blood," *follows* Dante's joyous observation of the universe smiling.

[4]Dorothy L. Sayers and Barbara Reynolds, trans., *The Divine Comedy 3: Paradise* (Penguin, 1962), 53.

Maker and Sustainer. Shifting from the martial glory of ancient elites to cosmic glory, however, frees up the last leg of Dante's epic to tell a different kind of story—one not concerned with battles, betrayals, fortunes rising and falling, the death of friends and foes, the ruin of cities. He uses that freedom to record an intellectual and spiritual quest: to investigate the vast circuitry of glories ever flowing from and to their eternal source.

*Paradiso* I.1-3, moreover, constitutes a dramatic moment of revision. At no point in the previous canticles, Dante is telling us, has God been absent. We have simply failed to see the glory variously reflected in all that is. *Paradiso* suggests that we suffer myopia regarding glory no less than evil, and Dante's wager in the final canticle is he can counter this shortsightedness by telling a story in which he interviews saints and visits God in heaven.

I have every confidence that those who have reached this point in the book will grant that Dante did a brave thing in taking the evil out his plot. But you may also be harboring, let's be honest, some misgivings. A story in which nothing bad happens and whose cast consists exclusively of saints doesn't promise much, does it? Where's the adventure? Where's the conflict? Where's the drama? And the prospect of heaven as a great big light show has a way of turning people off nowadays. Glory, simply put, is a problem.

C. S. Lewis admitted as much about himself. In his 1941 sermon "The Weight of Glory," Lewis takes up the topic of glory reluctantly: "There is no getting away from the fact that this idea"—the idea of glory—"is very prominent in the New Testament and in early Christian writings," Lewis writes. "Salvation is constantly associated with palms, crowns, white robes, thrones, and splendor like the sun and stars. All this makes no immediate appeal to me at all, and in that respect I fancy I am a typical modern." Glory, he goes on to note, suggests two more troublesome ideas: "fame" and "luminosity." The first seems to him "wicked," since it sounds like a "competitive passion," a grasping to be higher than others better suited to hell than heaven. "As for the second," he suggests, "who wishes to become a kind of living electric light bulb?"[5]

Lewis's confession clarifies that in our times the artist doesn't just have to help us to see the latent glory in creation; the artist also has to make Dante's sort of glory desirable. Dantist John Sinclair—a contemporary of our trio, and Williams's and Sayers's occasional correspondent—stated the matter well in regard to Dante's heaven by citing Lewis's own words. The issue was Beatrice's description of "the perfect life of the redeemed as light, love, and joy" (Sinclair's phrasing) in canto XXX:

> We have won beyond the worlds, and move
> Within that heaven which is pure light alone:
> Pure intellectual light, fulfilled with love,
> Love of the true Good, filled with all delight,
> Transcending sweet delight, all sweets above. (lines 38-42)[6]

In the notes to his 1939 prose translation of *Paradiso*, Sinclair explains that blessedness for Dante rests on the act of seeing things as they are through this "pure intellectual light," and that that vision will inspire love of the good and, in turn, surpassing joy among the blessed. He then cites Lewis's chapter on heaven in *The Problem of Pain*: "The suggestion of Mr. C. S. Lewis, made in another connection, is relevant here: 'The joys of heaven are for most of us, in our present condition, an acquired taste.'"[7] Twenty-three years later, as noted in chapter two, Barbara Reynolds alluded to the same line from Lewis in the opening sentence of her introduction to the Sayers-Reynolds *Paradise*, but she was more

---

[5] C. S. Lewis, "The Weight of Glory," in *The Weight of Glory and Other Addresses* (Macmillan, 1949), 8.

[6] Sayers and Reynolds, *Divine Comedy 3: Paradise*, 319. These lines are technically within the section of the text that Reynolds completed, but these lines use Sayers's rendering.

[7] John D. Sinclair, notes on canto XXX, *Paradiso*, by Dante (Oxford University Press, 1939), 442.

hopeful than Sinclair, continuing, "In a sense, Dante's *Paradise* is a story about the acquisition of that taste."

Dante wasn't the only one to attempt to tell a story to give readers a taste of glory—Sayers, Williams, and Lewis tried their hands at it too. Williams once again led the way. He examined Dante's treatment of glory in the specific figure of Beatrice and in the deep webs of existence, offering his friends a complex account of glory that operates on both the micro and macro scales. In the present chapter, I examine the dynamics of what Williams called the "Beatrician encounter," that is, the manifestation of divine glory in another. Sayers and Lewis, we will see, made valuable efforts to explain Williams's explanation and, following Williams's example, applied their findings in Beatrician encounters of their own devising. In chapter seven, we will travel through the spheres of the medieval heavens to reach God in Dante's version of the realm outside space and time, the Empyrean. In this spiritual ascent, our trio beheld, and in their own ways testified to, what Williams calls the "pattern of glory"—an order of gracious interdependencies extending throughout the universe, a magnificent, all-encompassing, and never-ending dance.

## BEATRICIAN ENCOUNTERS

Williams first discussed the "Beatrician encounter" in print in a chapter of *He Came Down from Heaven* (1938) titled "The Theology of Romantic Love."[8] In this first rundown, Williams focuses on *Vita Nuova* but frames Dante's revelatory encounters with premortem Beatrice as the beginning of a much larger "philosophical journey" that culminates in the *Comedy*.[9] In *The*

---

[8] The ideas had, of course, already been brewing for more than a decade at that point. See Charles Williams's unfinished *Outlines of a Romantic Theology*, ed. Alice M. Hadfield (Eerdmans, 1990).

[9] *HCDH*, 67.

*Descent of the Dove*, published the following year, Williams then elaborates on the journey—jogging through Dante's bibliography in a few pages and naming the poet the supreme chronicler of the Way of the Affirmation of Images (as detailed in chapter four). Four years later, *The Figure of Beatrice* offered a comprehensive account of the Florentine pilgrim's progress on the Affirmative Way.

Williams's unexpected death on May 15, 1945, meant that he did not have the opportunity to develop these ideas further. Luckily for him, he had two friends who not only his promoted his work but also elucidated it in the coming years.[10] In what follows, I will trace their reactions to Williams's notion of the Beatrician encounter in four stages: (1) Lewis explaining it in the context of Williams's verse, (2) Sayers explaining and expanding upon it in relation to Williams's prose, (3) Sayers crafting a Beatrician encounter, and (4) Lewis offering a creative response of his own.

## LEWIS EXPLAINS WILLIAMS

In what can only be called a heroic labor of friendship, Lewis published in 1948 a work whose full title runs *Arthurian Torso; Containing the Posthumous Fragment of The Figure of Arthur by Charles Williams and A Commentary on the Arthurian Poems of Charles Williams by C. S. Lewis.* As the title suggests, the book pulls together Williams's manuscripts for *The Figure of Arthur*, a study of the Arthurian legends, and Lewis's commentary, more than one hundred pages in length, on Williams's poems set in the world of Arthur and his knights.

---

[10]Their separate promotions were too numerous to list here. But on one occasion they teamed up. In May 1955, Lewis and Sayers submitted a letter to the editor of the London *Times* urging Williams's fans to mark the tenth anniversary of the death of the author—whom they refer to as "an outstanding figure in the world of English letters"—by attending public meetings in London, Oxford, and Cambridge or by "paying tribute" in their own manner elsewhere. C. S. Lewis and Dorothy L. Sayers, "Letter to the Editor," *The Times of London*, May 14, 1955, 9.

Unsurprisingly, Williams's treatment of the Arthuriad—in both his critical writing and his creative adaptations—circles around his distinctive theology of romantic love. "His master is Dante," Lewis writes in the commentary. "Love means to [Williams] something that begins with what he calls a 'Beatrician experience'—the sort of experience that Dante records in the *Vita Nuova*."[11] Lewis then provides his reader with a cogent definition of that experience, pulling together several strands of Williams's thinking expressed in his criticism and creative writing (more neatly than one suspects the original author could have done):

> The Beatrician experience may be defined as the recovery (in respect to one human being) of that vision of reality which would have been common to all men in respect to all things if Man had never fallen. The lover sees the Lady as the Adam [= original humanity] saw all things before they foolishly chose to experience good as evil, to "gaze upon the acts in contention." Williams believes that this experience is what it professes to be. The "light" in which the beloved appears to be clothed is true light; the intense significance which she appears to have is not an illusion; in her (at that moment) Paradise is actually revealed, and in the lover Nature is renovated.[12]

But the encounter isn't just a backward glance to the prelapsarian state of Adam and Eve or a glimmer of paradise. It is also, Lewis stresses, the beginning of a new "way of life" (i.e., the Affirmative Way):

> The great danger is lest he [the lover] should mistake the vision which is really a starting point for a goal; lest he should mistake the vision of Paradise for arrival there. He must follow this road

---

[11]C. S. Lewis, *Arthurian Torso: Containing the Posthumous Fragment of The Figure of Arthur by Charles Williams and A Commentary on the Arthurian Poems of Charles Williams by C. S. Lewis* (Oxford University Press, 1948), 116.

[12]Lewis, *Arthurian Torso*, 116.

till it leads him to the Byzantine precision. The immediate glory will dazzle him "unless he has a mind *to examine the pattern* of the glory." . . . The Beatrician experience, like the Wordsworthian experience, is the summons to a discipline and a way of life—the long way recorded in the *Divine Comedy* or *The Prelude*.[13]

To the suggestive final phrase the "pattern of the glory," we will return in chapter seven. For now I want to highlight two things happening here.

The first regards Lewis's love for Williams. Few scholars would give up so much of their precious writing time to publish their friends' unfinished work, and vanishingly few would accompany it with a commentary one hundred pages in length. That gift is even more pronounced when we consider the subject at hand, Williams's theology of romantic love. As discussed in chapter two, Williams's response to *The Allegory of Love* elicited a worried reply from Lewis, who staked out their different imaginative orientations as two sorts of "romanticism": that "which finds its revelation in love, which is yours, and another which finds it in mythology (and nature mythically apprehended) which is mine." Lewis's superb summary of the Beatrician encounter in 1948 demonstrates that, whatever his personal reservations, Lewis had been a faithful reader of his friend's work over the ensuing twelve years.[14] Here Lewis elucidates Williams's vision of the religious potential of *eros*; but the commentary's animating spirit is *philia*, friendship, of the truest sort.[15]

---

[13]Lewis, *Arthurian Torso*, 117.

[14]See Fiddes's chapter "Romantic Love and Arthurian Myth" regarding the ways that Lewis toned down the more risqué qualities of Williams's theology of romantic love in this commentary. Paul Fiddes, *Charles Williams and C. S. Lewis: Friends in Co-Inherence* (Oxford University Press, 2022), 173-222.

[15]Also germane is Lewis's poignant invocation of Williams and Dante in a single passage of his chapter on friendship in *The Four Loves* (1960). Because friends are united by common interest, Lewis reasons there, friendship is not limited to two parties (as erotic love is). Indeed, two "is not even the best." To explain why, he cites the impact of Williams's

Lewis's grasp of Williams's thought—my second point—made him an astute critic of Williams's poetry, which is, admittedly, not everyone's cup of tea. With Lewis's help, however, Williams's verses come alive, and Lewis is especially sharp regarding the ways in which Williams modifies the Beatrician experience in his Arthurian poetry.

For present purposes, Lewis's most important insight is that in Williams's imaginative world *anyone* can have a Beatrician encounter. Lewis, for example, takes a keen interest in an episode in the "Star of Percivale" segment of *Taliessin Through Logres* (1938), in which the knight-poet Taliessin takes up a harp and inspires a lowly listener:

> Taliessin stood in the court; he played
> a borrowed harp; his voice defined the music.
> Languid, the soul of a maid, at service in the hall,
> heard, rose, ran fleetly to fall at his feet.
>
> Soft there, quiescent in adoration, it sang:
> *Lord, art thou he that cometh? take me for thine.*
> The music rang; the king's poet leaned to cry:
> *See thou do it not; I too am a man.*

---

death on his friendship with Tolkien: "Now that Charles is dead, I shall never again see Ronald's reaction to a specifically Caroline"—Carolus being the Latin for Charles—"joke. Far from having more of Ronald, having him 'to myself' now that Charles is away, I have less of Ronald." Lewis then enlists Dante's help. Of new additions, old friends "can then say, as the blessed souls say in Dante, 'Here comes one who will augment our loves.'" Those words appear in the fifth canto of *Paradiso* where Dante likens the delight of the souls of the second sphere at Beatrice's approach to fish in a pond swirling around "some dropped-in morsel": "So I saw splendours draw to us in droves, / Full many a thousand, and from each was heard: 'Here now is one who will increase our loves.'" (trans. Sayers ll. 100-105). Dante's words set up Lewis's ensuing theological claim that a widening circle of friendship provides a foretaste of the economy of heaven: "In this, Friendship exhibits glorious 'nearness by resemblance' to Heaven itself where the multitude of the blessed (which no man can number) increases the fruition which each has of God." *Paradiso* offers an image of the heavenly society in which Charles now blissfully swims. Lewis, *The Four Loves* (Geoffrey Bles, 1960), 73-74; Sayers, Trans., *The Divine Comedy III: Paradise* (Penguin, 1962), 93.

The king's poet leaned, catching the outspread hands:
*More than the voice is the vision, the kingdom than the king:*
the cords of their arms were bands of glory; the harp
sang her to her feet; sharply, sweetly, she rose.

The soul of a serving-maid stood by the king's gate,
her face flushed with the mere speed of adoration.
The Archbishop stayed, coming through the morning to the Mass,
*Hast thou seen so soon, bright lass, the light of Christ's glory?*

She answered: *The light of another, if aught, I bear,*
*as he the song of another; he said: I obey.*
And Dubric [the archbishop]: *Also thy joy I wear.*[16]

What is going on here? Lewis, patiently, explains:

> Taliessin's song lifts to her feet a barbarian slave girl; she comes
> running to him in adoration. It is a thing that happens every day.
> The girl has had a Beatrician experience. In her untaught soul
> it becomes hero-worship, "calf-love"—can become whatever
> Taliessin chooses to make it; that is why a poet, a musician, an
> actor, has such advantage as a seducer if he wishes to adopt
> the role.[17]

These events "telescope" into a few minutes, Lewis writes, what
would "in real life" require weeks. Paradise is "momentarily
revealed" to the young woman through the poet's song—art
serves as vehicle for a glimpse at glory—but that places her in a
vulnerable position: She may mistake the "voice" of the poet for
the "vision" the song transmits.[18]

Taliessin responds courteously, neither "[snubbing] her" to
concentrate on his playing nor belittling her with "sensible advice."
He takes her hands and thereby directs her to "the true goal." Lewis

---

[16]Charles Williams, *Taliessin Through Logres* (Oxford University Press, 1938), 46.
[17]Lewis, *Arthurian Torso*, 136.
[18]Lewis, *Arthurian Torso*, 136.

continues, "She receives divine grace: none the less because she is bearing 'the light of another' as [Taliessin], after all, bore 'the song of another.' She is converted, saved in a labyrinth of vicariousness, 'a tangle of compensations, every joint a centre.' She has entered on the New Life." But the passage of joy does not yet end, nor need it ever end, in Williams's reckoning. The priest "wears her joy," Lewis relates, "as she wears Taliessin's who wears Percivale's, and all, Christ's."[19] Therefore, the Beatrician encounter, in Williams's rendering, is not just one revelation but an opening to many; through all of them the glory, and with it joy, may flow.

Lewis ranked Williams's verse among the chief poetic achievements of the century. Few have followed him in that judgment, but we can see here why he thought Williams was up to something that couldn't be found elsewhere (and certainly not in the poems of the modernists, above all Eliot, who seemed to him preoccupied with death and despair). Lewis wanted what Williams—like the Dante of *Paradiso*—offered: "glory or splendour; a heraldic brightness of colour, a marble firmness of line, and an arduous exaltation."[20]

## SAYERS EXPLAINS AND EXTENDS WILLIAMS

On October 22, 1948, one day after Oxford University Press officially released *Arthurian Torso*, Sayers wrote to Lewis to express her gratitude for the guidance he had provided to those perplexed by Williams's poems. She confided that she had "always found them exceedingly difficult," but with Lewis's help they appeared "much less so." She found the commentary a model of "straightforward interpretive criticism"—as opposed to the "creative" (her scare quotes) kind of criticism then in vogue. She

---

[19]Lewis, *Arthurian Torso*, 136.
[20]C. S. Lewis, preface, in *Essays Presented to Charles Williams* (Oxford University Press, 1947), vii.

cited a friend's complaint about "unintelligible books about modern poetry": One really just wants the critic to say, "This is a poem about a bus" and then go on to explain what the poem says, what stance the poet takes, whether the performance is good, and on what grounds the critic deems it well or poorly made.[21] Lewis had done just that: He had detailed the bus—no mean feat given how baffling Williams's poems could be.

She had been confronting the issue too, she then explained. In the lectures she was now giving on the *Comedy* (her exact phrase: "I now keep on having to give lectures"), she would begin with the sort of straightforward commentary her friend desired. She told her audiences about the bus, and the students seemed pleased with her, promising to "go away and read Dante." Nonetheless, Sayers confessed that she found herself occasionally "overcome by a dreadful conviction of shallowness and crudity in the presence of the 'modern' kind of critic, who is so clever and complicated that when he has done I understand him not at all" and his subject matter "even less than I did before."[22] What such a critic would make of Williams's Arthur poems, she feared to imagine; she was grateful that Lewis had stepped in to clear the thing up rather than cause more confusion.

What she didn't tell Lewis was that she was engaged in the same project in relation to Williams's Dante criticism. Previous chapters have traced his extensive influence on her *Hell* and *Purgatory* volumes. But in 1948—only a few months before she wrote to Lewis—she had taken another step: retracing the Affirmative Way. The context was the lecture "The Fourfold Interpretation of the *Comedy*." The lecture's ambition, as mentioned briefly in chapter four, was to make the standard medieval schema for biblical interpretation—with its literal, typological, moral, and anagogical

---

[21]Dorothy L. Sayers to C. S. Lewis, October 22, 1948, in *LDS*, 3:400-401.
[22]Sayers to Lewis, 22 October 1948, in *LDS*, 3:401.

senses—more accessible to a modern audience.[23] Her repackaging borrows heavily from Williams: Literal remains literal, but the typological becomes the Way of the City ("political"), the moral the Way of the Soul, and the anagogical the Way of Contemplation, the last, once again, subdivided into "Negative" and "Affirmative."

The last is what concerns us now.[24] Sayers believed that Williams had renewed the possibility of anagogical interpretation. In the introduction to *Introductory Papers on Dante* (1955), she names Williams the vanguard of "the next great movement in Dantism—an exploration of the long-neglected mystical signification."[25] (At this claim, we have heard Charles Singleton cough.) But she stressed in 1948 that the new movement was rooted in Dante's sort of contemplation, which differed from the practice of the best-known mystics—such as Teresa of Ávila and John of the Cross. In their form of contemplation, every "image of the Divine" that we might derive from our earthly existence is gradually "rejected" due to their immeasurable distances from the divine reality. "Dante's Way is different," Sayers told her audience in 1948. "It is the Affirmative Way, in which all of the images are accepted as valid, in so far, that is, as any finite image of the infinite can be valid."[26]

---

[23]As noted in chapter 4, the nomenclature differs over time and among commentators. For example, what I am calling the "typological" sense is also described by many medievals, at the cost of great confusion among undergraduate students, as the "allegorical" sense.

[24]Reviewing the functions of the other senses helps to clarify the fourth sense's function. The literal sense addresses the immediate goings-on in the biblical passage in question, be it a historical event, a commandment, or a claim about God. The typological sense maps the relationship between earlier and later events that reveal God's providential ordering of history—as in passages of the Old Testament that were understood to prefigure passages in the New. The moral sense deals with the soul's turning to God in this life ("the experience of the 'common Christian' in his passage from a state of sin to a state of grace," as Sayers puts it). The Greek root of *anagogy*, meanwhile, means "lift up." This sense considers the soul's ascent in heavenly things. For this reason, at this level commentators ponder the soul's flight from the corruption of this world in the afterlife, our ultimate beatitude in God, and the heavenly new Jerusalem.

[25]Dorothy L. Sayers, introduction, in *IPD*, xvi.

[26]Dorothy L. Sayers, "The Fourfold Interpretation of the *Comedy*," in *IPD*, 122.

Whether this somehow translates into a viable critical *method* (as Sayers hoped it would) is not our problem here. I bring all of this up because in the midst of her talk about interpreting Dante at four levels, Sayers launched into an exposé on the Affirmative Way and its travelers (note the plural). "This Way," she told her audience, "though it is more typically Western and might appear to be more typically Catholic and Incarnational than the other, has, I believe, never been fully mapped by any mystical theologian— unless we count Dante."[27]

Sayers here set out to be its cartographer. In the lecture, she goes on to argue that the Affirmative Way is "essentially the way of the artist and the poet" for whom images constitute their "very means to intellectual and emotional experience."[28] To reject images would be to reject their vocations. Dante she acknowledges as the "only real Doctor" of this school, but others have "mapped the Way in places."[29] She cites four English examples: seventeenth-century Anglican priest and religious writer Thomas Traherne, William Wordsworth (who made a good start on the way but didn't reach its end), William Blake, and Charles Williams—whom, as we saw in chapter four, would be named "master of the affirmations" in the dedications to her *Hell* and *Purgatory*.

After assembling her list, she narrates the stages of the way recounted in chapter five, observing that the first image—in which the beloved person, place, or thing is "bathed and suffused with the light of its true and eternal nature" (a.k.a. the Beatrician encounter)— may take different forms. To Dante, it is Beatrice. To Traherne, it is

---

[27]Sayers, "Fourfold Interpretation of the *Comedy*," 122.

[28]Reynolds astutely observes, "To someone of [Sayers'] temperament, with her hearty enjoyment of life, of all that writers and artists create, of the marvel and make-believe of the theatre, of the delights of the passionate intellect, the Way of the Affirmation of Images must have seemed a liberating sanction. No wonder she embraced it so joyously." Barbara Reynolds, *The Passionate Intellect: Dorothy L. Sayers' Encounter with Dante* (Kent State University Press, 1989), 173.

[29]Sayers, "Fourfold Interpretation of the *Comedy*," 122.

wheatfields and men and women. To Wordsworth, it is a landscape "apparelled in celestial light."[30] To Blake, is the heavenly host "crying, 'Holy, Holy, Holy'" at the sun's rising (where others see "a round disc of fire" resembling a gold coin).[31] Sayers was, in these suggestions, picking up on Williams's argument that the Affirmative Way has many tracks that all arrive at the same destination. She was at once explaining Williams's thought and extending it.

In the ensuing years, Sayers came back to the Affirmative Way repeatedly, delivering three lectures that discuss the topic at length: "The Poetry of the Image in Dante and Charles Williams" (1952), "Charles Williams: A Poet's Critic" (1955), and "The Beatrician Vision in Dante and Other Poets" (1956). (The last presents the core ideas found in a much-scribbled-in notebook laying out a book-length study of the topic—tentatively titled *The Burning Bush*—that would not come to fruition due to her death in 1957.[32]) Each of these addresses adds an important dimension; the last, for example, lines up further illustrations of "the Beatrician visions" in an array of documents—the book of Exodus, the Gospel of Matthew, the poems of Alfred Tennyson and Robert Browning, even the autobiography of Aldous Huxley. All of these texts, she argues, recount experiences that are "in the proper and technical sense mystical: what is experienced is the immediate and intuitive awareness of an eternal reality." She continues, "The thing that they have in common, and which distinguishes them from the mystical experience of the classical type, is that every one has a basis in the world of physical phenomena." It is the search for God in the things of the world rather than the interior of the soul—in short, "extravert" mysticism.[33]

---

[30]Williams Wordsworth, "Ode: Intimations of Immortality from Recollections of Early Childhood," in *The Major Works*, ed. Stephen Gill (Oxford World Classics, 1984), 297.

[31]William Blake, *Collect Poetry and Prose*, ed. David Erdman (Anchor, 1988), 565-66.

[32]Dorothy L. Sayers, "The Burning Bush," notebook, MS 234, Dorothy L. Sayers Library collection, Marion E. Wade Center, Wheaton College, Wheaton, IL.

[33]Dorothy L. Sayers, "The Beatrician Vision in Dante and Other Poets," in *PSPS*, 48, 51.

Sayers wasn't simply cataloguing specimens, however. She was also establishing theological grounds on which the Way of the Affirmation of Images could be recognized as legitimate. In the 1952 lecture, she argued that the Affirmative Way was more "*characteristically* Christian" than the Negative Way: "The Way of Affirmation— creative, incarnational, sacramental—asserting the relative validity of *all* images, from the lowest and simplest up to the highest and so to the one and only perfect and eternal Image—proclaims and depends on its Christian sanctions at every stage of the journey."[34]

What are those "sanctions"? Sayers names three in the lecture: the doctrine of a true creation, the doctrine of the Incarnation, and the doctrine of the Trinity. Regarding the first, Sayers contends that the Hebrew Bible's account of creation reveals that the universe is no mere "illusion," nor it is "a mere aspect" of God, nor the same thing as God, nor "a 'fall into matter' and an evil delusion." The cosmos was "*made* by God, as an artist makes a work of art."[35] As such, all of the constituents of creation are images of God. Her reason for invoking the Trinity has been previewed in previous chapters' mentions of the "*Deivrilis* . . . within the point of Godhead" (Williams's version) and the "Final Image—the Image of the Incarnate Christ in the very centre of the Unimaginable Godhead" (Sayers's version). The very nature of God, Sayers argues, means that the Affirmative Way may be carried right up to "the very confrontation of the soul with the immediate presence of God."[36] All other images may be negated in the soul's ascent, but that one we must affirm, and will do so joyfully when greeting it at our journey's end.

In her meditation on the Incarnation, Sayers calls first, appropriately, on the authority of Scripture: "In that [mortal]

---

[34]Dorothy L. Sayers, "The Poetry of the Image in Dante and Charles Williams," in *FPD*, 188.
[35]Sayers, "Poetry of the Image," 187, italics original.
[36]Sayers, "Poetry of the Image," 187.

flesh His glory dwelt, and was seen so dwelling by Peter and James and John at the Transfiguration, when their eyes were opened to behold it." Their eyes were *opened*, Sayers insists. The disciples' sight was changed, not he—the glory "was always there." She continues:

> From the Incarnation springs the whole doctrine of the sacraments—the indwelling of the mortal by the immortal, of the material by the spiritual, the phenomenal by the real. After an analogous manner, we all bear about with us not only the immortal soul but also the glorified body in which we shall be known at the Resurrection, though now it is known only to God, or to those to whom love may reveal it. It is this that lies at the bottom of Dante's whole Beatrician Vision: because he loved the mortal Florentine girl, it was given to him to behold her, as it were, walking the earth in her body of glory.[37]

She wraps up the lesson by pointing out that Dante's stress on *bodiliness*—his reveling in Beatrice's physical beauty—makes the *Comedy* disconcerting to those "who like their religion 'spiritual.'" Notice that, once again, Sayers is extending Williams, enlarging the application of the Beatrician encounter to encompass *anyone*. Sayers would tell you, dear reader, that at this very moment you bear about you a "glorified body" unseen. One of the many tragedies of the human condition is that we cannot see the glories seated across the table, passing us on the street, or facing us in the mirror.

Having studied these matters so closely, Sayers was, like Lewis, alert to the numerous ways Williams experimented with the Beatrician encounter in his fiction. In the same lecture, to cite one example, she examines Williams's character Pauline in his 1937 novel *The Descent into Hell*, a "supernatural thriller" (to use

---

[37] Sayers, "Poetry of the Image," 187.

T. S. Eliot's apt label) in which the staging of a play overlaps with
a series of metaphysical operations that blend past and present.
Pauline Anstruther, one of the locals cast in the play, deeply
admires the playwright, Peter Stanhope. As Sayers notes, Pauline
gazes on Stanhope with "the kind of devotion with which Dante
looks upon Beatrice" and so appears an ideal candidate for a
Beatrician encouter of the romantic (a.k.a. Dantean) sort.[38] But
that adoration doesn't inspire any special effects from Williams's
pen. Williams does something surprising, something new:
Pauline is the one "who visibly possesses a glorified 'other self,'"
and it is revealed not to her platonic lover Stanhope—as we would
expect—but to herself!

Williams puts a holy twist on the fantastic figure of the
doppelgänger in which one's eerie double is seen walking about.
When Pauline confronts her double, she perceives herself in
heavenly glory:

> She opened her eyes again; there—as a thousand times in her
> looking-glass—there! The ruffled brown hair, the long nose, the
> firm compressed mouth, the tall body, the long arms, her dress,
> her gesture. It wore no supernatural splendour of aureole, but
> its rich nature burned and glowed before her, bright as if mortal
> flesh had indeed become what all lovers know it to be. Its colour
> bewildered by its beauty; its voice was Pauline's, as she had wished
> it to be for pronouncing the imagination of the grand art.[39]

The double wears no halo or trails no radiant cloud, as in paintings.
This body has the same features as the one Pauline sees in the
mirror each morning, yet she beholds herself now as lovers their
beloveds—as thoroughly, irresistibly beautiful. Notice, too, that
its voice is richer too, Williams's point being that the *whole* person,

---

[38]Sayers, "Poetry of the Image," 195.
[39]Charles Williams, *Descent into Hell* (Faber & Faber, 1937), 170-71.

every fiber, has been glorified. She wishes she sounded like that when she read poems aloud.

Yet what she sees puts all human poetry to shame: "No verse, not Stanhope's, not Shakespeare's, not Dante's, could rival the original." Confronted by "the original," Williams writes, one realizes that poetry is "but the best translation of a certain manner of its [the object's] life. The glory of poetry could not outshine the clear glory of the certain fact, and not any poetry could hold as many meanings as the fact." The "fact" was Williams's way of talking about what God has *done* or *made* (what *factus* means in Latin).[40] "The glory of God is in facts," he wrote in a 1941 essay. "The almost incredible nature of things is that there is no fact which is not in His glory."[41] In this scene, then, Williams is asserting the priority of creation over even the best of human poetry because God's "facts" are images whose signifying power exceeds human invention.[42]

The scene stood out to Sayers, moreover, because Pauline's exposure to her own glory then allows her to minister to one of her ancestors (via some mystical time-bending whose implied conductor is God) as he prepares for martyrdom at the hands of Queen Mary. Sayers adored the way this plot created an "elaborate exchange of hierarchies" typical of Williams's thought in which the sacred authority "[moves] from man to woman, and from woman back to man, and from the present into the past and back again."

---

[40]Williams, *Descent into Hell*, 171.

[41]Charles Williams, "The Redeemed City," in *The Image of the City and Other Essays*, ed. Anne Ridler (Oxford University Press, 1958), 110. As in all things, Williams was picking up on a thread in Dante. In *Purgatorio* XVIII, the penitent Marco Lombardo, discoursing on love, explains, "Your apprehension draws from some real fact [*esser verace*] / An inward image, which it shows to you, / And by that image doth the soul attract" (lines 22-24; trans. Dorothy L. Sayers, *The Divine Comedy 2: Purgatory* [Penguin, 1955], 205).

[42]For a superb treatment of the imagination going horribly wrong in the same novel, see Sayers's discussion of the siren figures in *Purgatorio* and *Descent into Hell* in "The Cornice of Sloth," in *FPD*, 138-44.

All of this, Sayers stresses, has grown out of Dante, the scene's success revealing "what one original poetic mind [i.e., Williams] can do with the image implanted in it by another [i.e., Dante]."[43] Sayers wrote that about Williams, and she meant it; but her own mind was quite original too, and that image had been implanted in it, so . . .

## SAYERS WRITES A BEATRICIAN ENCOUNTER

Back in the barrage of letters that Sayers sent to Williams chronicling her transformative reading of Dante in 1944, she had wondered aloud whether Dante could play the role of Beatrice to someone else—a point that Williams had raised, inconclusively, in *The Figure of Beatrice*. The question stayed with Sayers over the ensuing years, and she referenced it more than once in her lectures.

Her most daring response to both Williams and Dante, though, came in a novel she began in 1953, provisionally titled *Dante and His Daughter*, and left unfinished at her death four years later.[44] One of the major sources of tension in the story is the apparent ability of Dante's daughter, who is named Beatrice, to see *him* as he saw the original Beatrice. When presented with this news by a family friend, Donna Margareta, Dante is incredulous—how could a girl do that? "Do you think that only men are capable of the vision of beatitude?" the lady asks. "Or that God has appointed only one human relationship to carry of the image of the glory?"[45] Dante is rattled when Margareta points out that the original Beatrice might not have enjoyed his "pestering" (her word) devotion. The poet panics: Could his great work, and his life, have been a lie?

---

[43]Sayers, "Poetry of the Image," 196.

[44]Again, this remarkable manuscript—spread across eight notebooks—is numbered among the Wade's holdings. Dorothy L. Sayers, "Dante and His Daughter Bice," DSP, MS-54-62.

[45]Sayers, "Dante and His Daughter Bice," DSP, MS-62d, notebook 8, p. MMM. I am indebted to archivist Robert Schuster for his invaluable transcriptions of the "Dante and His Daughter" notebooks.

Ultimately, he acknowledges that young Beatrice shares his gift, and this occasions a conversation between father and daughter about what she calls, echoing Sayers's critical writings on Dante and Williams, "the body of glory":

> "It is difficult to put into words. It is not light and it is not color, though it gives light and color to everything else. I do not see you with rays shooting out all round you like the saints in a holy picture, though I think that is what the men who paint the pictures are trying to show. It is more like light than anything else. It has the—what is that word the theologians use—of the works that God is known by?"
>
> "The effects?"
>
> "That is it. It has the effects of light."[46]

To this, the father replies, "Your name for it the right one. It is the body of glory. For it lies, does it not, in the flesh, and has the same features; yet though it is not distinct form the natural body it does not cover it, nor hover over it, nor separate from it, but indwells it." He goes on to explain that he perceives this to be the sort of body revealed to the disciples at the transfiguration and will be the body of "our resurrection."[47]

In this remarkable scene, Sayers is, first of all, drawing out the implications of Williams's expansion of the Beatrician encounter in his own creative writing—poetry and prose fiction—by setting it within the relationship between child and parent. She is, even more strikingly, taking the Beatrician vision back to its source, turning the tables on *Dante* to make him his daughter Beatrice's figural Beatrice. One might be tempted here to read this scene as a sort of Freudian wish fulfillment in which Sayers writes herself into Dante's daughter. But I'm more inclined to align her with the

---

[46]Sayers, "Dante and His Daughter Bice," DSP, MS-62d, notebook 8, p. MMM.
[47]Sayers, "Dante and His Daughter Bice," DSP, MS-62d, notebook 8, p. OOO.

sassy Donna Margareta. She is the vehicle through which Dante must undergo the kind of psychological crisis at which the realist novel—Sayers's form—excels. Dante is at once humbled and glorified in this book, as he is confronted by the complexity of *women's* perspectives.

## LEWIS WRITES A BEATRICIAN ENCOUNTER (GONE WRONG)

In chapter two, I observed that *The Great Divorce* has notable debts to *Inferno*, which Sayers caught and questioned Lewis concerning. I noted, too, Lewis's reply to Sayers that the book "owes more to the *Purgatorio* than to the *Inferno*." Once again, he informed her, "It all grew out of the Tragedian and the Lady: specimen of a meeting like that of Beatrice and Dante in the Earthly Paradise and what happens when one side won't play."[48] That scene is, in fact, one of two episodes in *The Great Divorce* in which Lewis responds not just to Dante but to Williams, offering in each case his own riff on the Beatrician encounter.

The first is so riddled with Dantean allusions that even the narrator wonders aloud—upon Sarah's entry, preceded by a procession of angels, children, and musicians—whether she is Beatrice:

"Is it? . . . is it?" I whispered to my guide.

"Not at all," said he [MacDonald]. "It's someone ye'll never have heard of. Her name on earth was Sarah Smith and she lived at Golders Green."[49]

The narrator is remembering Beatrice's advent in the Earthly Paradise—on a cart, attended by personified virtues and books of the Bible—as reported in *Purgatorio* XXX. But, as Lewis had learned from reading Williams, *anyone* can be a Beatrice. And

---

[48]C. S. Lewis to Dorothy L. Sayers, January 22, 1946, in *CLCSL*, 2:700.

[49]C. S. Lewis, *The Great Divorce: A Dream* (Geoffrey Bles, 1946), 98.

so Sarah was—to nearly everyone and everything she met in her earthly life. "Every beast and bird that came near her had its place in her love," MacDonald reports. "Every young man or boy that met her became her son," and every girl "her daughter." This was noncompetitive love: Every child returned "to their natural parents loving them more," and "Few men looked on her without becoming, in a certain fashion, her lovers. But it was the kind of love that made them not less true, but truer, to their own wives."[50] To love Sarah is to love everything else more, recalling the passage of joy in Williams's Arthurian poetry that Lewis so treasured.

The irony of the episode is that the *only* person on whom Sarah's loveliness fails to have its benevolent effect is the one who officially promised to love and cherish her: her husband. In their reunion, Frank tries, ineffectually, to pull Sarah back into the paltry shadow of love that was their married life, in which he manipulated her need for him. Again and again in *The Great Divorce*, the blessed souls offer their hellish counterparts luxury packages that would, if only they'd yield some idol, fulfill their most deep-seated desires. Frank is given the chance to forgive and be forgiven, to enjoy the heights of love for which we were made. He is invited to join Sarah in Love itself; but he refuses, and in seeking his revenge on her only annihilates what remains of his self. The Lady departs, serenaded with Lewis's rewriting of Psalm 91: "*The Happy Trinity is her home: nothing can trouble her joy,*" it begins, "*She is the bird that evades every net: the wild deer that leaps every pitfall.*"[51]

Sarah behaves herself as a perfect Beatrice in this scene, but Frank refuses to do as Dante had done in his own reunion scene atop Mount Purgatory, and that is to repent. Williams argues that the Beatrician encounter is a "moment of choice" between "action

---

[50]Lewis, *Great Divorce*, 98-99.
[51]Lewis, *Great Divorce*, 109.

and no action, intellect and no intellect, energy and no energy, romanticism and pseudo-romanticism."[52] Will the one beholding the image drive further into the reality that lies behind it? Or will one turn aside?

Lewis's version of the scene suggests that he took that lesson to heart. In Frank, he shows us the consequences of exercising our freedom poorly. But Frank's disastrous choice is the reader's gain, for it illustrates where the bad habits we form in ourselves or encourage in others ultimately lead. There is no question which life, Sarah's or Frank's, comes out looking the better. To return to the issues with which this chapter began, *The Great Divorce* presents in one scene after another the choice of between evil and glory, the one self-enclosing and self-defeating, the other filled with life and love. In the process Lewis slyly refreshes the New Testament's portrayals of glory as fame and luminosity. *The Great Divorce* might in this way be understood as "The Weight of Glory, Part II."

Of fame, we need only continue the conversation in which the narrator discovers that Sarah is not Dante's Beatrice: "She seems to be . . . well, a person of particular importance?" To which the MacDonald figure replies, "Aye. She is one of the great ones. Ye have heard that fame in this country and fame on Earth are two quite different things."[53] Through Sarah, Lewis would show us that behind the New Testament's robes and crowns and talk of fame lies, ultimately, an altogether attractive ethic of local love—love at the street level. Sarah Smith was a nobody by any worldly measure— just a resident of a London suburb. But if you introduce a different measure, say the standard of neighbor-love that Jesus commands

---

[52]*FB*, 123. In the same passage, Williams argues that when we choose to accept the image, "that Imagination in action becomes faith, the quality by which the truths within the image are actualized within us."

[53]Lewis, *Great Divorce*, 98.

in Matthew 22:39, hers was a life of surpassing greatness. She was, and is, a celebrity in the kingdom of God.

Her luminosity, meanwhile, occasions a memory lapse in the narrator. Was she naked or clothed? "Only partly do I remember," the narrator claims, "the unbearable beauty of her face." Lewis takes this move straight out of Dante's playbook in *Paradiso* I:

> Within that heav'n which most receives His light
>> Was I, and saw such things as man nor knows
>> Nor skills to tell, returning from that height;
> For when our intellect is drawing close
>> To its desire, its paths are so profound
>> That memory cannot follow where it goes. (lines 4-9)[54]

Reynolds helpfully comments, "As it draws near to God the intellect penetrates so deeply into the knowledge of the Supreme Good that when the experience is ended human memory is unable fully to recall it."[55] Lewis takes advantage of the "bad memory trope" (as Dante scholars call it) to have it both ways. If Sarah were naked, the narrator suggests, she nonetheless seemed clothed with "the almost visible penumbra of her courtesy and joy." Her character adorns her. If clothed, the narrator could see through her raiment to her "inmost spirit" shining—there could be no hiding the true person. "Clothes in that country are not a disguise," Lewis writes. "The spiritual body lives along each thread and turns them into living organs. A robe or a crown is there as much one of the wearer's features as a lip or an eye."[56] The imagery of Revelation that Lewis confessed to finding off-putting in 1941—the white raiment, the crowns—is here renewed, in part

---

[54]Sayers and Reynolds, *Divine Comedy 3: Paradise*, 53.

[55]Reynolds, notes on canto I, in *Divine Comedy 3: Paradise*, 58. She continues, provocatively: "This is an awareness common to the mystics and it is not impossible that Dante underwent a mystical experience of which Paradise is the reasoned, logical, humanized expression in terms of poetry."

[56]Lewis, *Great Divorce*, 97.

by turning, creatively, to an image provided by Scripture: Sarah is truly *robed in righteousness* (Ps 132:9; Is 11:5; 61:10; Job 29:14; etc.), and her spiritual attire allows her to appear more than a holy light bulb. The whole scene, I'm suggesting, is designed to slip past those watchful dragons in our modern sensibilities that make the traditional iconography of glory unattractive.

## LEWIS WRITES A MACDONALDIAN-
## BEATRICIAN ENCOUNTER (GONE RIGHT)

Now, in a broad-brush sort of way, *The Great Divorce* may be said to constitute a series of Beatrician encounters in which figures of glory try to coax hellions out of their self-enclosed shadows and into the life-renewing light. The book, simply stated, is about the ever-present opportunity for glory that lies before us all. But against the background of Williams's specific account of the Beatrician encounter, there is one other scene that stands out. To recognize it, we need to recall two observations I made earlier: (1) that the original Beatrician encounter occurs in Dante's *Vita Nuova* (*New Life* in English), and (2) that, in Lewis's reckoning, Williams's sort of romanticism belonged to "the bridal chamber" and his own to "the wood beyond the world."[57]

The scene in question is George MacDonald's entrance into the story. Upon discovering the spirit's identity, the narrator "[tries], trembling, to tell this man all that his writings had done for me." He continues, "I tried to tell how a certain frosty afternoon at Leatherhead Station when I first bought a copy of *Phantastes* (being then about sixteen years old) had been to me what the first sight of Beatrice had been to Dante: *Here begins the New Life.*" He goes on to

---

[57]The phrase "the wood beyond the world" is an allusion to the name and chief setting of a groundbreaking 1894 fantasy novel by William Morris. In *Surprised by Joy*, Lewis recalls his childhood self as "a boy soaked in William Morris." C. S. Lewis, *Surprised by Joy* (Geoffrey Bles, 1955), 138.

explain to his host that after lingering "in the region of imagination," he ultimately came to know that "the true name of the quality which first met me in his books is Holiness."[58] In *Surprised by Joy*, Lewis speaks of this as the moment in which his imagination was "baptised."[59] In this episode, Lewis rewrites the Beatrician encounter on his own terms, a fantasy book taking the place of Beatrice as the glorious beginning of the "New Life" that leads, if faithfully pursued, to fellowship with God. Both Lewis's and Williams's sorts of romanticism—the romanticism of myth and fantasy and longing and that of romantic love—come to the same paradisical end. If there were ever a literary wink at a friend, this is it.[60]

There may be a second wink later in the book when MacDonald at last responds to the narrator's repeated questioning as to why "the Solid People" (as in the redeemed) "since they were full of love did not go down into Hell to rescue the Ghosts."[61] MacDonald plucks a blade of grass to serve as a "pointer" and then directs the narrator to "a crack in the soil so small that I could not have identified it without this aid. 'I cannot be certain,' he said, 'that this *is* the crack ye came up through. But through a crack no bigger than that ye certainly came.'" He then reveals, "All Hell is smaller than one pebble of your earthly world: but it is smaller than one atom of *this* world, the Real World."[62] The image bears a striking resemblance to Williams's measurement of hell's dimensions in the final pages of *The Figure of Beatrice*, which Lewis likely read while, or perhaps immediately before, composing *The Great Divorce* for serialization. There Williams explains that the bottom of

---

[58]Lewis, *Great Divorce*, 60-61.

[59]Lewis, *Surprised by Joy*, 171.

[60]Recall that the book ran serially in late 1944 and early 1945—before Williams's death. Lewis read portions of it to the Inklings before serialization began earlier in 1944. Alas, as far as I know, there is no record of what Williams made of this scene.

[61]Lewis, *Great Divorce*, 66.

[62]Lewis, *Great Divorce*, 112.

hell, "low hell," as he called it, "however enormous it may seem to those in it," would appear "very narrow for most—and very small to the redeemed, no more than a little snake slipping for a moment out of a rocky cleft into a grassy valley."[63] The two authors were making the same profound theological point, and both were knowingly indebted to Dante: that sin narrows our worlds down to the cramped spaces of hell, whereas redemption opens to us the vast expanses of divine creation.

It is from *that* journey that the "bright spirits" have come, MacDonald informs the narrator. "Every one of us lives only to journey further and further into the mountains," he tells the narrator. "Every one of us has interrupted that journey and retraced immeasurable distances to come down to-day on the mere chance of saving some Ghost." What's out there? Whither do the redeemed venture? With another wink, this time to the devoted reader of Lewis's fiction, MacDonald calls it *"Deep Heaven"*—Lewis's term in his space novels *Out of the Silent Planet* (1938) and *Perelandra* (1943) for what we call "outer space."[64] In calling the expanses "Deep Heaven," Lewis was attempting to reenchant our cosmology by borrowing materials from medieval authors—including, of course, Dante. To follow Dante and his trailing trio to the end, we now venture into those deep heavens.

---

[63]*FB*, 230.
[64]Lewis, *Great Divorce*, 66, italics original.

**Figure 7.1.** Illustration for *Paradiso XXVII*, in Dante's *La comedia di Dante Aligieri con la nova espositione di Alessandro Vellutello* (Venice, 1544)

# 7

# PATTERNS OF GLORY

*I think [Paradiso] reaches heights of poetry which you get nowhere else: an ether almost too fine to breathe. It is a pity that I can give you no notion of what it is like. Can you imagine Shelley at his most ecstatic combined with Milton at his most solemn and rigid? It sounds impossible I know, but that is what Dante has done.*

C. S. LEWIS, LETTER TO ARTHUR GREEVES, JULY 8, 1930

*Excitement about getting to Heaven is not rare in works of literature; excitement about being in Heaven is a much rarer thing. Few poets venture to linger very long after the first trumpet-blast that heralds the opening of the gates.*

DOROTHY L. SAYERS, ". . . AND TELLING YOU A STORY"

*Besides being an image of the whole redeemed universe, [Paradiso] is also an image of the redeemed Way.*

CHARLES WILLIAMS, *THE FIGURE OF BEATRICE*

DOROTHY SAYERS DIED AND went to heaven, or so Lewis saw reason for her friends to hope, before she completed her rendition of *Paradiso*. Reynolds nobly stepped in, as we have seen, adding thirteen cantos to the twenty Sayers had left in solid shape as well as composing the front matter, back matter, and commentary for the dangling *Paradise* installment. Yet as informative as those materials are, they lack the stylistic verve and startling insight of the inimitable Dorothy L. Sayers. Reynolds would have readily admitted as much. They had been friends; Reynolds knew what had been lost. Sayers, however, left clues about what she likely would have said about *Paradiso* if given the chance to write an introduction and notes; indeed, we can already see an interpretive line taking shape in her very first piece of Dante criticism. That would be, once again, ". . . And Telling You a Story," that harvest of the vivid first impressions she shared with Williams, which considers Dante from the perspective of a fellow practitioner of the art of storytelling.

You'll recall that one of Sayers's chief observations—one that her editor, Lewis, singled out for praise—was that Dante's techniques in the first two canticles "mirror" their subject matter. *Inferno*, whose arena is a pit of "grossness," *feels* overcrowded and tight-fitting. It induces a kind of claustrophobia that makes the reader want to get out. In *Purgatorio*, the poet "purges" the style and the landscape just as the penitents purge their vices through prayers and spiritual calisthenics. Sayers noticed, moreover, that across the second canticle the story relies less and less on "agitating incidents" and "exterior props." In *Paradiso*, Dante then quickly strips away one traditional support of the storyteller's art after another: "In so far as it is possible for a narrative style to be 'transhumanised,' the thing is done." "Landscape vanishes," Sayers observes, "The whole outward aspect of things is resolved into light and motion; landscape becomes a dance of geometrical patterns, touched in from a palette of pure light." "Incident vanishes" as well—"no *event*, in the ordinary sense of the word, takes place." Dante gives us "only soaring flight into Heaven after Heaven—all of which (it is explained to us) are in fact one and the same Heaven; a continuous pressing closer to the heart of reality."[1]

Amid this metamorphosis, Dante replaces the "excitements" on which the story depended at the start—run-ins with beasts and mythical monstrosities, close squeezes, unexpected turns of events, and so on—with a "a steadily increasing exhilaration, a piling-up of that *stupor* which, as a younger Dante had pointed out, comes over us in the presence of great and wonderful things." She was juxtaposing the cheap thrills of "excitement"—where one gets stirred up—with the gladdening effect at the etymological heart of *exhilarate* (which we can still hear in *hilarious*). To dedicate thousands of lines of verse to "the mere exploration of Paradise, without assistance from celestial conflicts, terrestrial judgments, or Olympian fun and games," Sayers rightly names "a cracking test of the poet's confidence both in his skill and his theme."[2] I have called it the problem of glory.

But how, we want Sayers to tell us, does the poet pull it off? Alas, as she was writing this piece in the mid-forties, Sayers was not prepared to go any further. Immediately after outlining the daunting challenge Dante set for himself, she flatly states, "But the thing is done: the possibility of enduring delight is grasped and presented in a way that the adult intellect can accept."[3] Thankfully, her later writings offer hints as to what exactly the adult intellect may find savory about Dante's third canticle, and the strongest come in her last public lecture on Dante, "Dante the Maker," delivered on May 8, 1956, while she was in the thick of translating *Paradiso*. Yet that lecture is, undoubtedly, but a fragment of what Sayers would have said had she once again been given the platform of a Penguin introduction, canto-level

[1]ATYS, 28, 30-31.
[2]ATYS, 30-31.
[3]ATYS, 31.

commentary, and appendixes in which to expatiate. Thus, we must look elsewhere for supplementary criticism to grasp, however tentatively, *how* the "thing is done." How does the mirroring work in this case? And, more importantly, how does Dante make his celestial journey to God *exhilarating*? To answer these questions, we must also consult, for the final time, that great aficionado of the third canticle, C. S. Lewis, and the man whom Lewis believed had "learned much" from "the Dante of the *Paradiso*," Charles Williams.

## A HAPPY MARRIAGE OF INCOMPATIBLES

At some point, all three members of my cohort threw up their arms and pronounced *Paradiso* to be sui generis, an incomparable poetic achievement. When speaking to students about it (as we have heard him tell Sayers), Lewis invoked the massiveness of Milton and the airiness of Percy Bysshe Shelley—somehow present at the same time and *better* than Milton and Shelley at their best. It also exhibited, Lewis told Sayers, a "grave processional movement— that devout *canzone*-ish, demure stateliness—, and the factual, first-person science-fiction narrative quality."[4] Sayers, once again, was so delighted with Lewis's "pregnant words" that she told him that she might quote them in her *Paradise* introduction in order to win sympathy for the translator. There was simply no way to carry across every particle of this magnificent stylistic amalgam. At the beginning of the *Paradiso* chapter in *The Figure of Beatrice*, meanwhile, Williams warns the reader that the third canticle is especially difficult for moderns because we arrive so poorly prepared: We have little to which to compare the subject (beatitude) and the method ("continual variation in light"), and we may not even grasp that this was intended to be "very advanced poetry" that even Virgil could not understand.[5]

---

[4]C. S. Lewis to Dorothy L. Sayers, August 5, 1955, in *CLCSL*, 3:638.
[5]*FB*, 191.

Perhaps without realizing it (though I suspect they did), they were playing a game in these pronouncements of which Dante was the master—what scholars call the inexpressibility trope (or ineffability topos). Though Dante makes such statements sporadically throughout the *Comedy*, he does so with increasing frequency in *Paradiso*. It is on display, for example, in canto XXXI's description of the glory of Mary. As the new dawn surpasses the beauty of the last sunset, the passage begins,

> So, mounting as from vale to mountain-crest,
> > These eyes beheld, at the remotest rim,
> > A radiance surpassing all the rest.
> As here, where we await the pole, to him
> > Entrusted once who drove so ill [i.e., Phaeton of Greek myth], the sky
> > Flames brighter and the adjacent light grows dim,
> So there, that oriflame of peace on high
> > Was quickened at the heart, diminishing
> > Its flame in equal measure outwardly.
> About the heart I saw an outstretched wing
> > More than a thousand angels jubilant,
> > Distinct in radiance and functioning.
> Their gladsome sporting their festive chant
> > Diffused, it seemed, a loveliness so gay
> > That joy was in the eyes of every saint.
> Were I endowed with wealth of words to say
> > All I imagine, yet I dared not try
> > The least part of their gladness to convey. (lines 121-38)[6]

Notice that Dante claims to be lacking words to express what his imagination had taken in *immediately after* demonstrating what that imagination could do—a series of stanzas in which he layers

---

[6]Dorothy L. Sayers and Barbara Reynolds, trans., *The Divine Comedy 3: Paradise* (Penguin, 1962), 330-31.

one breathtaking image atop another, that set the glorious scene around the Blessed Virgin. In other instances, Dante deploys the trope first and then describes, memorably, exactly what he had just claimed was indescribable. In this case, Dante follows a verbal triumph with a descriptive "defeat." The overarching rhetorical point is well taken: The gladness that angelic and human onlookers experience when gazing upon Mary exceeds earthly language. Yet our sense of the height of that gladness hinges on the detailed pictures of light and festivity that Dante has just shown.

We have witnessed Lewis adopt such maneuvers in relation to *Paradiso* throughout this book. In the first epigraph—shared with Greeves after Lewis and Owen Barfield had returned to *Paradiso* in June 1930—he does so directly: "It is a pity that I can give you no notion of what it is like," he says, before going on to argue (for the first time) that Dante beats both Milton and Shelley at their own games simultaneously. Lewis returned to the comparison a few years later in the lecture "Shelley, Dryden, and Mr. Eliot" (published in 1939), elaborating on Milton's massiveness as "the sense that every word is being held in place by a gigantic pressure" and Shelley's "air and fire" as "the untrammelled, reckless speed through pellucid spaces which makes us imagine while we are reading him that we have somehow left our bodies behind."[7] Taking all of this, and mixing in what Lewis told Sayers in 1955, we can begin to develop a profile of Dante's richly paradoxical "final style": It is at once massive and airy, stately and factual, ecstatic and rigid.

I say *begin* because this list leaves out what Lewis disclosed in his enraptured first dispatch to Greeves regarding the "new world" that *Paradiso* had opened for him. Dante, he once again reported, somehow mixes "intense, even crabbed, complexity of language

---

[7]C. S. Lewis, ""Shelley, Dryden, and Mr. Eliot," in *Rehabilitations and Other Essays* (Oxford University Press, 1939), 38.

and thought" with "a feeling of spacious gliding movement, like a slow dance, or like flying." Lewis likened *Paradiso* to the stars—"endless mathematical subtility of orb, cycle, epicycle and ecliptic, unthinkable and unpicturable, and yet at the same time the freedom and liquidity of empty space and the triumphant certainty of movement." He instructed Greeves to think of the "complexity and beauty" of Catholic theology, which brought to Lewis's mind the wheels within wheels beheld by the prophet Ezekiel ("but wheels of glory," Lewis emphasized).[8]

In these lists of "incompatibles" (to borrow a word from our author), Lewis reveals important aspects of the poem's appeal to an "adult intellect" like his. In *Paradiso*, one encounters the sort of complexity that usually bogs the mind down while being uplifted by a feeling of swift, pleasing motion (like flying or dancing); mathematical convolutions that fascinate astronomers along with the sense of outer space's allowance for free floating so captivating to the poet and science fiction writer; as well as the density *and* elegance of a theological system centuries in the making whose intricacy recalls the nested flames of Hebrew prophecy.

There is still more going on here. Lewis proposed these combinations as reference points, and yet, as we have seen before in this book, what appears at first a *likeness* turns out to be an *identity*. As Greeves probably already knew, and if not would learn shortly after liftoff in *Paradiso* I, Lewis's comparisons are assembled out of the final canticle's furnishings. For its plot follows Dante and Beatrice as they fly through the universe, observing many wheels of fire and discoursing on the movements of heavenly bodies and Christian doctrine.[9] In other words, to describe *Paradiso*'s

---

[8]C. S. Lewis to Arthur Greeves, January 13, 1930, in *CLCSL*, 1:857.

[9]At one point in canto XXIX, Dante even mentions Ezekiel, intervening in a theological dispute concerning the number of wings possessed by the creatures representing the Gospels, siding with the John of Revelation over the Hebrew prophet.

style, Lewis invoked its content—each "mirrors" the other. He was previewing the fact that as the soul advances on the last leg of its journey to God, it faces not evil nemeses but the great cosmic questions—where did it all come from? how does the universe hang together? what is the human place in it? and where, oh where, is God in all this? You can understand why Lewis counseled Greeves not to try to read *Paradiso* "in long stretches" with foot on fender—as he might a novel or history—but in small portions, "in rather a liturgical manner, letting the *images* and the purely intellectual conceptions sink well into the mind."[10]

## IMAGES BROAD AND DEEP

*Images*—there's that troublesome word again. It has served my trio in various ways across this book, and I have tried to keep their distinct meanings straight. We must be especially careful now not to handle it cavalierly, since the members of the cohort applied the word in three distinct ways in relation to *Paradiso*, and all are weighty. Thus, as each sense arises in the ensuing pages, we must pause to mark it. Here Lewis is speaking of images in the normal way that literary critics talk about them—as arrangements of words that appeal to the reader's physical senses (i.e., words that form pictures in our heads). True to his advice to Greeves, Lewis meditated on the imagery of *Paradiso* in the years to come, leaving behind two extended discussions and scattered notes elsewhere in his writings.

Those two accounts were referenced in chapter four: the two papers Lewis read to the Oxford Dante Society, "Dante's Similes" (1942) and "Imagery in the Last Eleven Cantos of Dante's *Comedy*" (1948). These were, undeniably, professional performances. In the first, Lewis ranges freely across the poetic canon, making comparisons to passages of Homer, Virgil, Milton, and John

---

[10]C. S. Lewis to Arthur Greeves, 30 January 1930, in *CLCSL*, 1:876, italics original.

Donne, and taking for granted the audience's acquaintance with Aristotle, Thomas Aquinas, and historian Thomas Babington Macaulay. In the second, he alludes to a catalog that he has made that classifies scores of images that appear in the final cantos of *Paradiso* according to categories of his own devising (including "smell," "childhood," and "meteorology"). Yet behind all this scholarly fanfare lies the dedicated reader's desire to understand why something has so powerfully affected him. To recall Sayers's language, Lewis wanted to know "how the thing is done," and in each case he sheds light on not only how *Paradiso*'s imagery works but also why it is so intellectually satisfying.

In the 1948 paper, Lewis may have been directly following Sayers's lead. At the close of ". . . And Telling You a Story," she turns to Dante's similes and observes that they are "earthy, homely, concrete" throughout the *Comedy* and likens them to "strong holding-pins, pegging [the poem] immovably to daily experience." She stresses, moreover, that because Dante is concerned, first and foremost, about precision, the images used as sources (a.k.a. what follows *like* or *as* in the simile) represent an exception to the rule of mirroring: "We do not find all the gross similes in the gross bits and all the noble similes in the noble bits; the images are neither dehumanized in Hell nor transhumanised in Heaven."[11] Lewis does not mention Sayers in the paper, but the piece takes aim at exactly these issues, as if Lewis wished to run the experiment himself on a favorite track of *Paradiso*. He casts his net wider, though, examining any image that would *not* "appear on the screen if anyone (God forbid) made a film" of *Paradiso*—in other words, any image that crops up in a casual comparison, clearly delimited simile, metaphor, or allusion.[12]

---

[11]ATYS, 35.

[12]C. S. Lewis, "Imagery in the Last Eleven Cantos of Dante's *Comedy*," in *Studies in Medieval and Renaissance Literature*, ed. Walter Hooper (Cambridge University Press, 1966), 78.

Thanks to the learned doctor's thorough accounting, we discover that the last eleven cantos—in which Dante and Beatrice head to the outer rim of the cosmos and then cross over into the still more foreign environment of the Empyrean, where the souls bathe in God's light and love—contain more than two hundred images dug from the stuff of the earth. We have already seen three in the excerpt from *Paradiso* XXXI above: a sunrise, a mountain climb, and the standard that the French kings carried into battle (the Oriflamme). Lewis also calls our attention to, among many other things, a blanket, garments, a ring, raindrops, a flower bed, a fountain, a nursing infant, a student preparing for a test, a traveler jumping on a ramshackle road—images that belong to country life along with those of the city ("as Charles Williams would have delighted to note," Lewis observes). Examining the images of "weight," Lewis highlights how strange it is that as the poem reaches the farthest point in the universe from earth one finds so many "ponderosities": "I have always felt that no poet—least of all, any poet whose theme is so unearthly as Dante's—has such an admirable solidity." Arriving at the largest classes, he again underscores how Dante defies our expectations. There are as many images of horticulture and agriculture as of "heat and light": "The poetry of the *Paradiso* is full of roots and leaves and growth as it is of lights—and far fuller of both than jewels and crowns." And both are outdone by "technical" images dealing with "the arts, crafts, manufactures, and skilled occupations."[13]

Having reviewed all his tallies, Lewis concludes the piece with a powerful, though understated, observation: "It is, perhaps, this continual reference both to the quiet, moistened earth and to the resonant pavements, workshops, and floors, which support

---

[13]Lewis, "Imagery in the Last Eleven Cantos," 84, 92.

and make convincing his invention of a heaven which, in the obvious sense, makes very few concessions to the natural man."[14]
Sayers had been correct about the pervasive "earthy" imagery—it
is there right up to the end of the poem. What she hadn't recognized, as Lewis shows here, is the role of that "concrete" imagery
in accommodating earthbound readers to a heaven of "pure intellectual light, fulfilled with love" (XXX.40).[15] Even as Dante strips
away the world of ordinary experience in the narrative ("trans-
humanises" it), he freely imports goods from the material world
we know. Working with both hands, as it were, Dante presents us
with a heaven that is at once alien, even shockingly so, and a place
surprisingly like home.

*Paradiso*'s imagery is not only broad but deep—that was the
lesson of Lewis's 1942 paper. Once again, Lewis recognized that
Dante's seemingly lazy habit of comparing one thing to another
of the same kind is, within the specific conditions of his epic,
*Paradiso* in particular, anything but. The sliding of "likeness" into
"sameness" can initiate a kind of chain reaction—a cascade of
correspondences to the poem's other events, overarching themes,
and master symbols, with each new interaction enhancing the
significance of the original image and all the others in the chain.
The result, as Lewis told us in chapter four, is that the longer
one looks at the analogy the deeper it becomes, the more richly
intertwined with everything else in the poem, and "the more
fruitful in thoughts that are interesting as long as you live."[16]

Take one more look at the images in the *Paradiso* XXXI passage.
Mary is likened to the new dawn, a fitting image, we might say,
given her role in salvation history. But the resonances are deeper:
Medieval commentators often associated her, allegorically, with

---

[14]Lewis, "Imagery in the Last Eleven Cantos," 93.
[15]Sayers and Reynolds, *Divine Comedy 3: Paradise*, 319.
[16]C. S. Lewis, "Dante's Similes," in *Studies in Medieval and Renaissance Literature*, 72.

Aurora (the mythological Dawn). That includes Bernard of Clairvaux, the saint who directs Dante to attend to Mary a few lines before the quoted passage begins. Meanwhile, the Oriflamme was a banner that bore the image of the sun, which is already suggestive (God is light); but it was also a *sacred* article, associated with the Abbey of St. Denis (and so its saintly protector) in Paris and a symbol of divine intervention. Image after image beckons us onward to others and circles back again to refresh those we've already seen. These buzzing similes are honey to the "adult intellect," too.

## A POET OF STATEMENT

In her aforementioned last Dante lecture, "Dante the Maker," Sayers made her own inquiry into how the poet could, with a lean image or even a single word, set the whole network "vibrating in unison" (to borrow Lewis's language). In an earlier lecture, she had named Dante a "Poet of the Image" (alongside Williams), which she defined as a writer who generally avoids making "overt, rationalised *statements* about the reality" that the writer's images are designed to express.[17] By this method, she suggested, Dante was being at once vivid and economical, involving the reader's senses and intuition (not just intellect) and appealing to both personal and communal experience. A statement is reasoned over (and then done with); an image is an invitation to extended reflection.

But in 1956, in the throes of translating *Paradiso*, Sayers recast Dante as a "Poet of Statement." This was not exactly an about-face. The poet of statement is not framed as the opposite of the poet of the image but the "poet of search," the one writing to relate "what he knows," the other to discover "what he feels."

---

[17]Dorothy L. Sayers, "The Poetry of the Image in Dante and Charles Williams," in *FPD*, 193.

(In another lecture later in the year, she cites Keats as the model "searcher," and calls Dante a convert from searching to stating.[18]) The shift would seem to be explained when one remembers how many "rationalised statements" *Paradiso* contains (such as, for example, Beatrice's lengthy discourse on the density of the moon in canto II).[19] Yet that is not the larger point Sayers sought to make in 1956. Dante is a poet of statement because he could see the big picture—of his culture and his work—with unusual clarity. Because he already knew what he was about before he set to work, he was able to construct elaborate scaffolding in advance and thereby "[know], while writing, exactly what every word and line means to the whole poem." And because he wrote against the background of an audience that shared his beliefs, he could leave much unsaid or half-expressed, "[relying] on his reader to fill in for himself all of the implications latent in an apparently simple phrase."[20]

Most of the lecture is dedicated to demonstrating that this is exactly what we see in the famous first and last lines of the poem: *La gloria di colui che tutto move* ("The glory of him who moves all things") and *L'amor che move il sole e l'altre stelle* ("The love that moves the sun and the other stars"). In the opening line, she locates "the two great seminal words out of which the whole articulated structure of the cantica is built"—*glory* (i.e., light) and *move*—and in the closing line she finds that structure's satisfying resolution in the notable "change of wording"—the addition of love. What is the structure resolving? On Sayers's telling, in *Paradiso* Dante turns to his advantage the two conceptions of God that the medieval world inherited from the ancients: Greek philosophy's "abstract, mathematically static" notion of a "First Cause" and the

---

[18]Dorothy L. Sayers, "The Poetry of Search and the Poetry of Statement," in *PSPS*, 9.
[19]To use the language of chapter 5, numerous are *Paradiso*'s sermons.
[20]Dorothy L. Sayers, "Dante the Maker," in *PSPS*, 21.

"actively personal God" of the Bible. The progression of the poem, she argues, is the gradual movement from the abstract (God as remote Cause) to the personal (God is Love). The whole poem, she memorably adds, is constructed like a bridge to get one from the first line to the last, and "roads from all the other parts of the poem run together to one point from which to pass over that bridge."[21]

Amid all of this passage to and fro, Sayers underscores how Dante's command of his dual inheritance allows him to build up rich patterns of images and to animate the most pedestrian of words. Lewis, as seen in chapter four, made the second point as well in "Dante's Similes," noting how "light, love, up, down, high, low, sun, star, and earth" are so freighted with meaning in the *Comedy* that they seem to become poetry of their own accord. Sayers here wonders over what Dante can make of *move*.

Both authors emphasized, Lewis in 1942 and Sayers in 1956, that Dante achieved these effects not by being original (as we expect great poets to be) but by being traditional. His genius lay in inhabiting his tradition fully and activating it imaginatively on the grand scale. He made music out of physics and theology. He conjured images to render difficult concepts mentioned in the old books. He spied connections across fields and ages. For those who share in Dante's tradition, Sayers suggests, the great "poem of Statement" that is *Paradiso* gives pleasure not by its startling novelty (though Dante does advance some provocative claims). Rather, the adult intellect enjoys here the satisfaction of observing countless strands of its inheritance woven together within an artistic unity—one vast, dynamic, and glorious image encompassing the cosmos.

---

[21]Sayers, "Dante the Maker," 22-23.

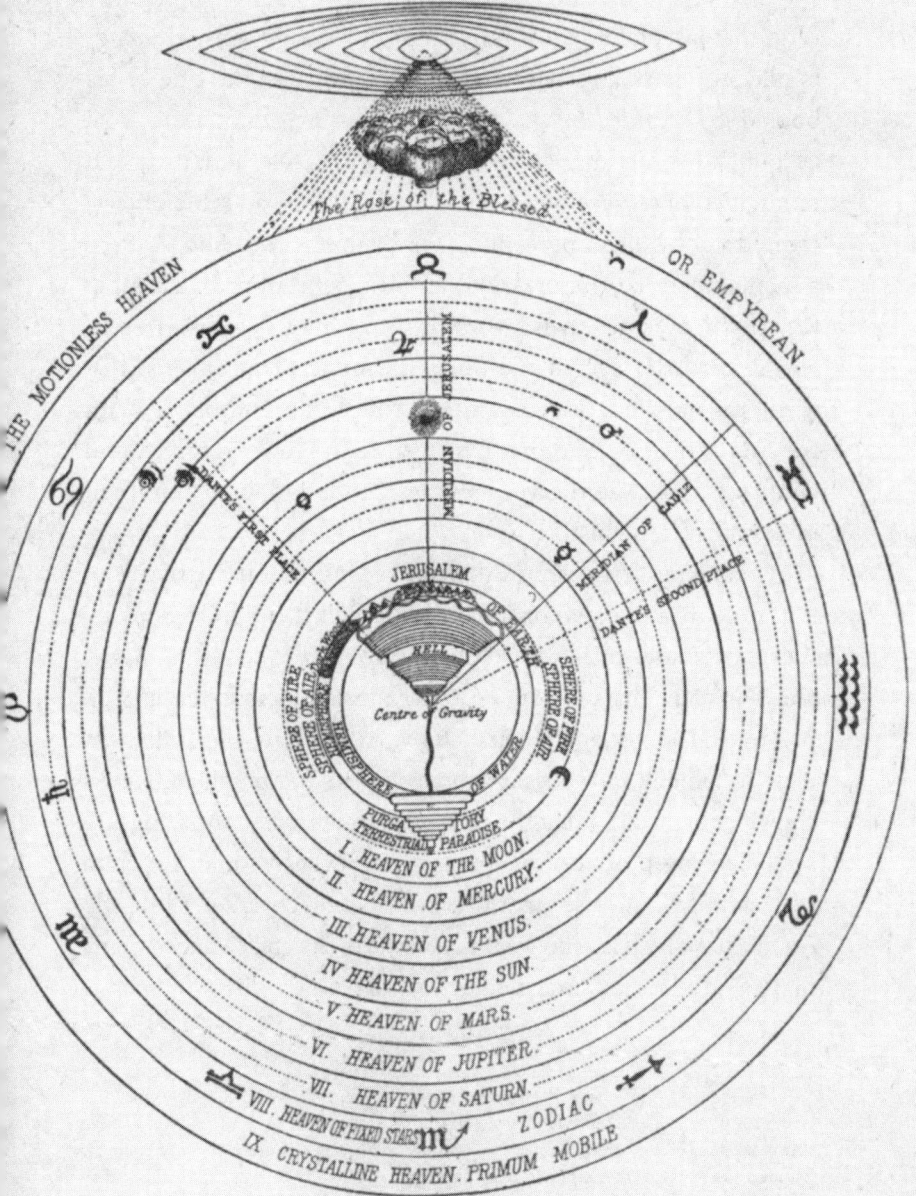

**Figure 7.2.** "The Universe," in Maria Francesca Rossetti's *A Shadow of Dante* (Longmans & Green, 1894 edition)

## THE DISCARDED COSMIC IMAGE

With that last statement, I move into the second sense of *image* in play in this chapter—the one Lewis placed in the title of his book *The Discarded Image* (1964). That is image not as a verbal account of something seen, heard, smelled, felt, and/or tasted but "a mental representation of something (esp. a visible object) created not by direct perception but by memory or imagination; a mental picture or impression; an idea, conception."[22] Another word for it, the one Lewis favors inside the book's covers, is *model*. The "discarded image" in question is the model of the universe that medieval and Renaissance authors from Dante to Milton (with the merry host of Geoffrey Chaucer, John Gower, Donne, and company in between) carried in their heads and wrote into their poems, plays, and histories.[23]

Whereas moderns assume that such a model should derive from experiments and equations, medievals built theirs from books— the authoritative ones passed down through the centuries, pagan and Christian. That might not sound like an auspicious jumping-off point, given how far apart their Platonic, Aristotelian, Old Testament, New Testament, and patristic sources are on some points. Yet Lewis shows, convincingly, that the medieval genius for synthesizing and systematizing produced a "single, complex, harmonious mental Model of the Universe" that deserves to be recognized alongside Aquinas's *Summa* and the *Comedy* as one of the great achievements of the period, "a supreme medieval work of art."[24]

---

[22]"Image," sense 5a, in *Oxford English Dictionary*, "image (*n.*)," March 2025, https://doi .org/10.1093/OED/8522035192.

[23]As mentioned in the introduction, the book began as lectures that Lewis wrote to equip his students so that once they set off into the *Comedy* or *Canterbury Tales* or *Paradise Lost*, they would not feel the need to make frequent visits to the commentators. He likened the book to a map that one looks at in advance so that you don't have to bury your head in one while on the trail. C. S. Lewis, *The Discarded Image* (Cambridge University Press, 1964), vii.

[24]Lewis, *Discarded Image*, 11-12.

The model is, *The Discarded Image* shows, nearly all-embracing, covering the heavens above, the soul within, and even how history was told. Dante is the indisputable star of Lewis's review of the parts of the universe (though he is named regularly and reverentially throughout the study). Two points of that review stand out for present purposes. The first concerns the contrast between the medieval and modern outlook on the night sky. When "modern eyes" look up, we perceive "a sea that fades away into mist," and the notion of "space" promulgated by astronomers induces in us "terror or bewilderment or vague reverie." Not so the medievals. "Pascal's terror at *le silence éternel de ces espaces infinis*," Lewis argues, "never entered [Dante's] mind." When our poet passes through the heavens, he is instead "like a man being conducted through an immense cathedral."[25]

While a superb analogy in its own right, it also leads naturally (and I suspect intentionally) to the second point: the unique fusion Lewis locates in the *Comedy* between poetic cosmology and Christian spirituality. "One class of experts" in medieval society, Lewis writes early in the book, "ignore the model almost completely": "the great spiritual writers" (including St. Bernard, whom he names directly). Lewis ventures two reasons why this was so. First, the spiritual writers dealt with "practical" matters concerning the care of souls; contemplating the starry heavens was not a favored remedy for lust or gluttony. Second, while solidly theistic, the model was not conspicuously Christian. It did not occasion a "conflict between religion and science" as erupted in the Victorian period, Lewis stresses. The two, rather, belonged to separate spheres, with the result that one rarely observes the fusion of joyful "contemplation of the Model and intense religious feeling of a specifically Christian character . . . except in the work of Dante."[26]

---

[25]Lewis, *Discarded Image*, 100. See also Sayers's lecture "Dante's Cosmos," in *FPD*, 78-101.
[26]Lewis, *Discarded Image*, 19.

The "cathedral tour" is an apt characterization of the unique journey through the heavens that Beatrice takes Dante on in *Paradiso*. Leaving earth—the center of the universe, yes, but a *tiny* place in the medieval understanding—they pass through nine concentric spheres. In ascending order, those spheres belong to the moon, Mercury, Venus, the sun, Mars, Jupiter, Saturn, the fixed stars, and, finally, the Primum Mobile (meaning the "First Movable"). Simply narrating all these crossings would seem an impressive enough feat, but Dante gives each sphere a spiritual twist. The ancients taught the medievals that the spheres influence human psychology and history. Dante-the-plot-maker plays with those personalities in his selections of the souls that Dante-the-pilgrim and Beatrice interview at each level.[27] Lewis clearly enjoyed this idea, listing each of Dante's choices when offering his reader a general rundown of the characteristics of each planet in the medieval imagination. This table provides a compact summary:

**Table 7.1.** Lewis on the planetary temperaments and their representatives in *Paradiso*

| PLANET | PERSONALITY | DANTEAN DELEGATION |
|---|---|---|
| Moon | tendency to wander | those who abandoned religious vows "for some good or pardonable reason" |
| Mercury | "Skilled Eagerness" | "Beneficent men of action" |
| Venus | beauty/amorousness | "Those, now penitent, who loved recklessly and lawlessly" |
| Sun | wisdom/liberality | theologians and philosophers |
| Mars | "Martial Temperament" | martyrs |
| Jupiter | "Cheerful" yet "Tranquil" | "Wise and just princes" |
| Saturn | melancholy | contemplatives |

Source: C. S. Lewis, *The Discarded Image* (Cambridge University Press, 1964), 105-9.

Our poet—with his spreadsheet of a mind—also coordinates, sphere by sphere, topically appropriate scientific, historical, and

---

[27]These delegates are not *physically* present, mind you; they remain altogether in God's immediate company in the Empyrean. Their selves are projected—like the images of a magic lantern—out to the sphere in question for pedagogical purposes.

theological talking points, thereby conferring on Dante-the-pilgrim training in the higher learning of his age, a stellar liberal arts education.[28]

The upshot of all of this elegant arrangement—both in the general casting of the model and Dante's supplements to it—Lewis spells out toward the end of *The Discarded Image*. Today's artists, Lewis laments, find no easy comforts in reality. They may face "a reality whose significance [they] cannot know, or a reality that has no significance; or even a reality such that the very question whether it has a meaning is itself a meaningless question."[29] Thus, modern artists must, by their own powers and proclivities, unearth that meaning or bestow one on the universe. By contrast, Lewis argues, "the Model universe of our ancestors had a built-in significance." When the medievals looked on the starry sky, they saw the "admirable design" of the heavens and stood in awe of "the wisdom and goodness that created it" all. They did not need to "make" meaning for themselves: "The achieved perfection was already there. The only difficulty was to make an adequate response." On Lewis's telling, Dante had made such a response in *Paradiso*. While reading it, Lewis enjoyed a double pleasure. Here was the best poetic representation of the model—"an object in which the mind can rest, overwhelming in its greatness but satisfying in its harmony"—coupled with the "high religious ardour" that he shared with the poet.[30]

## PATTERNS OF GLORY

Now is a good moment to take stock of what we have gleaned from Lewis and Sayers, for we have already gone a long way

---

[28] Accordingly, the figure of Beatrice is transformed in *Paradiso*. She is still glorious to behold but now has *lots* to say on topics on which medieval women were rarely, if ever, given a hearing, and she proves a patient, if also somewhat bemused, professor of the natural sciences and divinity.

[29] Lewis, *Discarded Image*, 204.

[30] Lewis, *Discarded Image*, 100, 120.

toward understanding both "how the thing is done" and why someone possessing an adult intellect would find this poetic ride exhilarating. It is tempting simply to list the features we have reviewed—Dante's impossible combination at the level of style, his smuggling of earthy imagery into heaven, his buzzing similes, his activation of the most commonplace words, his bridging of cultural inheritances, his spiritual adaptation of the age's cosmic image—and then present Dante with one blue ribbon after another.

That would be a mistake, however, because all these qualities are entangled. The thickness of Dante's language derives from his tradition, as Sayers would have us see, including his meaning-ridden mental model of the universe, as Lewis pointed out. Those chain reactions in his imagery, too, are functions of his mastery of received materials. He lived in the time—as Sayers and Lewis taught us in chapter five—before travel writing, philosophy, religious allegory, and poetic self-reflection had split and gone their separate ways. Countless are the local satisfactions that *Paradiso* provides. Yet, as all three members of my cohort saw clearly, Dante's greatest achievement was to hold it all together— all the styles, feelings, ideas, images—within the vast, three-tiered architecture of his epic. *Paradiso* is its crown, for here, in the clear light of heaven, one may see how the parts fit together, how they mirror and elaborate on one another, how running through the whole work are great and elegant patterns whose satisfactions to the adult mind far surpass the agitating incidents of hell.

Sayers, Williams, and Lewis all remarked on the "patterned" pleasures of *Paradiso*, both within itself and in relation to the previous canticles. As noted above, Sayers was struck by the landscape's transformation into "a dance of geometrical patterns, touched from a palette of pure light" in the mid-forties. Ten years later, in "Dante the Maker," she noted, again with relish, that *Paradiso* is intensely patterned. Whereas in hell the "pattern of movement" is the (monotonous) circle, and in purgatory the circle and the line (through time), heaven offers the circles of the spheres, the line of the ascent, and "the celestial dance" (more on this in the coda).[31] She discerns, too, a correspondence between the light imagery that dominates *Paradiso* with the canticle's overarching spiritual concern: "As this visual music proceeds through its shimmering variations upon the theme of light, to resolve itself finally into one harmony of recovered form, we begin to see the outline of a single over-riding pattern impressed on the whole poem, which is the pattern of salvation."[32]

Williams called it "the pattern of glory." The term did not apply exclusively to Dante, though the *Comedy* was a prime example of it. In Williams's view, most of us have glory wrong. "The word glory, to English ears," he writes in *He Came Down from Heaven*, "usually means no more than a kind of mazy bright blur." Glory *is* bright, and it is a maze, Williams counters, but we don't know what we are saying. "The maze should be, though it generally is not, exact, and the brightness should be that of a geometrical pattern." Understood in this way, glory "becomes a kind of key problem—what is the web of the glory of heaven as a state?"[33] In other words, how do we *live* that way? How is glory instantiated on the ground, among the people?

As Charles Hefling observes, for Williams, "Glory is like what you see through a kaleidoscope rather than what you see through a fog. It is precise and regular, like a solemn liturgy or an intricate dance, which are two images Williams uses in his novels for the all-inclusive orderliness that bespeaks the divine."[34] Williams believed that glory wasn't just a personal attribute but a way

---

[31] Sayers, "Dante the Maker," 33-34.
[32] Sayers, "Dante the Maker," 27.
[33] *HCDH*, 33.
[34] Charles Hefling, introduction, in *Charles Williams: Essential Writings in Spirituality and Theology* (Cowley, 1993), 5.

that things hang together, *cohere*, within larger patterns that are discernible in the natural order, the social order, and the order of history. "The glory of God is in facts," we heard him say in the last chapter. "The almost incredible nature of things is that there is no fact which is not in His glory." He could make that last statement with confidence because he had read the final canto of *Paradiso*.

## THE FINAL VISIONS

"This also is Thou; neither is this Thou"—such, Williams proposes in the opening pages of *The Figure of Beatrice*, was "the maxim of [Dante's] study, as regards the final Power."[35] The first half of the formula has been our study throughout this book, as we watched Dante experiencing glory through the mediation of what Williams taught Sayers and both of them have taught us to call "images." To pursue images in this third and final sense is to undertake the Affirmative Way, to open the eyes of the soul outward on creation in hopes of catching mediated rays of the divine light. In *Paradiso*, as the third epigraph of this chapter suggests, Williams saw not only the image of the redeemed universe but also an image of the redeemed way—a vast network of *proper* relations, a web of glory woven by God in which all the nodes happily take their stations and the innumerable links between them tingle endlessly, joyously.

But the second half of the formula is equally true, and for this reason Williams never denigrated the Negative Way, that is to say, the traditional way of the mystics by which all images are rejected as falling immeasurably short of God. Even the pilgrim on the Affirmative Way, Williams stressed, must keep moving—never severing one image from the network, never mistaking the image for the original, never crediting the pilgrim's own powers for the gift. All is preparation for the final vision—which Sayers previewed for us in chapter five—"in which all the shining Images are seen 'transhumanised' and summed

---

[35]*FB*, 8.

up in the final Image—the Image of the Incarnate Christ in the very centre of the Unimaginable Godhead."[36]

Thus, in the end, Beatrice must, and joyfully does, turn her eyes from Dante back to her most Beloved, and Dante turn his eyes from her. After looking upon Mary, the supreme "God-bearer" whose humility allowed Love to trespass among us, Dante fixes his gaze (*ficcar lo viso*) on the divine light. There follow two visions. The first is cosmic:

> O grace abounding, whereby I presumed
>> So deep the eternal light to search and sound
>> That my whole vision was therein consumed!
> In that abyss I saw how love held bound
>> Into one volume all the leaves whose flight
>> Is scattered through the universe around;
> How substance, accident, and mode unite
>> Fused, so to speak, together, in such wise
>> That this I tell of is one simple light.
> Yea, of this complex I believe mine eyes
>> Beheld the universal form—in me,
>> Even as I speak, I feel such joy arise. (lines 82-90)[37]

The "universal form" is, Reynolds explains, "the feature, property, or nature of the universe, that which makes it what it is. To glimpse that would be to read in the mind of God Himself the divine idea of all things."[38] Reading God's mind might sound absurd, but Reynolds gestures to Dante's helpful metaphor of a book in the passage above. Within the divine light, the cosmos, which appears a chaotic mix to us on the earth floor, is now revealed as so many pages gathered together in a single volume. In her 1947 lecture "The Meaning of Heaven and

---

[36]Dorothy L. Sayers, "The Fourfold Interpretation of the *Comedy*," in *IPD*, 123-24.

[37]Sayers and Reynolds, *Divine Comedy 3: Paradise*, 345.

[38]Barbara Reynolds, note on canto XXXIII, in Sayers and Reynolds, *Divine Comedy 3: Paradise*, 348.

Hell," Sayers cites these lines in answer to every child's concern that one would run out of things to do in heaven. The eternity that Dante envisages here is anything but "an unmeaning stretch of endless time." He offers instead a vision in which one beholds "all times and places known in one deathless and ecstatic present."[39]

The Way of the Affirmation of Images, Sayers told us in chapter six, is underlaid by three doctrinal warrants: true creation, Incarnation, and Trinity. Sayers had no doubt pulled down several theological tomes before making those assertions. Yet she also knew that she had Dante's support in the form of canto XXXIII, for here, at the end of the Affirmative Way (indeed, of all ways), Dante *knows* the three doctrines experientially. The subject of the first vision is the *truth* of creation. Dante sees the cosmos from the divine point of view, fulfilling his long quest to spy God through his works. Yet creation is *not* God: "Neither is this Thou." The pious scandal of the last canto is to image the Trinity and Incarnation. To render the first, Dante draws on the elementary school kit of shapes and colors:

> That light supreme, within its fathomless
>> Clear substance, showed to me three spheres, which bare
>> Three hues distinct, and occupied one space:
> The first mirrored the next, as though it were
>> Rainbow from rainbow, and the third seemed flame
>> Breathed equally from each of the first pair.[40]

It is so surprisingly simple, the first-time reader says. And yet, the veteran replies, so many of the dominant images and ideas of the *Comedy* recur here—in the light, in the circles, in the fire, in the numbers three and one—that one can only wonder at Dante's planning (à la Sayers's "Poet of Statement"). But it is also an *inhuman* image—a god fit for mathematicians (as critics have long

---

[39]Dorothy L. Sayers, "The Meaning of Heaven and Hell," in *IPD*, 55.
[40]Sayers and Reynolds, *Divine Comedy 3: Paradise*, 346.

complained). In "Dante the Maker," Sayers astutely observes that the Godhead (or, better said, Godsphere) is shown here "under the same impersonal aspect" it wore in *Paradiso*'s opening lines—"an abstraction of multidimensional geometry." It may not seem "like an object of love."[41] For an awkward second, Sayers argues, the synthesis that Dante has spent so many thousands of lines constructing— between the "Aristotelian All-Mover" and the "Living God" of biblical witness—seems in danger of collapse. But then, "in the flash of a single line they are fused into a single identity."[42]

That line occurs as Dante studies the second sphere—the one whose light reflects the first's—and reports: *mi parve pinta de la nostra effige,* or "it seemed to me painted with our image." Within the Trinity, Dante faces, blissfully, the Incarnation, the everlasting union of the divine image ("the express *image* of His Person" of whom Heb 1:3 speaks) and the human image.

As Williams, echoing the curious locutions of Dante's heaven, liked to say: The poet beheld the in-manning of God and experienced the in-Godding of man. Accordingly, beholding the Glory moves Dante. The spectacle invites his participation, and ours. We may join the stars in their ardent circling of Love itself. Dante tells us so in the *Comedy*'s closing lines:

> High phantasy lost power and here broke off;
>  Yet, as a wheel moves smoothly, free from jars,
>  My will and my desire were turned by love,
> The love that moves the sun and the other stars.
>  (lines 142-45)[43]

---

[41]I can vouch from pedagogical experience that it often does not—though students often miss the simile in the Trinity described in line 126.

[42]Sayers, "Dante the Maker," 39.

[43]My attribution of these lines to Reynolds is a best guess. Reynolds may have been working off Sayers's notes. My judgment call is based on the fact that I could find no full translation of these lines in Sayers's published works. See Sayers and Reynolds, *Divine Comedy 3: Paradise,* 347.

**Figure C.1.** Fra Angelico, *The Last Judgment* (ca. 1425), Museo di San Marco, Florence

# CODA

DANTE HAS SENT US OFF with love in our hearts and stars in our eyes. One is tempted to leave it at that. Many books do. The members of my cohort would not be content with that arrangement, however, because they were convinced that many people didn't fully grasp what Dante was up to in the *Comedy's* last words. Williams says so directly in *The Figure of Beatrice*, pointing out that the final line—so often quoted in isolation—contains a subordinate verb ("that move"), which should direct our attention back to the sentence's main verb ("were turned"). Dante was less worried about the loveliness of the stars, Williams insisted, than the fact that "Love rolled his own desire and will." There is a challenge in that, Williams saw: Around what do your will and desire turn?

Here Professor Lewis would pipe up to make sure that we comprehend the particular character of the love in question. Dante "is speaking of love in the Aristotelian sense," he explains in *The Discarded Image*. God "moves" the heavens not by force but by attraction—"as an object of desire moves those who desire it."[1] Sayers meditated on the same issue in "Dante the Maker" and further worried that readers would miss the reference in the concluding wheel simile. It is no mere "earthly mechanism," she

---

[1] C. S. Lewis, *The Discarded Image* (Cambridge University Press, 1964), 113.

argues, but a recapitulation of the image of the *magne rote* ("great wheels") seen many times across the *Comedy*.[2]

Within the cohort's collected papers, though, the most daring attempt to bring modern readers into the experience related by Dante in *Paradiso*'s culminating canto appears not in a piece of criticism but a work of fiction—Lewis's *Perelandra* (1943). The author openly acknowledged Dante's influence on the novel, telling an American correspondent in 1944 that his female Venusian, Tinidril, "owes something to Matilda at the end of *Purgatorio*," referring to the woman Dante meets in the Earthly Paradise atop Mount Purgatory prior to Beatrice's entrance.[3] On Lewis's substantial debt to *Paradiso*, however, no one appears to have questioned him.

The moment comes, fittingly, in the very last pages of the novel. There Ransom, the Earthman and philologist hero of Lewis's Space Trilogy, and the unfallen first humanoids of Venus converse with the angelic overseers of Mars and Venus about cosmology and the flow of time into eternity. Again and again the conversation circles around the topic of the "Great Dance," the angelic characters making cryptic statements such as this: "The Great Dance does not wait to be perfect until the peoples of the Low Worlds are gathered into it. . . . The dance which we dance is at the centre and for the dance all things were made. Blessed be He!"[4]

And yet for the reader who arrives armed with copies of *Paradiso* and *The Discarded Image*, this angel-speak is not difficult to decipher. In the latter book, Lewis enumerates the image of a "celestial dance" among the ancients' benefactions to the assemblers of the medieval model. He points to the fourth-century

---

[2]Dorothy L. Sayers, "Dante the Maker," in *PSPS*, 40.

[3]C. S. Lewis to Charles Brady, October 29, 1944, in *CLCSL*, 2:530. See also Jason Baxter's superb reading of *Perelandra* against the background of *Purgatorio* in *The Medieval Mind of C. S. Lewis: How Great Books Shaped a Great Mind* (IVP Academic, 2022), 59-61.

[4]C. S. Lewis, *Perelandra* (Bodley Head, 1943), 246.

philosopher Calcidius, who wrote of a *caelestis chorea*, and cites Pseudo-Dionysius's account of the angelic hierarchies "[facing]" God "ἀμέσως, *nullius interiectu*, with nothing between, encircling Him with their ceaseless dance."[5] Dante depicts those hierarchies in *Paradiso* XXVIII, where the pilgrim witnesses the angelic orders circling God and singing hosannas, and many readers, including Reynolds, have characterized their exultant orbiting as a dance.[6] Reynolds was following her friend Sayers's lead. As noted in chapter seven, Sayers recognized the "celestial dance" as the new dimension of movement that *Paradiso* adds to the circle (*Inferno*'s motion) and line (*Purgatorio*'s addition).

In *Perelandra*, Lewis joins this celestial dance with the choreographic spin on the divine life that that develops across his writings in the early forties.[7] The best-known articulation of the latter idea appears in *Beyond Personality* (1944), which was then recycled in *Mere Christianity* (1952). In the passage, Lewis argues that "God is not a static thing—not even a person—but a dynamic, pulsating activity, a life, almost a kind of drama. Almost, if you won't think me irreverent, a kind of dance." He goes on to propose that it should be personal to us: "The whole dance, or drama, or pattern of this three-Personal life is to be played out in each one of us: or (putting it the other way round) each one of us has got to enter that pattern, take his place in that dance."[8]

---

[5]Lewis, *Discarded Image*, 71.

[6]The line in question announces the last of the three subgroupings of angels. Reynolds renders it "The dances which remain display to view / Princedoms, Archangels, and one circle more" (ll. XXVIII.124-125). The word rendered "dances" is *tripudi*, which derives from a Latin word for a three-step dance (*tripudium*). Charles Singleton, for one, reads it that way. But other modern translators and commentators prefer to read it as "rejoicing" or "festivity." Reynolds, *Divine Comedy 3: Paradise*, 304.

[7]To cite another example, in *The Problem of Pain* (1940), Lewis suggests that the joy of the "eternal dance"—in which each player gives herself to the others—does not exist for joy, or good, or love, though it conveys all three: "It is Love Himself, and Good Himself, and therefore happy. It does not exist for us, but we for it." C. S. Lewis, *The Problem of Pain* (Centenary, 1940), 141.

[8]C. S. Lewis, *Beyond Personality* (Geoffrey Bles, 1944), 26.

This second notion of the dance—as joyful pattern that each of us must enter—also has obvious Dantean precedents. Many are the frolics of the saints in *Paradiso*, but among the most boisterous, amusingly enough, are the scholars of the sphere of the Sun. Upon their entry in *Paradiso* X, they form an ecstatic circle around Dante and Beatrice, whose rising and falling song reminds Dante of women in a dancing chain:

> So carolling, that ardent aureole
>> Of suns swung round us thrice their burning train,
>> As neighbouring stars swing round the steady pole;
>
> Then seemed like ladies, from the dancing chain
>> Not loosed, but silent at the measure's close,
>> Listening alert to catch the new strain. (ll. 76-81)[9]

Of this and other heavenly revels, Reynolds superbly observes, "The spheres of heaven whirl, dizzy with delight; the angels and rejoicing souls weave their fantastic dance; there is laughter, inebriation, a riot of charity."[10]

At the close of *Perelandra*, the synchronizing of the two dances—cosmic and interpersonal—resolves the anxieties that Ransom expresses regarding the seeming insignificance of humanity due to the vastness of the universe and what he has learned of God's creative projects away from earth. In light of what he has seen, not only do humans seem small, Ransom confesses; the Incarnation no longer appears the central event of *all* history.

In the vision of the Great Dance, Ransom—and Lewis's reader—gets an overpowering answer, and as Reynolds could see decades ago, that vision derives from Dante. She well named it a "descant" upon Dante's third canticle, alluding to a form of

---

[9]Sayers, Divine Comedy 3: *Paradise*, 137.

[10]Barbara Reynolds, "Dante's Vision of Heaven," in *Journey to the Celestial City: Glimpses of Heaven from Great Literary Classics*, ed. H. Wayne Martindale (Moody Press, 1995), 48.

medieval music in which one singer intones a fixed melody while others accompany it with improvisations.[11] If we listen closely to Lewis's account of the Great Dance, we can hear Dante's melody playing throughout the later writer's offshoot.

I should acknowledge that the elements of the dance vision are not strictly Dantean; like Lewis's cherished medieval model, the Great Dance draws together modern and ancient ideas, Platonic and patristic, scientific and poetic. It likely owes much to Williams, too, for Lewis's friend had twice written—in *The Greater Trumps* (1932) and the book that so impressed Lewis in 1936, *The Place of the Lion* (1931)—cosmic visions that mix elements of ancient and modern cosmology (in the former case referring to it as a "great dance").[12] The debts to Dante, though, are the heaviest, being tonal, imagistic, and procedural (or maybe it's better to call the last quality "processional"). The dance vision unfolds a cosmic order in which *everything* coheres before trailing off into a direct encounter with the Godhead that Lewis wisely does not detail. In short, this is Lewis's adaptation of Dante's envisioning of beatitude in *Paradiso* XXXIII.[13]

It does not begin as a vision but as speech, the words conjuring images so vivid that at a certain point Ransom (who is reporting all of this to the narrator) "thought he saw the Great Dance." The dance, the account begins, "seemed to be woven out of the intertwining undulation of many cords or bands of light, leaping

---

[11]Reynolds, "Dante's Vision of Heaven," 55.

[12]For more on Lewis's debts to Williams as well an array of theological insights into Lewis's construction of the Great Dance, see Paul Fiddes's superb chapter "The Great Dance in C. S. Lewis's *Perelandra*," in *Charles Williams and C. S. Lewis: Friends in Co-Inherence* (Oxford University Press, 2021), 320-37.

[13]I avoid using the phrase "beatific vision" because Lewis does not show us the beatific vision, as traditionally defined, directly (God in his essence). It is also notable that Lewis, like Sayers, describes the cosmic image (the universe in a book) as the "beatific vision"—or at least part thereof. See C. S. Lewis, "Imagery in the Last Eleven Cantos of Dante's *Comedy*," in *Studies in Medieval and Renaissance Literature*, ed. Walter Hooper (Cambridge University Press, 1966).

over and under one another and mutually embraced in arabesques and flower-like subtleties."[14] It is light, dancing light, light that recalls a ballerina (or elaborate characters in a book?) interlaced with floral movements. We know why it is made of light: It is the divine light that pervades the universe in *Paradiso* I and becomes the "visual music," the dominant theme (in the musical sense), of the third canticle. We know why it leaps, dances, and embraces. *Paradiso*'s abundant floral imagery, too, suggests why Ransom immediately perceives flowering shapes.

In Dante's first vision in *Paradiso* XXXIII, he sees, once again, "substance, accident, and mode unite," thereby enjoying an apprehension of cosmic harmony that only the divine perspective can provide. The episode, as I argued in chapter seven, draws to a satisfying conclusion Dante's ascent from local to cosmic patterns of glory. In this scene, Lewis sends Ransom on that adventure, the earthling gradually coming to grasp experientially the doctrine of divine omnipresence. Because God is everywhere, and because God delights in and confers significance on all his habitations, *everywhere is the center of the universe*. Accordingly, everywhere Ransom looks within the evolving pattern of the dance, his vision is enticed, discovering at once novelty and continuity. "Each figure," we are told, becomes temporarily "the master-figure or focus of the whole spectacle, by means of which his eye disentangled all else and brought it into unity"—only to be then "entangled" by what lies on the margins, which exerts in turn its own claim on his eye.[15] He observes pattern within pattern opening out onto yet larger patterns—a never-ending web of glory that comes to include inanimate matter, animate life, personal beings, universal truths: Everything is swept up into the joyful movements of the dance.

---

[14]Lewis, *Perelandra*, 251.
[15]Lewis, *Perelandra*, 251.

And still Ransom goes deeper, the vision "[passing] altogether out of the region of sight as we understand it"—into the realm, as Lewis well knew, where only the great mystics have ventured. The Dantean resonances, in turn, become even more pronounced. Here, Lewis writes, "the whole solid figure of these enamoured and inter-inanimated circlings was suddenly revealed as the mere superficies of a far vaster pattern in four dimensions,"—and, having toured *Paradiso*, we know why Lewis wanted the figure to be solid, why it is suffused with *amor*, why there is so much circling, why the author is stringing words together in wilder and wilder ways. The sentence continues, "and that figure as the boundary of yet others in other worlds: till suddenly as the movement grew yet swifter, the interweaving yet more ecstatic"—we know why it was growing swifter, why more ecstatic, why Ransom's powers of reason and remembrance (as Lewis now reports) begin to fade, why, too, he found next—that "at the very zenith of complexity, complexity was eaten up and faded, as a thin white cloud fades into the hard blue burning of the sky, and a simplicity beyond all comprehension, ancient and young as spring, illimitable, pellucid, drew him with cords of infinite desire into its own stillness."[16] We know the style that Lewis was aiming for in this passage: "the sense that every word is being held in place by a gigantic pressure" and "the untrammelled, reckless speed through pellucid spaces which makes us imagine while we are reading him that we have somehow left our bodies behind" (as Ransom feels he has).

We know, moreover, why after the exhilaration of ever-increasing velocity and ever-heightening intensity of light, after peering into the very depths of time and space, the dance's crescendo is not disconcerting *infinite* complexity but a lush simplicity. All those motions, dimensions, the countless tesserae

---

[16]Lewis, *Perelandra*, 252-53.

within innumerable mosaics that comprise creation, culminate in clarity, quietness, everlasting freshness, an enveloping that answers desires too old and deep to name. And we know why Lewis recast the Dantean vision: because he, like Sayers, had tasted the bread of angels at Dante's table and wanted to share the feast with his contemporaries. Dante had been a "scientifictionist" (as Lewis told Sayers in 1949).[17] Lewis was his heir. In this visionary translation of Dante, Lewis refurbishes the discarded medieval image, weaves modern strands into ancient patterns of glory, and, with appropriate modesty, shows just the fringe of the garments of the eternal One.

Yet this vision, like that of Lewis's favorite poet, fades. Dante must come back to earth, and so must Ransom, and so must we. What then? What are we to *make* of these heavenly visions? One answer is embodied in *Perelandra*, and all the other adaptations, major and minor, we have reviewed across this book: We may distribute what we have received through new channels. We may strive to renew our inheritance—following the example of the four authors examined in this book.

At the close of his "Weight of Glory" sermon, Lewis suggests another, more immediate application. He admits that one may wonder "what practical use there is" in the sort of "speculations" that his sermon had "indulged" in concerning human longings and the New Testament's promises of glory.[18] The same question may legitimately be asked about Dante's speculations on glory in the *Comedy* and Sayers's, Williams's, and Lewis's in their responses to Dante, critical and creative.

---

[17]In *The Discarded Image*, Lewis also credits Dante with inventing the first "science-fiction effect" in literary history for the moment when Dante and Virgil, after passing through the center of the earth, shift from passing down to Lucifer's waist to climbing up to his feet (142).

[18]C. S. Lewis, "The Weight of Glory," in *The Weight of Glory and Other Addresses* (Macmillan, 1949), 14.

Lewis suggests "one such use," and I think it applies to the speculations of all the members of the literary quartet assembled in this book. He argues that while we may spend too much time considering "our own potential glory," we cannot do so "too often or too deeply" regarding our neighbors': "The load, or weight, or burden of my neighbour's glory should be laid daily on my back, a load so heavy that only humility can carry it, and the backs of the proud will be broken." Lewis is recalling the terrace of the proud in *Purgatorio*, where we learned that humility was the virtue that paves the way for the others. (It even made a way for Love to enter the world, as the sculpture on the first terrace teaches.) With this assignment, Lewis sends us out in the world to dwell among "possible gods and goddesses." "The dullest and most uninteresting person you talk to," he observes, "may one day be a creature which, if you saw it now, you would be strongly tempted to worship, or else a horror and a corruption such as you now meet, if at all, only in a nightmare."[19]

The *Comedy*, Lewis knew, is equipment for such encounters. Sayers knew it too. Dante taught her that we are already invested with the glorified bodies "in which we shall be known at the Resurrection."[20] Sayers held, with Williams, that we inhabit a world of images and that one day we may be confronted by glory as we walk down the street or glance in the mirror. "Look, look well," Williams charges us accordingly. *The Figure of Beatrice* closes, fittingly, by quoting Beatrice on this theme: "*Riguarda qual son io*"—"See what I am." To this, Williams adds in the last words of his study of Dante: "we have hardly yet begun to be looked at or to look."[21] The Way of Dante was not one man's path; it lay open even now.

---

[19]Lewis, "Weight of Glory," 14-15.
[20]Dorothy L. Sayers, "The Poetry of the Image in Dante and Charles Williams," in *FPD*, 187.
[21]*FB*, 232.

Dante took Dorothy Sayers, Charles Williams, and C. S. Lewis through hell, and they thanked him for his infernal instruction in how not to live. But they loved the medieval poet because the pit is only the first stage of his epic pilgrimage. Dante made "art for seeing evil." My trio testified that the *Comedy* is also, and to a far greater extent, art for experiencing glory.

# Afterword

## PURGATORIO

THE WAY OF MARY AND THE WAY OF THE ARTIST

NICOLE MAZZARELLA

AFTER A FRIEND SPENT HOURS on hold with an insurance company, she texted me, "Dante forgot this circle." I'd received similar texts over the years from others naming the circles that Dante forgot: the DMV, an academic conference, and our family van (my daughter sending this text from the back seat after a twenty-two-hour drive with the entire family, including our dog). This is how we most often think of Dante's circles of hell, as a place where we are trapped.

This is the inferno, the reality of hell, where we have no hope of leaving. At the very core of Dante's hell are those confined in ice, whereas Dante's *Purgatorio* is a place of hope. *Purgatorio* reminds us that prior to final judgment, we are not trapped, even in our deepest patterns of sin. Transformation through Christ is possible.

When Richard Hughes Gibson invited me to engage with *Purgatorio* as an artist, he shared with me Charles Williams's fascination with the phrase "look well." In Gibson's examination of this phrase, he lauds Williams for finding in *Purgatorio*

> possibly "the greatest line in Dante and therefore in all poetry." That would be Beatrice's line in canto 30: "*Guardaci ben: ben sem, ben sem, Beatrice,*" or, "Look well: we are, we are, Beatrice."

These were to Williams words to read by, to see by, to live by; he inscribed them in notebooks, in letters, in three of his published books. In *The Figure of Beatrice*, he finds in these words the ethical core of the way of Dante: "The general maxim of the whole way in Dante is *attention*; 'look', 'look well.'"[1]

Gibson also draws our attention to Purgatorio as a place where the arts in collaboration with liturgy are "vehicles through which we may see God's reality clarified."[2]

When Richard first sent me this highlighted passage, I wondered what it meant to "look well" in *Purgatorio* as a place where art and liturgy meet and to take seriously Dorothy Sayers's charge to take hold of "what [this great poem] truly means to us" in its "true and eternal meaning." What would it mean to invite this work of art to offer us a liturgy to look well? It was here I discovered a path and prayer for artists to reorient our imaginations by traveling with Mary through *Purgatorio*.

The questions for contemplation below are written in the spirit of a St. Ignatian Examen. In *Stretched to Greater Glory*, George A. Aschenbrenner, SJ, offers approaches to the exercises that guide my approach to this liturgy for the artist; Aschenbrenner describes how the exercises should be "initiated by and intermesh with the power of God's word" as "a matter of prayer with the word of God."[3] The questions for contemplation for each terrace of *Purgatorio* are not intended as a self-help tool by which we identify flaws and try to correct them by sheer will.

The following liturgy inspired by *Purgatorio* is intended as a prayerful invitation for God to awaken us to our need for his grace and our need for his love to bring restoration.

---

[1] Richard Hughes Gibson, "Purgatorio: The Ascent of Love," Wade Center (Ken and Jean Hansen Lectureship), Wheaton, IL, February 15, 2024.
[2] Gibson, "Purgatorio."
[3] George A. Aschenbrenner, *Stretched for Greater Glory: What to Expect from the Spiritual Exercises* (Loyola Press, 2004), 5.

## THE WAY OF MARY: AN ARTIST'S PRAYER OF SELF-EXAMINATION

On each terrace of *Purgatorio*, these prayers of self-examination invite us to consider the posture of the penitent, the path of Mary, and questions to contemplate that we might "look well" with what we make.

While Dante's *Purgatorio* is an ode to the fine arts as part of a reordering disordered loves, it also speaks to any who do not consider themselves artists. Dante portrays creative acts that are not limited to the fine arts, including images of Mary at the wedding feast calling for more wine and Mary at the temple caring for her child. Each of us has a way of making that invites others to glimpse God's reality. Thus I refer to making as a way to broadly consider all the creative acts in our lives.

Entering *Purgatorio*, we remember that we are not in hell, where we have to remain. Even if a pattern of sin has deadened a part of us, *Purgatorio* reminds us of the promise of interior spiritual freedom that comes through the transforming love of God. *Purgatorio* asks us whether we see rightly, and it stirs in us a prayer for the grace to turn away from hell's "fierce embrace of unreality."

## THE WAY OF MARY ON THE FIRST TERRACE: PRIDE

On the first terrace, the terrace of pride, we find the penitent hunched over from heavy rocks that keep them from looking up. We encounter those so encumbered with themselves they are truly unable to look well. The annunciation, carved onto the mountain, is a reminder for how to look well. Those bowed down by pride are reminded of Mary's response, "I am the Lord's servant."

## QUESTIONS TO CONTEMPLATE

1. Whom do I serve in my making?

2. What prideful postures encumber me from looking well at God and others?

3. What do I need to release in order to say, "I am the Lord's servant"?

## THE WAY OF MARY ON THE SECOND TERRACE: ENVY

On the terrace of envy are those deprived of sight; their eyes are sewn shut with iron wire. They hear voices telling them of examples of love, including Mary informing Jesus, "They have no wine." Those who are envious are reminded of Mary's loving concern for others, reminding us that our love of others may influence our ability to look well.

## QUESTIONS TO CONTEMPLATE

1. In what ways does my envy blind me from a loving concern for others?

2. In what ways might I notice and tend to the needs of others, in particular those I envy?

3. In what ways might I find spiritual freedom in celebrating the works of other artists?

## THE WAY OF MARY ON THE THIRD TERRACE: WRATH

On the terrace of wrath, Dante is caught up in a vision of a temple in which Mary says, "O my son, why have you done this to us? You can see how we have sought you—sorrowing, your father and I." After seeing this, he encounters a vision of wrath and a thick smoke, "as black as night," that overtakes his eyes with "such rough—textured stuff / as smoke that wrapped us there in Purgatory; my eyes could not endure remaining open."

On this terrace of wrath, another place where we struggle to see, we learn from Mary when she asks, "Why have you done this to us?" She does not give way to wrath but instead asks the question at the heart of it all. "Why have you done this to us?" She names her sorrow.

## QUESTIONS TO CONTEMPLATE

1. How in my making do I bring my real questions before the Lord?
2. What is at the core of the question that I have for Jesus? For example, in my anger, where is there grief or fear?
3. What questions have I avoided exploring in my work?

## THE WAY OF MARY ON THE FORTH TERRACE: SLOTH

On the terrace of sloth is "the love / of good that is too tepidly pursued." Sloth, or acedia, is a state of not caring, or as Father Jean-Charles Nault describes it: ignoring "the giftedness of the moment." In a 2024 sermon, Pope Francis warned that acedia is "a little like dying in advance" as "the demon of acedia wants precisely to destroy the simple joy of the here and now, the grateful wonder of reality; it wants to make you believe that it is all in vain, that nothing has meaning, that it is not worth taking care of anything or anyone."

On this terrace, those who gave way to sloth now run. As they run, they hear examples of the virtuous, including Mary, running to Elizabeth to share in her news after the annunciation.

## QUESTIONS TO CONTEMPLATE

1. In what ways have I given up the wonder of the giftedness of the moment or given way to believing that my creative work is in vain?

2. When I avoid making, what is the true reason I distract, numb, or avoid it?

3. Dorothy Sayers said, "A loose and sentimental theology begets loose and sentimental art-forms. Let us, in heaven's name, drag out the divine drama from under the dreadful accumulation of slipshod thinking and trashy sentiment." Where have I been slothful in looking well?

## THE WAY OF MARY ON THE FIFTH TERRACE: AVARICE

On the terrace of avarice, the face-down penitents confess that they did not look well. For "just as we did not lift our eyes on high / but set our sight on earthly things instead, / so justice here impels our eyes toward earth." Here they acknowledge how their preoccupations separated them from God, as one describes his earthly self "a squalid soul, / from God divided." The penitents call us to consider where we set our gaze and what distracts us from "lifting our eyes on high." In their "outstretched and motionless" state, they also speak of the virtuous and Mary who "In that hostel where / you had set down your holy burden, there / one can discover just how poor you were." They consider this place where she chose "indigence / with virtue rather than much wealth with vice."

## QUESTIONS TO CONTEMPLATE

1. Contemplating all that led Mary to the lowly place of Jesus' birth, what is an open, humble stable that is currently available for my creative work? How might I enter the space available today rather than pining for a more exalted space?

2. What gives my making a sense of purpose or value?

3. What are reasons to pursue making, even if I gain neither attention nor material gain?

## THE WAY OF MARY ON THE SIXTH TERRACE: GLUTTONY

On the terrace of gluttony, we find agonizing hunger and thirst under two trees from which the penitents cannot partake. They circle the trees whose fragrance "kindles in us / craving for food and drink; and not once only, / as we go round this space, our pain's renewed." But on this path they discover that this is not pain but a solace, as they identify with Christ, who has come "to free us through the blood He shed / and, in His joyousness, called out: 'Eli.'" Here they are also reminded of Mary at the wedding feast as she tells Jesus they have no wine. The penitents' transformation is to cry out for the needs of others rather than for their own satiation.

### QUESTIONS TO CONTEMPLATE

1. In what ways have I been gluttonous in consuming others' creative work rather than making my own creative work to share with others?
2. Do I hunger and thirst for righteousness through my making, or do I seek momentary satiation instead?
3. In what ways do I consider the needs of others in my making?

## THE WAY OF MARY ON THE SEVENTH TERRACE: LUST

Finally we enter the raging fires on the terrace of lust, where "the mountain hurls its flames; / but, from the terrace side, there whirls a wind / that pushes back the fire and limits it." Here the penitents "from the heart of that great conflagration" confront their misplaced longings and cry out the words of Mary, "I know not man."

Here we consider the ways that our longings are actually fulfilled:

1. How does my making reveal what I desire?
2. What deeper longing does it reveal?

3. In what lesser ways or ways of excess do I seek to fulfill those longings through my making?

## THE WAY OF THE ARTIST: THE WAY OF MARY

On this ascent of love through *Purgatorio*, we gain an awareness of the love that God has for us and our need for his restoration. As we hold forth our making before God, the path of Mary reminds us that it is on God's love that we ought to look well.

# ACKNOWLEDGMENTS

DANTE TEACHES HIS READERS to treat others' generosity toward us with the utmost seriousness. His warning against the failure to do so is dire: betraying a benefactor gets you sent to the ninth circle of hell to shiver through eternity in the lake of ice. Though this book be little, its development has made me a debtor many times over, and the following list of helpers, sponsors, promoters, and encouragers is surely incomplete. My first word of gratitude must go to Walter and Darlene Hansen, who endowed the lecture series of which mine was the suitably Dantean ninth installment. Thank you for supporting public-facing scholarship. May you be blessed for honoring the fifth commandment with your gift. Marj Mead has been this project's shepherd from first to last; she helped transform my short proposal into three lectures and three lectures into a seven-chapter book. Great thanks are due, too, to Laura Stanifer and Jill Walker, who endured my jibber-jabbering in the reading room without complaint and proved indefatigable archival spelunkers, even when confronted with a request for an artifact of uncertain date titled simply "Me." Xander Park, my Swiss-army-knife of a research assistant, was also indispensable in dealing with the overwhelming riches of the Wade. David and Crystal Downing, now emeritus Wade directors, were gentle in reminding me about the intended length of the lectures and generous in forgiving me for surpassing that limit every time. May this book pay you back for your forbearance.

Jeremy Botts, Nicole Mazzarella, and David Hooker earned stars in their heavenly crowns for their kind and dexterous fielding of my barrages of Dante-themed text messages and emails (sometimes as many as five in a day). Thank you for venturing into unexplored artistic terrain in your responses.

I have dedicated this book to the late poet and Renaissance scholar Brett Foster and his still adoring friend among the quick, the historian Timothy Larsen, but so many other friends' names deserved to hang at the front of this book. That includes Jeffrey Barbeau, a Hansen alum, and Jim Beitler, an upcoming Hansen lecturer. You two were the cheerleaders that I didn't realize I needed when I began assembling the notes into the first lecture. Alan Jacobs has also been a tireless friend to my person and my work and a resource upon whom *all* of my books have drawn. To Jay Wood, with whom I began the Dante seminar on campus, and Adam Wood, his son, with whom the seminar continues, I am also deeply indebted.

The team at InterVarsity Press, foremost Jon Boyd and Rebecca Carhart, have been given a few too many opportunities to show patience with the author, and they have conducted themselves most charitably in them all.

The final word of gratitude here, as in all my books, goes to Dr. Alison Ruth Caviness Gibson, my colleague, co-parent, and best beloved. Your ability to endure lectures on Dante, public and private, has reached epic proportions. In you, I behold the Glory daily.

# IMAGE CREDITS

Figure I.1. Wikimedia Commons

Figure 1.1. Library of Congress, Rare Book and Special Collections Division

Figure 2.1. National Gallery of Art, Gift of the Christian Humann Foundation

Figure 3.1. Cornell University Library, PJ Mode Collection of Persuasive Cartography

Figure 3.2. Hathi Trust

Figure 4.1. Special Collections, Firestone Library, Princeton University

Figure 5.1. Hathi Trust

Figure 5.2. Hathi Trust

Figure 6.1. Wikimedia Commons

Figure 7.1. Cornell University Library, Division of Rare and Manuscript Collections

Figure 7.2. Hathi Trust

Figure C.1. WikiArt

# INDEX

*The Marion E. Wade Center*

Founded in 1965, the Marion E. Wade Center of Wheaton College, Illinois, houses a major research collection of writings and related materials by and about seven British authors: Owen Barfield, G. K. Chesterton, C. S. Lewis, George MacDonald, Dorothy L. Sayers, J. R. R. Tolkien, and Charles Williams. The Wade Center collects, preserves, and makes these resources available to researchers and visitors through its reading room, museum displays, educational programming, and publications. All of these endeavors are a tribute to the importance of the literary, historical, and Christian heritage of these writers. Together, these seven authors form a school of thought, as they valued and promoted the life of the mind and the imagination. Through service to those who use its resources and by making known the words of its seven authors, the Wade Center strives to continue their legacy.

# THE HANSEN SERIES

The Ken and Jean Hansen Lectureship is an annual lecture series named in honor of former Wheaton College trustee Ken Hansen and his wife, Jean, and endowed in their memory by Walter and Darlene Hansen. The series features three lectures per academic year by a Wheaton College faculty member on one or more of the Wade Center authors with responses by fellow faculty members.

Kenneth and Jean (née Hermann) Hansen are remembered for their welcoming home, deep appreciation for the imagination and the writings of the Wade authors, a commitment to serving others, and their strong Christian faith. After graduation from Wheaton College, Ken began working with Marion Wade in his residential cleaning business (later renamed ServiceMaster) in 1947. After Marion's death in 1973, Ken Hansen was instrumental in establishing the Marion E. Wade Collection at Wheaton College in honor of his friend and business colleague.